The New York Times

PARENT'S GUIDE
TO THE BEST
BOOKS FOR
CHILDREN

THIRD EDITION, FULLY REVISED AND UPDATED

The New York Times
PARENT'S GUIDE TO THE BEST BOOKS FOR CHILDREN

THIRD EDITION, FULLY REVISED AND UPDATED

Eden Ross Lipson

THREE RIVERS PRESS
NEW YORK

Published by Three Rivers Press, New York, New York. Member of the Crown Publishing Group.

Originally published in different form by Times Books in 1988 and 1991.

Random House, Inc. New York, Toronto, London, Sydney, Auckland
www.randomhouse.com

THREE RIVERS PRESS is a registered trademark and the Three Rivers Press colophon is a trademark of Random House, Inc.

Permissions acknowledgments appear on pages 521–530 and are an exten-sion of the copyright page.

Printed in the United States of America

Design by Lindgren/Fuller Design

Library of Congress Cataloging-in-Publication Data
Lipson, Eden Ross.
    The New York times parent's guide to the best books for children /
Eden Ross Lipson.—3rd ed.
        p.   cm.
Includes bibliographical references and index.
1. Children's literature—Bibliography.   2. Best books.   3. Read-ing—Parent participation.   4. Children—Books and reading.   I. Title:
Parent's guide to the best books for children.   II. New York times.
III. Title.
Z1037 .L724   2000
[PN1009.A1]
011.62—dc21   00-037727

ISBN 0-8129-3018-5

10 9 8 7 6 5 4 3 2 1

Third Edition

This edition is for the next generation,
the children of the twenty-first century.

[624]

CONTENTS

ACKNOWLEDGMENTS

The children's publishing industry in the United States has gone through tremendous upheavals and consolidation since the first edition of this guide appeared. Within the multi-imprint houses belonging to multinational corporations, a generation of editors, publishers, and marketers have come of age. Determined small houses continue to appear. The scene has been complicated by the rise of the chain stores, the battering of library budgets, and the impact of computers. Yet the courtesy and collegiality offered by senior figures in the field, skilled editors, and the young assistants and associates who have helped me in ways large and small have not diminished. I am grateful to all of them for taking my calls and helping me to make corrections. The errors of fact that remain are all mine and I apologize for them.

Special thanks to the great teachers who have taken time over these years to show me better ways to look at and think about children's books, especially Margaret K. McElderry, Janet Schulman, and Lauren Wohl.

Within the large, fascinating, and rapidly growing institution that is *The New York Times,* the *Book Review* remains a tiny, rather protected enclave. I owe thanks to the five editors I have worked with. My friend John Leonard hired me; Harvey Shapiro twice feared I would have a baby in the office; Mike Levitas thought, correctly, that I would have fun handling children's books. Rebecca Pepper Sinkler, as a mother and grandmother, brought special supervisory insight to the children's coverage and Charles McGrath was surprised to meet children's books again just as his youngest child left for college.

If "friendship is a sheltering tree," as a little sampler says, then I have been blessed to live in a lush and verdant grove. I feel the strength and support of many friends whom I hardly see in the rush of daily life. E-mail has a delightful catch-up immediacy, but mostly it's still fleeting phone calls, postcards, letters, pictures of growing children, and now grandchildren. Life is rushing by ever faster, and somehow we are all still overscheduled and overworked. But because the supporting bonds of friendship carry energy back and forth, they endure. We have helped each other over time, made life not just bearable but fun.

Neal Johnston questioned me closely about how I wanted this guide to work and he is the person who deserves all the credit for the system of coding that has worked so well and makes the book so easy to use. He gave up waiting for a Hardy Boys entry many years ago. Technology overtook the simple system we used on the first and second editions. Special thanks to Jude Biersdorfer, that Gen X stylist and production genius who helped me so calmly through the technical parts of this edition even as her own career burgeoned. Thanks to the Gen Y support troops as well: Allison Steele, who spent part of her freshman year at NYU doing update research, Irina Levin, who worked on the indexes, and Garth Johnston, who understood the computers at home and grasped the issues of consistency.

INTRODUCTION

This book is for people who care about honest-to-goodness children and who want to instill in them a love of reading. It is for adults who understand that reading is the key to the future—indeed, to the preservation of civilization—but who also read for their own entertainment and hope their children will, too.

In other words, as I said a dozen years ago when the first *New York Times Parent's Guide to the Best Books for Children* was finished, "This book is for the converted."

That much hasn't changed, but a great deal else has.

The youngsters I knew best back then are nearly all grown now, and within the breadth of their memories, the childhood experience changed as surely as it did when the radio and then television first entered the home. I wrote that edition on the first computer in our house, a large contraption that occupied the space of honor in the living room, just the way those other newfangled machines had in earlier times.

The new world—for children as well as adults—is filled with batteries and magical electronics, with computers, cell phones, beepers, interactive activities and games, and elaborate merchandise tie-ins. It is also a world in which many American children lead far more restricted lives than their parents did. They move about less freely; they have less unstructured time; they are bombarded by commercial entertainment.

One of the pleasures of being a parent—grand, god, surrogate, or just Mom and Dad—is helping to choose books. They are wonderful gifts. They cost more or less the same as old-fashioned (i.e.

[211]

nonelectronic) toys, last much longer, and give boundless satisfaction. But the worlds of publishing and book buying and borrowing have also changed. Giant international conglomerates have swallowed up and eliminated many smaller imprints, though brave, independent publishers do still exist. (Indeed, there seem to be new ones each season.) For a time, there were hundreds of independent "children's only" bookstores in the United States. Now the chains so dominate that few of those specialty shops survive. The Internet offers endless goodies, only a click away. Libraries, hit hard by budget cutbacks during the early '90s, are regaining acquisition budgets, although as a nation we are not training or supporting enough librarians.

And then there is Harry Potter. It is difficult to overestimate the importance of the surprising success of J. K. Rowling's series of adventure fantasy novels about that orphan wizard. It has brought hundreds of thousands of adults—directly, not just vicariously—back to the pleasures of children's books. Curious about the phenomenon, they find themselves rediscovering the delight of a galloping adventure. Without sex or violence!

Part of the sheer delight of the Potter phenomenon is that the focus was solely on the books, at least during the reign of the first four. Each reader or listener imagined it all. Each had an intense personal vision, for example, of what a game of quidditch, that sky-high broomstick game they play at the Hogwarts School, looked and sounded like. Chris Van Allsburg said in his 1982 Caldecott Medal speech that children give a book "life" by understanding it, that they can "possess a book in a way they can never possess a video game, a TV show, or a Darth Vader doll." He was, is, right. As an insightful eleven-year-old told *The New York Times:* "You know how they make books and movies for TV? I've read the books, and my mom would get the video. I've noticed that every single time the book is better than the video." It is a variation on the mantra I taught my own children: the book is always better than the movie. Of course, as Katherine Paterson, the Newbery Medal winner, has pointed out, "If we prescribe books as medicine, our children have a perfect right to refuse the nasty-tasting spoon."

Use this guide to choose books for birthdays, for holidays, for spring, for school, for Saturday, for laughter, for tears, for finding out what happened next, or for thinking about what if. . . . Try to find titles that children can embrace now, that they can seize and not shove away for some deferred gratification they're supposed to "grow into," like a big sister's cast-off winter coat. As Beverly Cleary, the author of the beloved Ramona series, once recalled:

"When I was a child, a relative gave me *Ivanhoe* to grow into. I was so disappointed that I still have not grown into it."

To help you fend off such disappointments and find books that will intrigue and delight the kids you know, this is a selective guide to 1,001 books published in the United States. Almost all are from the twentieth century. It is a mixture of classic, standard, and solid new titles. There are lots of books for lap-listening babies and toddlers, books to read aloud with preschoolers, books for beginning readers to read to themselves, books for middle-school children to devour or dabble in as they begin to sort out their lives, and a few books for teenagers as they struggle into maturity. Some are noble veterans and some are just fun; others may be helpful directly or indirectly as they address real issues children face.

You may be surprised to learn that there are truths and tricks to choosing and that you have an active, crucial role in the process. As the sign in Manhattan's Gotham Book Store says, "So many books, so little time."

If we met, say, on a street corner, and you asked me to help you find a book for your child (just the way people really do ask, incidentally), like a teacher or librarian or a clerk in a good bookstore, I would quickly turn the questions back to you: How old a child? A boy or a girl? Where does he or she live? Siblings? Intact family?

[697]

Special interests? A book to read aloud, or a book for a child to read to herself? I would go on asking questions until I could make an educated guess of an appropriate recommendation.

In the same way, I have organized the guide with its dozens of special indexes so that you can tailor your choices to a child's particular tastes and interests, or to your own tastes. Remember that the same title may appear in many indexes—easily half a dozen—because the ways we see and understand books change as we ourselves grow.

Karla Kuskin, the artist and poet, said about a picture of a large number of sleeping animals in one of her books: "Over there on the right, one cat with one eye open . . . looking at a mouse. A two-and-a-half or three-year-old will spot that cat immediately; a six-year-old will take longer; a twelve-year-old may miss it." And, she added, "At thirty-seven, you hardly have a chance." Similarly, the themes and subthemes of many stories or novels are not obvious on first reading to either adults or children; rather, they are suggested by haunting phrases, images, and ideas, all of them more powerful precisely because they are subtle.

As you browse through the listings and the indexes, or as illustrations catch your eye, I hope you find many books you already know or even just vaguely remember. If you are a baby boomer and came of age after World War II, you will discover nearly 170 titles published before 1966. I have a theory that it takes between fifteen and twenty years for a book to become a classic—the living, or rather growing-up, time between when you first read a book *as* a child and when you first read a book *to* a child. Some of the more recent titles I have included will have that lasting power, but only a few. If they reach that magic realm, they develop a special immortality, the kind that every day allows a seven-year-old, somewhere, to first meet Fern Arable and the baby pig she calls Wilbur.

This edition includes more recent books about real people—biographies and autobiographies and therefore history—and more books about science. There are more titles from the '90s that deal with minorities, both broadly and specifically defined, reflecting an enthusiasm for diversity that should not be denigrated as "political correctness." Indeed, there is a generous tradition in American children's books of inclusivity, a totally praiseworthy tradition.

For the purpose of this guide, I have included only a few young-adult titles. Teenagers have many independent paths for finding their own books; young children are much more dependent on adult assistance. I have not included books published for adults that are now considered children's titles and found on standard reading lists.

It is sometimes a very fine judgment, and today it is often a marketing or business decision whether a book is published for adults or children. *Catcher in the Rye* and *To Kill a Mockingbird,* though originally adult titles, have become identified as school books. (Indeed, the only adults who read them today, it seems, are parents.) I have also confined the guide to titles issued by children's trade book publishers because I wanted these selections to be accessible to ordinary readers, to people who regularly browse in ordinary bookstores and libraries. The great help of the Internet here is in finding out-of-print books.

[601]

THE GUIDE

The 1,001 main titles are numbered consecutively and divided into groups according to text level from wordless through picture books; story books; books for early readers, middle, and advanced readers. Remember that wordless books are not necessarily for babies, and children can pleasurably listen to stories that are much too hard for them to read by themselves.

Within each section, books are listed alphabetically by title. Each main title carries important bibliographic information—author, illustrator, and publisher in hardcover and paperback, and date of original publication. To help you in stores, libraries, and on-line, where appropriate, I have consolidated the hardcover publisher's name to the modern incarnation. For example, all books published by Harper & Row now say HarperCollins. There are also notations of certain important prizes.

The John Newbery and Randolph Caldecott medals, endowed by Frederic G. Melcher and his family and administered by the Association for Library Service to Children, are the best-known children's book prizes in the United States. Each year a changing committee of children's librarians gives a medal to the author of "the most distinguished contribution to American literature" (Newbery) and to the artist of the "most distinguished American picture book for children" (Caldecott), as well as a variable number of Honor Books. In bookstores and libraries you can recognize the winners because they usually have gold or silver stickers on their jackets.

Since 1952, *The New York Times* has annually asked a changing panel of judges to choose what they consider to be the best illustrated books of the year. They usually pick around ten, but the number varies. In recent years the *Times* has given each of the artists a certificate and made sticker labels available to the publishers.

Cheering for the home team, I have included mention of *The New York Times* Best Illustrated winners where appropriate.

I have also tried to describe each book as succinctly as possible, in one paragraph that also refers to other books in the series or related titles. The voice in the entries is mine. While there are no negative reviews, my tone, of course, reflects my own taste and enthusiasms. Since you need to establish a baseline of familiarity with any critic—and that is what I am here—why don't you begin by looking up a half-dozen of your own favorite children's book titles. If you find them, and the descriptions jibe with your memory, then this is a book you can use with a reasonable expectation of success and satisfaction. If the descriptions don't seem appropriate to you for any reason, this may not be the guide for you.

AVAILABILITY

Publishing in the United States, including the children's publishing industry, has been in a tremendous state of flux, with titles going in and out of print at a great and unpredictable rate. There has been a dramatic consolidation of publishing houses since I prepared the first edition of this book. Then, as now, I had the help of members of the Children's Book Council, the nonprofit trade organization of the children's publishing industry. I talked to editors, writers, teachers, librarians, and journalists, not to mention parents and children. The selections reflect my judgment and opinions, and errors of omission are entirely mine.

When I began work on this new edition two years ago, almost all of the older titles I selected were in print, which means in theory available for bookstores, libraries, and Internet catalogs to order for you if they don't have them in stock. But, alas, many have gone officially out of print. At first this made me frantic, but I realized that even as I was checking with Amazon.com for print status, I was also checking with the major out-of-print catalogs such as Alibris.com and finding the titles. If I had to choose a moment to be inclusive, with the knowledge that a determined individual could find a children's book—even an out-of-print children's book if she really wanted—the moment is now.

Good libraries are your best friend. It's not popular to say this, but you don't need to buy many children's books. Children need to read them, to flip through them, to digest quickly the important information they need. But many books, like a moth to a flame, give children everything they need in one reading. Go to the library as a regular ritual and take home as many books as you can. The books to buy are the ones children take out over and over, study, and really love.

THE INDEXES

The key to the indexes lies in the fact that each of the 1,001 main title books has a permanent record. Every reference to the book, including the illustrations, carries the record number, and you can use it to go back into the guide and get bibliographic information for ordering, or refresh your memory of the book's description.

The first index includes EVERY book mentioned in the guide, main titles, series titles, and related titles using the record number of the main title as the reference number. The related titles are in italic. Then follow indexes by author and illustrator, which will help you find another book by someone whose work you have enjoyed. The books in the guide are listed by reading level, but a special set of indexes suggests listening levels and suitability of books for younger children. Some books almost ask to be read aloud, so there is also an index of those pleasurable titles.

The subject indexes cover a wide range of special interests. But a word of warning. Bibliotherapy—looking to a book to solve a problem—is a little like over-the-counter cold remedies: It may help, but it isn't likely to solve the problem alone. I have included some fine books about sibling rivalry, death, divorce, and health issues. Loving families work with children to address those problems by integrating such books into their lives. The books just help. It's the family attention that really counts.

There are indexes of familiar categories—folktales, ghosts, grandparents, cats, and dinosaurs—and some specialized ones as well: minorities, science, and music.

I don't think the indexes of boys' and girls' books are particularly controversial or troublesome; if I did I wouldn't have included them. The last decade has produced a lot of rhetoric about girls' development (*Reviving Ophelia*) and boys' development. Children ARE different. There are many books directed specifically to boy readers or girl readers, and my simple purpose is to encourage reading by appealing to children's enthusiasm. The two categories are suggestions, not rules or orders, and, heaven knows, they are not exclusive. Boys love *The Wizard of Oz* and girls love *Harry Potter*. Parents of older children might, however, spend more time poking around in the middle reading books and books for young adults,

[760]

looking for specific titles that might interest their youngsters this afternoon or tonight, when it seems those hormones are starting to run faster and some fresh ideas might be handy.

Please take some time to play with the guide and the indexes. A reference book can be full of serendipitous surprises if you let it fall open to random pages. If you are working your way, book by book, through a special index, flip occasionally to another, or scout around for a new book by a writer you admire.

DESIGN AND ILLUSTRATIONS

The illustrations scattered throughout the guide are from the books I review. Each one carries the record number of the book it is from. The record numbers run consecutively through the book and will lead you back to the entry in the main text, where you will find the full bibliographic information.

The guide has unusually wide margins. We always tell children NOT to write in books, and generally speaking, that's right. But if you are really using this guide and you buy and borrow books for more than one child, take a pencil and make notes in the margin about which books you give to those children, at what age, and for what occasion and how they were received. That way the guide goes forward with your family, and also becomes a meaningful reading record. Favorite cookbooks are stained with greasy fingerprints and notations of recipe adjustments. May this guide be as useful.

BEST WISHES

The most important way we teach children the value of books is by reading ourselves. Reading picture books and story books with very young children establishes a wonderful ritual that all too often dissipates when youngsters learn to read. It is particularly difficult to persuade school-age children that they should use their precious leisure time reading to themselves if they see the adults who tell them to "go read" parked in front of the television or computer screen.

Continue to read with children as they grow. If you can, read ahead of them, even if just a chapter a night. Their books are generally short and interesting. You will honor the children with your attention to their concerns and will be happily surprised by the writers you meet.

I end where I began, hoping that your children will learn to enjoy reading books as much as you and I do. Have fun.

[26]

Wordless Books

The reader supplies the language to accompany these all-picture books. But please do not assume that because there are no words, the titles in this section are all for very young children. Some are extremely sophisticated and meant for older readers.

〔1〕

ANNO'S JOURNEY [1]

Written and illustrated by Mitsumasa Anno

Cloth: Philomel
Paper: Paper Star
Published: 1978

[1]

One man in a small boat arrives at an unknown shore. The reader has a kind of bird's-eye view of the wordless pages as the traveler sets off and the shore gives way to meadows, forest, farmlands, and a European city. This is a good book to begin with if you are not familiar with the remarkably complex picture books by the great Japanese children's book artist. With their extraordinary detail and elaborate construction yet simple narrative movement, they are for all ages. Indeed, children tend to accept a richness of detail and cross-cultural complexity in his work that adults often find awesome. If this example intrigues you, then look for the brilliant "guidebooks" *Anno's Britain, Anno's Italy,* and *Anno's Medieval World.* Most of the great Anno math books (they are both inspired and inspiring)—*Anno's Counting Book, Anno's Hat Tricks, Mysterious Multiplying Jar, Anno's Math Games I, II and III*—are officially out of print or difficult to find, but well worth the effort.

THE BEAR AND THE FLY [2]

Written and illustrated by Paula Winter

Cloth: Crown
Published: 1976   **Prizes: New York Times Best Illustrated Book**

Three bears at dinner. Enter one fly. Chaos ensues. Hilarious, ridiculous, undignified, amusing chaos. No need for words in this three-color caper.

A BOY, A DOG AND A FROG [3]

Written and illustrated by Mercer Mayer

Cloth: Dial
Paper: Dial
Published: 1967

In the first of four droll and appealing books for preschoolers, some discoveries and adventures are spelled out in simple illustrations. The other titles include *A Boy, a Dog, a Frog; A Friend; One Frog Too Many; Frog on His Own;* and *Frog, Where Are You?*

[3]

[4]

BUILDING [4]

Written and illustrated by Elisha Cooper

Cloth: Greenwillow
Published: 1999

Here, in a small, pleasant-to-hold book, is a detailed account of how a vacant lot near an urban downtown was transformed by the construction of a modest building. It is illustrated with airy, impressionistic watercolors; and while there are a few unclear steps, an attentive young reader can work out the chronology of construction. Invaluable for young engineers.

CHANGES, CHANGES [5]

Written and illustrated by Pat Hutchins

Cloth: Macmillan
Paper: Aladdin
Published: 1971   **Prizes: New York Times Best Illustrated Book**

A delightful wordless adventure involves the transformation and reconfiguration of two wooden figures, a man and a woman, and brightly colored blocks that turn into a boat, a wagon, and eventually a home.

[6]

CLOWN [6]

Written and illustrated by Quentin Blake

Cloth: Henry Holt
Paper: Henry Holt
Published: 1996   **Prizes: New York Times Best Illustrated Book**

As is often the case, this is a wordless story that speaks volumes. The clown is just one of the cast-off toys thrown in a trash can. Somehow he alone pulls himself to life and sets off in high-top sneakers to explore the world. He ends up with his pals in the home of an impoverished family that is extremely pleased to have him. The illustrations are spare and deft and poignant.

THE GREY LADY AND THE STRAWBERRY SNATCHER [7]

Written and illustrated by Molly Bang

Cloth: Four Winds
Paper: Scholastic
Published: 1980   **Prizes: Caldecott Honor**

This eerie adventure involves a basket of strawberries, a skateboard, and more. The full-color illustrations of the gray lady and the green creature with a purple hat who follows her through swamp and wood are lush and startling.

[6]

LOOK-ALIKES [8]

Written and illustrated by Joan Steiner

Cloth: Little, Brown
Published: 1998

Using words undermines the engrossing complexity of eleven dioramas made from hundreds of everyday objects combined to become a train station, a circus, a general store, a harbor, a diner. There's a little boy who leads the reader along, but no plot, yet the compositions are so rich they hold the attention of adults as well as children. Indeed, the real audience is composed of those old enough to appreciate the scenes. *Look-Alikes Jr.* is less elaborate but still great fun.

NAUGHTY NANCY [9]

Written and illustrated by John S. Goodall

Cloth: Margaret K. McElderry
Published: 1971/1999

The heroine of this lush, full-color, full- and half-page book is a beautifully dressed young mouse with a romantic sensibility. The ingeniously conceived half pages speed the action along. *Shrewbettina* and *Paddy Pork* are two other characters whose adventures are also told in the same format. The color reproduction in the reissues of the later 1990s is a little harsh, but these remain books as appealing to adults as to children for their whimsy and interactive pleasure.

PETER SPIER'S RAIN [10]

Written and illustrated by Peter Spier

Cloth: Doubleday
Paper: Picture Yearling
Published: 1981

It's a clear, fair summer's day as a young girl and her younger brother go out to play in the yard. Soon the sky darkens and it begins to rain. The storm lasts all day and the children and their dog are in and out of the house. They explore in the garden, splash out to the park, and study their neighborhood. A delightful book of closely observed details of daily life and the magic of rain. The full-color illustrations are affectionately drawn and appeal to preschoolers as well as to their older siblings.

PICNIC [11]

Written and illustrated by Emily Arnold McCully

Cloth: HarperCollins
Paper: Harper Trophy
Published: 1984

It's a perfect summer day, so the mouse family sets off in a red pickup truck to have a picnic by a lake. One child falls out and the family doesn't notice that she's missing till late afternoon. No real damage is done and there is a happy ending. A wordless charmer. The companion books are *First Snow, School,* and *New Baby.*

[9]

SECTOR 7 [12]

Written and illustrated by David Wiesner

Cloth: Clarion
Published: 1999   **Prizes: Caldecott Honor**

Imagine a class trip to, say, the Empire State Building, one that ends up in a magical place, Sector 7, where clouds are made and dispatched into the skies. A schoolboy wearing a long red scarf leaves

[12]

his class on the viewing deck and, traveling on a puffy cloud, enters a spectacular wordless fantasy. In the old-fashioned factory, stern workers send off normal clouds right on schedule. Then everything changes and creatures of the sea take to the skies as clouds.

THE SNOWMAN [13]

Written and illustrated by Raymond Briggs

Cloth: Random House
Paper: Random House

Published: 1978

A boy builds a snowman that comes to life in his dreams. This book has unusual, almost haunting power. Perhaps it comes from the snowman's wise expression throughout the full-color cartoon format. *Building a Snowman* is a version of the story with text.

WHAT GOES AROUND COMES AROUND   [14]

Written and illustrated by Richard McGuire

Cloth: Viking Press
Published: 1995

A doll flies out the window and sets off on a trip that takes it around the world before it ends up—guess where? The wonderfully witty, stylish illustrations make the story so appealing.

WILL'S MAMMOTH   [15]

Written by Rafe Martin
Illustrated by Stephen Gammel

Cloth: Putnam
Paper: Paperstar
Published: 1989

Sometimes grown-ups just don't know anything. Will's parents told him that "all the mammoths had disappeared ten thousand years ago." But out in his own backyard, in the snow, Will finds a glorious, seething mass of mammoths. It's an essentially wordless book of joyful adventure.

[13]

ZOOM [16]

Written and illustrated by Istvan Banyai

Cloth: Viking Press
Paper: Puffin
Published: 1995

Turn each page and discover that the image is a world within a world. In these detailed drawings an overhead view of a farmyard turns out to be a child playing with a toy farm set, which in turn is a catalog cover held by a boy who is on a cruise ship, which turns out to be on a poster. Hypnotically interesting as you go back and forth moving through space. In *Re-Zoom* the element of time is added.

[16]

9

Picture Books

 These books have simple texts, and for the most part, a very young child can study them and understand what they are about. The narrative is clear in the illustrations. Some picture books can be grasped at a glance; others will continue to reveal detail and nuance as a child studies them, and perhaps take on personal meaning as treasured favorites. Picture books are principally for preschool-age children, but school-age children often continue to enjoy them.

faster

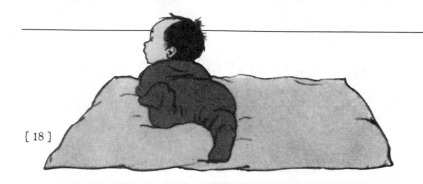

[18]

10 MINUTES TILL BEDTIME [17]

Written and illustrated by Peggy Rathmann

Cloth: Putnam
Published: 1998

Every family has going-to-bed rituals, but there's a family of hamsters determined to keep this lad awake. Hilarious complications spin almost out of control.

101 THINGS TO DO WITH A BABY [18]

Written and illustrated by Jan Ormerod

Cloth: Lothrop, Lee & Shepard
Paper: Puffin
Published: 1984

A catalog of activities is also a record of a day in the life of a family with a father, an active older sister, a dear baby, and a black cat. Mother is the loving artist. The three-color illustrations and gentle domestic ideas are both enchanting and encouraging. A book for siblings of many ages.

17 KINGS AND 42 ELEPHANTS [19]

Written by Margaret Mahy
Illustrated by Patricia McCarthy

Cloth: Dial
Paper: Pied Piper
Published: 1987   **Prizes: New York Times Best Illustrated Book**

A glorious nonsense verse about royalty and pachyderms trundling through the jungle one mysterious night, illustrated handsomely in batik fabric designs.

A FIREFLY NAMED TORCHY [20]

Written and illustrated by Bernard Waber

Cloth: Houghton Mifflin
Published: 1999

All lights are not the same. Little Torchy grew up on the same diet as the other fireflies, but when he turned his light on, the forest turned bright as day and all the sleeping creatures woke up. But, Torchy discovers, there are places where bright lights, many different kinds of them, hold sway. Torchy goes to the city.

A TEENY TINY BABY [21]

Written and illustrated by Amy Schwartz

Cloth: Orchard Books
Paper: Orchard Books
Published: 1994

The teeny tiny baby tells us he can get anything he wants, and the illustrations show his doting adults and nice schedule and world in what is clearly Brooklyn Heights. We see the baby peacefully sleeping and then awake—oh, so awake—as all the others in the household flag. The illustrations are hilarious, but preschoolers poring over the book for information about their own infancy and preciousness will see the humor rather differently from their parents, who remember the fatigue.

AARDVARKS, DISEMBARK! [22]

Written and illustrated by Ann Jonas

Cloth: Greenwillow
Published: 1990

There they were on the top of Mount Ararat; the flood was over, the water had receded. Noah opened the door and sent the animals off, calling out their names. He and his family left last, and as they walked down the mountain they passed many animals now extinct or endangered. This remarkable picture book—read sideways, for everyone is coming down the mountain—is at one and the same time an alphabet book and an annotated catalog of more than 125 named creatures, most of which no longer exist.

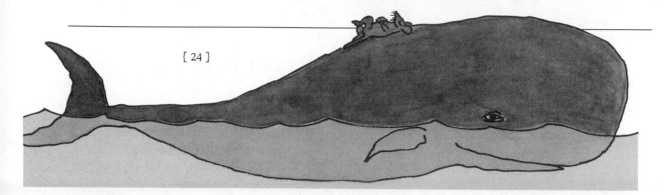

[24]

ALPHABET CITY   [23]

Written and illustrated by Stephen T. Johnson

Cloth: Viking Press
Paper: Puffin
Published: 1995   **Prizes: Caldecott Honor**

Startlingly realistic paintings of the shapes of letters hidden in various structures around New York City—the fire escape is a Z, a lamppost is a J. Very beautiful, sophisticated, and mysterious. The mysterious companion book is *City by Numbers,* in which, for example, trash cans align to make an 8.

AMOS & BORIS   [24]

Written and illustrated by William Steig

Cloth: Farrar, Straus & Giroux
Paper: Sunburst
Published: 1971   **Prizes: New York Times Best Illustrated Book**

This splendid and affecting story of true friendship between a whale and a mouse shows, rather than announces, the merits of cooperation and helpfulness. It is also, of course, funny, and the illustrations are playful.

AN ALPHABET OF ANIMALS   [25]

Written and illustrated by Christopher Wormell

Cloth: Dial
Published: 1990

In this large, sumptuously printed abecedarian, the handsome animal illustrations, including a narwhal, a quetzal, and a xenops, were carved from linoleum blocks, and successive printings created the unusually rich colors.

ANGELINA BALLERINA [26]

Written by Katharine Holabird
Illustrated by Helen Craig

Cloth: Clarkson N. Potter/Pleasant Company
Published: 1983/2000

The first in a series of books about a little mouse who wants to be a ballerina and gets her heart's desire. The rather English full-color illustrations are particularly whimsical.

ANGRY ARTHUR [27]

Written by Hiawyn Oram
Illustrated by Satoshi Kitamura

Cloth: Farrar, Straus & Giroux
Paper: Sunburst
Published: 1989

Arthur wants to stay up and watch television, and when his mother says no, he has a tantrum. What a tantrum! It ends up being a universe quake. The brilliant illustrations are jagged and tense and explosive, like Arthur's temper. And when it's over . . . he can't remember what upset him so.

ANIMAL CRACKERS [28]

Written and illustrated by Jane Dyer

Cloth: Little, Brown
Published: 1996

An enchantingly pretty collection of familiar poetry and verse, both traditional and contemporary—particularly suitable for younger listening children.

[26]

ANIMALS SHOULD DEFINITELY NOT WEAR CLOTHING [29]

Written by Judi Barrett
Illustrated by Ron Barrett

Cloth: Atheneum
Paper: Aladdin
Published: 1970

Some things are just silly to think about—for example, a walrus in a tie and jacket. Many other such possibilities are included in this book. The illustrations are, well, suitable. *Animals Should Definitely Not Act Like People* is the funny companion volume.

[30]

ANTLER, BEAR, CANOE: A NORTH-WOODS ALPHABET YEAR [30]

Written and illustrated by Betsy Bowen

Cloth: Little, Brown
Published: 1991

The author-illustrator lives in northern Minnesota near the Canadian border, and her colored woodcut images and annotations capture the seasons she knows so well—with kayaks, minnows, outboards, and wolves. *Tracks in the Wild* is another interesting way of looking at her region, and *Gathering: A Northwoods Counting Book* is full of information.

APE IN A CAPE: AN ALPHABET OF ODD ANIMALS [31]

Written and illustrated by Fritz Eichenberg

Cloth: Harcourt Brace
Paper: Voyager
Published: 1952   **Prizes: Caldecott Honor**

An alphabet book with original rhymes—dove in love, goat in a boat—involving relatively unusual animals in amusing situations. The illustrations may seem old-fashioned to adult eyes, but their large size and simplicity remain appealing to the very young.

[31]

APPLEBET [32]

Written by Clyde Watson
Illustrated by Wendy Watson

Cloth: Farrar, Straus & Giroux
Paper: Sunburst
Published: 1982

The organizing principle of this cheerful rhyming alphabet book is that a farmer and her daughter, Bet, are taking apples to a country fair.

ARLENE ALDA'S 1 2 3: WHAT DO YOU SEE? [33]

Written and illustrated by Arlene Alda

Cloth: Tricycle
Published: 1998

A delightful counting book using photographs of unexpected objects and things.

B IS FOR BETHLEHEM: A CHRISTMAS ALPHABET [34]

Written by Isabel Wilner
Illustrated by Elsa Kleven

Cloth: Dutton
Published: 1990

The wonderfully disciplined text uses an alphabet of rhymed couplets to tell the story of the Nativity. The ebullient, richly detailed illustrations incorporate a variety of techniques and contain much to discuss.

BABOON [35]

Written by Kate Banks
Illustrated by Georg Hallensleben

Cloth: Farrar, Straus & Giroux
Published: 1997

Lushly painted illustrations and simple text make the baby baboon's first walk with his mother into a wondrous journey. One idea at a

time, the baby learns that some of the world is green, some parts are slow (like the turtle) or fast (like the gazelle), and all in all, it is big.

BARK, GEORGE [36]

Written and illustrated by Jules Feiffer

Cloth: HarperCollins
Published: 1999

George the puppy has a problem—he just can't bark. He can meow, quack, oink, moo, but not bark. The doctor extracts George's troubles and then, it turns out, George speaks English. It's not quite a shaggy dog story, but the spare illustrations and minimal text suit the joke perfectly.

THE BEAUTIFUL CHRISTMAS TREE [37]

Written by Charlotte Zolotow
Illustrated by Yan Nascimbene

Cloth: Houghton Mifflin
Published: 1970/1999

[32]

The new edition of a fine story of urban renewal in the largest sense has been given elegant, stylized illustrations. Mr. Crockett buys the

19

neglected and empty house on the block and keeps to himself. One year he buys a small misshapen tree, plants it in front of his house, and proceeds to nurture it. He also befriends a neighborhood boy; together they watch the tree grow and, another year, befriend a whole chorus of multicolored birds.

THE BIGGEST BOY   [38]

Written by Kevin Henkes
Illustrated by Nancy Tafuri

Cloth: Greenwillow
Paper: Mulberry
Published: 1995

Billy's parents embroider a fantasy he loves about what a big boy he is—so big he can go to school and ride a bike, wear the house like a jacket, grow up . . . and still be a little boy safe at home in his own bed. Another good story about feeling large and small at the same time is *Big Boy*.

BLACK CAT   [39]

Written and illustrated by Christopher Myers

Cloth: Scholastic
Published: 1999

A sinewy black cat, "cousin to the concrete," moves through New York City by day and by night. The stunning illustrations, a com-

[39]

[41]

bination of photographs, collage, ink, and gouache, are richly tex-tured and give the settings a sometimes uncanny depth. The cat, always sleek and subtly patterned, is a fascinating guide.

BLACKBOARD BEAR [40]

Written and illustrated by Martha Alexander

Cloth: Dial/Candlewick Press
Published: 1969/2000

One of the best stories about a helpful imaginary buddy features a docile blackboard bear, best friend to a little boy who wants to play with the big kids. It is back in print in a charming edition, the other titles in the series, including *And My Mean Old Mother Will Be Sorry, Blackboard Bear* and *You're a Genius, Blackboard Bear* may be hard to find.

BLUEBERRIES FOR SAL [41]

Written and illustrated by Robert McCloskey

Cloth: Viking Press
Paper: Puffin
Published: 1948

Prizes: Caldecott Honor

[41]

Here are the memorable parallel adventures of a little girl and a baby bear, both of whom go hunting blueberries with their mothers one summer morning in Maine. They each lose track of time and

follow the wrong mothers. Suffice it to say they end up with the right ones. The story is as appealing to contemporary blueberry pickers as it was to their parents and grandparents.

THE BOY WHO ATE AROUND [42]

Written and illustrated by Henrik Drescher

Cloth: Hyperion
Published: 1994   **Prizes: New York Times Best Illustrated Book**

Displeased by the strong bean-and-cheese soufflé on the table, Mo turns himself into a monster and attacks the larger problems by eating everything in his way—Mom and Dad, the table and chairs, the house, and the neighborhood. He eats and eats until the inevitable happens. And then he turns back into a little boy, and, amazingly, is rewarded with a banana split. Deliciously gross, but also immoral— i.e., tantrums work.

BRINGING THE RAIN TO KAPITI PLAIN: A NANDI TALE [43]

Written by Verna Aardema
Illustrated by Beatriz Vidal

Cloth: Dial
Paper: Dial
Published: 1981

A cumulative story (like *The House That Jack Built*) from East Africa about how Ki-pat brought the rain to the "dry, oh so dry, Kapiti Plain." The rhythms and repetitions in the text are so engaging the story almost asks to be read aloud, and the full-color pictures evoke the widest and driest of plains.

[44]

BROWN BEAR, BROWN BEAR, WHAT DO YOU SEE? [44]

Written by Bill Martin, Jr.
Illustrated by Eric Carle

Cloth: Henry Holt
Paper: Henry Holt
Published: 1962/92

Who sees what? Brown Bear, Brown Bear sees the Blue Horse who sees the Green Frog. The large-format bright white book with dazzling collage animals and the singsong questioning text has been a favorite with very young lap listeners for generations, and it's easy to understand why. So much to discuss, so many things to label and laugh at. A classic.

BROWN COW, GREEN GRASS, YELLOW MELLOW SUN [45]

Written by Ellen Jackson
Illustrated by Victoria Raymond

Cloth: Hyperion
Paper: Hyperion
Published: 1995

The illustrations are painted three-dimensional clay constructions, and complemented by playful typography. Here's a story about a brown cow who eats green grass and makes white milk, and the granny who churns the milk into yellow butter that is smeared on big brown pancakes for a little boy to eat. In other words, how color works, told in a playful, entertaining way.

BUDDHA [46]

Written and illustrated by Susan L. Roth

Cloth: Doubleday
Published: 1994

The illustrations for this retelling of the early life and spiritual experiences of Siddhartha Gautama are collages made of brilliantly colored cut paper.

BUNCHES AND BUNCHES OF BUNNIES [47]

Written by Louise Matthews
Illustrated by Jeni Bassett

Cloth: Dodd, Mead
Paper: Scholastic
Published: 1978

The bunches of bunnies, lots and lots of them, are arranged across these pages to help teach the principles of multiplication.

CAN I KEEP HIM? [48]

Written and illustrated by Steven Kellogg

Cloth: Dial
Paper: Dial
Published: 1971

The narrator, a little boy, is so desperate for a pet that he tries to persuade his mother to let him keep a succession of creatures—a dog, a bear cub, a tiger, and even another little boy. The full-color cartoon-style illustrations capture his longing perfectly.

CAN'T SLEEP [49]

Written and illustrated by Chris Raschka

Cloth: Orchard Books
Published: 1995

Watch carefully: In this story of a little dog's wakefulness in the night the mysterious moon rises in the sky and then sets protectively, finally going to sleep secure that the little dog is awake and taking a turn keeping watch. Lovely, almost abstract illustrations.

CAPS FOR SALE [50]

Written and illustrated by Esphyr Slobodkina

Cloth: HarperCollins
Paper: Harper Trophy
Published: 1947

A peddler dozes under a tree and the naughty monkeys snatch his wares, the pile of caps, right off his head. A wonderful, classic pic-

[51]

ture book, endlessly entertaining for generation upon generation. Acting out the story or just playing monkey is a very satisfying preschool game. There is also a big edition suitable for classroom use and an enchanting version of the story set in Africa called *The Hatseller and the Monkeys*.

THE CARROT SEED [51]

Written by Ruth Krauss
Illustrated by Crockett Johnson

Cloth: HarperCollins
Paper: Harper Trophy
Published: 1945

[52]

Such a simple story, so peacefully told. A little boy plants a seed, waters and tends the seedling, and eventually . . . there's a carrot. The small fellow is a close cousin to Harold of purple crayon fame, and his story is as soothing and as memorable.

CAT IS SLEEPY [52]

Written and illustrated by Satoshi Kitamura

Cloth: Farrar, Straus & Giroux
Published: 1996

The marmalade cat searches the household of a musical boy and a literary girl, and finally finds a place to nap. One of a series of finely thought out, beautifully illustrated concept board books for toddlers and others. Other books are about dog, duck, and squirrel.

CAT UP A TREE [53]

Written by Ann Hassett
Illustrated by John Hassett

Cloth: Houghton Mifflin
Published: 1998

Nana Quimby is baking when she looks out her window and sees a cat in the tree, then five, then ten, eventually forty of them. The fire department has all sorts of excuses for refusing to help. But then, when the town needs help catching mice, it's another story. The illustrations are delightful with many things and creatures, colors and patterns to find and count.

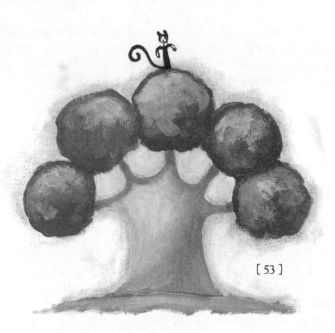

[53]

CATCH ME & KISS ME & SAY IT AGAIN [54]

Written by Clyde Watson
Illustrated by Wendy Watson

Cloth: Philomel
Published: 1978

This bubbling collection of short rhymes and verses has cheerful three-color illustrations of sturdy children and a winsome cat. The title verse refers to a bathtub escapade and is perfect for reciting while drying off.

CHICKA CHICKA BOOM BOOM [55]

Written by Bill Martin, Jr.
Illustrated by Lois Ehlert

Cloth: Simon & Schuster
Published: 1989

[54]

What with A telling B to meet at the top of the coconut tree, and the other letters of the alphabet joining them, guess what? The coconuts fall out of the tree and the sound they make when they land is . . . *Chicka Chicka Boom Boom*. Big bright illustrations and great fun for reading aloud.

[58]

THE CHOSEN BABY   [56]

Written by Valentine P. Wasson
Illustrated by Glo Coalson

Cloth: HarperCollins
Published: 1939

A gentle book about adoption for very young children that has been in print for more than half a century.

CITY DOG   [57]

Written and illustrated by Karla Kuskin

Cloth: Clarion
Paper: Clarion
Published: 1994

[57]

A lighthearted verse tells about taking the dog to the country, and the equally lighthearted illustrations follow the progress from city leash to country romp, ending in the dark under a smiling "melon yellow moon." The full verse is printed on the last page, perhaps to help the reader-out-loud to practice the cadences, or young poets to learn about form.

CLOUDY WITH A CHANCE OF MEATBALLS   [58]

Written by Judith Barrett
Illustrated by Ron Barrett

Cloth: Atheneum
Paper: Aladdin
Published: 1978   **Prizes: New York Times Best Illustrated Book**

It's a wild story Grandpa makes up. He says that in the magical land of Chewandswallow, meals come from the sky. But what happens when the weather changes? Silly to even think about. The illustra-

tions are both sophisticated and outrageously funny, and appeal most to school-age children. The sequel is called *Pickles to Pittsburgh*.

COLOR ZOO   [59]

Written and illustrated by Lois Ehlert

Cloth: HarperCollins
Paper: HarperCollins
Published: 1989   **Prizes: Caldecott Honor**

Exotic animals hide in the shapes and cutouts that pile up and rearrange on each succeeding page, so, for example, a tiger becomes a mouse. The companion book to this one is *Color Farm*, but all the artist's work is brilliant-hued and distinctive.

COME ALONG DAISY!   [60]

Written and illustrated by Jane Simmons

Cloth: Little, Brown
Published: 1998

Amazing just how much expression Daisy duckling's two pin-dot eyes can convey. In the delightful toddler series, Mama urges Daisy to hurry up, then to *Go to Sleep, Daisy*, and in *Daisy and the Egg* she anxiously waits for a sibling.

[62]

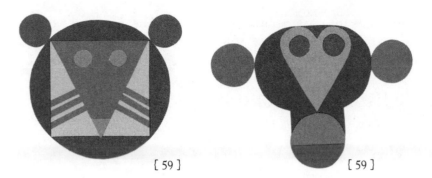

[59]   [59]

COME ON, RAIN!   [61]

Written by Karen Hesse
Illustrated by Jon J. Muth

Cloth: Scholastic
Published: 1999

Oh, it's hot! The page fairly shimmers. Four little girls and their mother wait for the sweet summer rain—come on, come on!—and then enjoy it. Deft illustrations capture the heat and the relief.

CORDUROY   [62]

Written and illustrated by Don Freeman

Cloth: Viking Press
Paper: Puffin
Published: 1968

Corduroy is a small stuffed bear waiting in a department store; he eventually goes home with a little girl named Lisa. His adventures continue in *A Pocket for Corduroy*. Although the story is complete and understood by young children, there are some appealing abridgments available, including a board book.

COUNT WITH MAISY   [63]

Written and illustrated by Lucy Cousins

Cloth: Candlewick Press
Published: 1997

It's hard to choose just one of the dozens of books about the perky little mouse. The distinctive use of primary color backgrounds, the simple text, and the appealing use in many of lift-the-flap surprises

[60]

have made them enormously popular. This one, in which Maisy counts things, including flowers and fleas, is delightful.

[64]

CURIOUS GEORGE   [64]

Written and illustrated by H. A. Rey

Cloth: Houghton Mifflin
Paper: Houghton Mifflin
Published: 1942

The first of a series of books about a small monkey captured in Africa by a man wearing a yellow hat and brought back to live in a city. George's curiosity leads him to wreak havoc everywhere he goes. But he is always well-meaning, rather like many of his most devoted preschool admirers. Other original titles include *Curious George Gets a Medal* and *Curious George Rides a Bike*. There are also titles with illustrations taken from the animated television series in which the color and drawings are not as vibrant as in the original books, and board books and merchandise.

DANCE   [65]

Written by Bill T. Jones and Susan Kuklin
Illustrated by Susan Kuklin

Cloth: Hyperion
Published: 1998

Jones, a dancer and choreographer, is caught in movement in a series of inviting photographs with captions that suggest some of the joy and energy that come from his opening phrase: "I am a dancer. I want to dance."

DANCING IN THE MOON: COUNTING RHYMES   [66]

Written and illustrated by Fritz Eichenberg

Cloth: Harcourt Brace
Paper: Voyager
Published: 1955

Verses with ridiculous premises for counting from 1 to 20, accompanied by large, distinctive, eccentric illustrations.

DAWN [67]

Written and illustrated by Uri Shulevitz

Cloth: Farrar, Straus & Giroux
Paper: Sunburst
Published: 1974

The text of this lovely picture book comes from a Chinese poem about an old man and his grandson. They are asleep by the shore of a mountain lake and dawn approaches. The full-color illustrations capture the subtle changes of light in the early morning.

THE DAY JIMMY'S BOA ATE THE WASH [68]

Written by Trinka Hakes Noble
Illustrated by Steven Kellogg

Cloth: Dial
Paper: Pied Piper
Published: 1980

The day Jimmy's pet snake goes along on the class trip to the farm makes a memorable story. The full extent of the mayhem is revealed in the dizzy, funny illustrations. *Jimmy's Boa Bounces Back* tells about what happens when the boa goes to a proper tea party. Just try and guess what happens in *Jimmy's Boa and the Big Splash Birthday Bash*.

DO NOT FEED THE TABLE [69]

Written by Dee Lillegard
Illustrated by Keiko Narahashi

Cloth: Doubleday
Published: 1993

Tiny poems, marvels of wit and economy, celebrate kitchen implements such as the toaster, the microwave, and the humble spatula,

while charming sunlit watercolor illustrations capture the details of one little boy's daily rituals.

[72]

DRUMMER HOFF   [70]

Written by Barbara Emberley
Illustrated by Ed Emberley

Cloth: Prentice Hall
Paper: Simon & Schuster
Published: 1967   **Prizes: Caldecott Medal**

The simplest cumulative rhyme and precise, funny illustrations describe the firing of a cannon by a gaggle of soldiers dressed in the style of the American Revolution. Needs to be read aloud together.

EACH ORANGE HAS 8 SLICES   [71]

Written by Paul Giganti, Jr.
Illustrated by Donald Crews

Cloth: Greenwillow
Paper: Mulberry
Published: 1992

The genius of this entertaining introduction to arithmetic and mathematics is that youngsters of a considerable age range can count or add or multiply to find out answers to the questions nimbly posed and stylishly illustrated. The orange has eight slices and two seeds in each slice . . . how many seeds? The author and artist collaborated on *How Many Snails?*

EACH PEACH PEAR PLUM   [72]

Written by Janet and Allan Ahlberg
Illustrated by Janet Ahlberg

Cloth: Viking Press
Paper: Puffin
Published: 1979

An enchanting picture book set on a summery afternoon in the countryside in which semi-hidden nursery rhyme characters, such as Goldilocks, the Three Bears, Bo Peep, and Jack and Jill, can be spotted by sharp-eyed readers.

ERNEST AND CELESTINE [73]

Written and illustrated by Gabrielle Vincent

Cloth: Greenwillow
Paper: Mulberry
Published: 1982

The first in an out-of-print series of books from a Belgian author about Ernest the bear and Celestine the little mouse. The affection between them, the delicacy of the illustrations, and the plausibility of their adventures are all endearing. In this story, Celestine loses her duck-doll in the snow and Ernest tries to solve the problem. Other titles include *Ernest and Celestine at the Circus, Ernest and Celestine's Picnic,* and *Merry Christmas, Ernest and Celestine.*

THE FATHER WHO HAD 10 CHILDREN [74]

Written and illustrated by Benedicte Guettier

Cloth: Dial
Published: 1999

Father has a scratchy beard and wears a suit and takes good care of his ten babies, which, when you think about it, is exhausting. He tries to take a vacation from them, but discovers that he misses them too much. Wouldn't you?

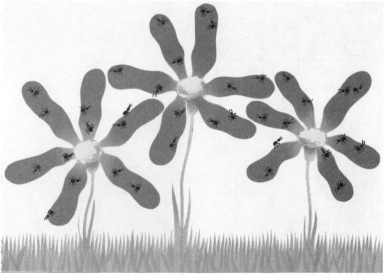

[71]

FEELINGS [75]

Written and illustrated by Aliki

Cloth: Greenwillow
Paper: Mulberry
Published: 1984

A catalog of emotions—witty illustrations of faces showing sorrow, joy, love, hate, pride, fear, frustration, and more. Since some children have difficulty explaining their emotions—often because they don't have the words for them—this is a useful as well as an entertaining book, and excellent for shared reading. *Manners* is a companion title.

FINDERS KEEPERS [76]

Written and illustrated by Will and Nicholas Mordvinoff

Cloth: Harcourt Brace
Paper: Voyager
Published: 1951   **Prizes: Caldecott Medal**

Who owns the bone two dogs have found? It's a funny story with funny pictures, just right for lap listeners and small children, never mind that adults may see the illustrations as old-fashioned.

[80]

FINGER RHYMES [77]

Written and illustrated by Marc Brown

Cloth: Dutton
Paper: Puffin
Published: 1996

Finger rhymes are those rhymes and games you do with babies and very young children in which everyone ends up laughing. The animal-filled illustrations in this pleasing collection include such familiar favorites as the Eensy Weensy Spider and This Little Piggy. The illustrations are encouraging for older readers, who may have to follow the instructions. The companion volumes are *Hand Rhymes* and *Party Rhymes*.

"FIRE! FIRE!" SAID MRS. MCGUIRE [78]

Written by Bill Martin, Jr.
Illustrated by Richard Egielski

Cloth: Harcourt Brace
Paper: Voyager
Published: 1996

The simplest kind of plot summary would be: An engine company responds to a neighborhood fire alarm. But add the call-and-response text, adapted from an old nursery rhyme, the urban setting and characters that the illustrator has provided, and the bucket brigade pileup of characters shouting the alarm, and it's lots of fun. There are some tired stereotypes in some of the illustrations, but also some refreshing new visions.

FIRE TRUCK [79]

Written and illustrated by Peter Sis

Cloth: Greenwillow
Published: 1999

A little boy named Matt so loves fire trucks that one day he wakes up and discovers that he's turned into one. He careers around the house in clever disguise doing daring deeds until the possibility of pancakes causes him to turn back into a little boy. The drawings are deft and full of possibility. Related titles are *Truck, Truck, Ship Ahoy!* and *Dinosaur*.

FIREMAN SMALL   [80]

Written and illustrated by Wong Herbert Yee

Cloth: Houghton Mifflin
Paper: Houghton Mifflin
Published: 1994

Fireman Small would like to get some sleep, but, as the rhyming text explains, emergencies keep interrupting—Farmer Pig's cat is stuck up a tree; Little Bunny falls down the well; there's a fire in the hippopotamus's bakery. Charming watercolor illustrations. Then there's *Fireman Small to the Rescue*.

FIRST FLIGHT   [81]

Written and illustrated by David McPhail

Cloth: Little, Brown
Paper: Little, Brown
Published: 1991

A little boy goes on his first airplane trip to visit his grandmother. His teddy bear turns into a traveling companion who acts out every behavioral fantasy and neurosis. Stylishly done, with both humor and sympathy.

THE FIRST NIGHT   [82]

Written by B. G. Hennessy
Illustrated by Steve Johnson

Cloth: Viking Press
Paper: Puffin
Published: 1993

The apparently simple illustrations to this very spare account of the Nativity are acrylic paintings on butternut wood, which gives them

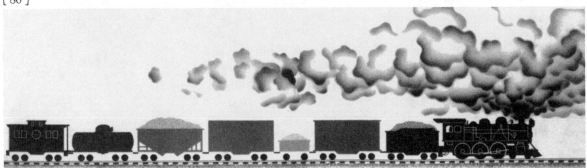

a quiet lushness that suits the story. It's a small book, one very young lap listeners can hold and hear.

FISH EYES: A BOOK YOU CAN COUNT ON [83]

Written and illustrated by Lois Ehlert

Cloth: Harcourt Brace
Paper: Harcourt Brace
Published: 1992   **Prizes: New York Times Best Illustrated Book**

Deep in the cobalt-blue sea of these pages there are amazing, brilliant flip-flopping fish. Their shapes and colors and numbers increase imaginatively. The simple rhymed text and the cutout holes for little fingers on each page invite the very young reader or listener to chant aloud and help turn the page. The distinctive collage style can be found above ground in *Growing Vegetable Soup, Planting a Rainbow, Feathers for Lunch,* and other titles.

FIVE LITTLE FOXES AND THE SNOW [84]

Written by Tony Johnston
Illustrated by Cyndy Szekeres

Cloth: HarperCollins
Published: 1987

It starts to snow the week before Christmas, and in the cozy den, Gramma Fox has her hands full trying to manage the five little foxes as well as her knitting project. All is revealed on Christmas morning. A delightful story of anticipation with funny full-color illustrations. The text has a nice cadence for reading aloud.

FREDERICK [85]

Written and illustrated by Leo Lionni

Cloth: Pantheon
Paper: Random House
Published: 1967   **Prizes: Caldecott Honor**
New York Times Best Illustrated Book

The first of the wonderful books about Frederick the mouse, a daydreamer and poet who, when winter comes, is also an entertainer.

[85]

The artist works in a distinctive full-color collage style. (There is a one-volume hardcover collection entitled *Frederick's Fables: A Treasury of 16 Favorite Leo Lionni Stories.*)

FREIGHT TRAIN [86]

Written and illustrated by Donald Crews

Cloth: Greenwillow
Paper: Mulberry
Published: 1978   **Prizes: Caldecott Honor**

A freight train hurtles across the pages through day and night from the city into the countryside, with a sense of speed that is quite magical as the train becomes almost an abstraction of color. It's a wonderful book to read with young children, and a case where the board-book version is satisfying. *Trucks* and *Flying* are also exciting.

FRIENDS [87]

Written and illustrated by Helme Heine

Cloth: Margaret K. McElderry
Paper: Aladdin
Published: 1982

A rooster, a mouse, and a pig are best friends and have a fine time together. The witty and lighthearted full-color illustrations are ebullient. The companions also appear in *Friends Go Adventuring,* and if you go to the library, you may find some other stories such as *The Alarm Clock, The Visitor,* and *The Racing Cart* that are now out of print.

[87]

GEORGE SHRINKS [88]

Written and illustrated by William Joyce

Cloth: HarperCollins
Paper: Harper Trophy
Published: 1985

In this beautifully realized dream fantasy, George wakes up to find that his parents are out, he has shrunk to tiny size, but he must nevertheless deal with a whole list of household chores. The illustrations capture the problems of scale perfectly—the toothbrush, the cat, the garbage, and a tiny George. There is a board-book version that captures the essence of the story.

GILA MONSTERS MEET YOU AT THE AIRPORT [89]

Written by Marjorie Weinman Sharmat
Illustrated by Byron Barton

Cloth: Macmillan
Paper: Aladdin
Published: 1980

Moving is bad enough, but what if you are from the big city and when the airplane lands, giant lizards meet you? The little boy meets a boy out west who has similarly outlandish fantasies about life in New York.

GINGER [90]

Written and illustrated by Charlotte Voake

Cloth: Candlewick Press
Published: 1997

As a rule, orange cats are very set in their ways and not particularly friendly. Ginger is no exception, and is not amused when the family brings home a little gray kitten. If the story is predictable to adult eyes, or suggests lessons about sibling rivalry, the delicate, airy illustrations are so enchanting that young readers are not likely to notice, but very likely to be delighted.

THE GINGERBREAD BOY [91]

Written and illustrated by Richard Egielski

Cloth: HarperCollins
Published: 1997

Once upon a time a clever artist took the folktale about the childless couple who baked up a Gingerbread Boy and transported it to modern Manhattan. The chase now begins as the Boy leaps out the window of a tenement, boards a bus, switches to the subway, and

[88]

ends up in Central Park, where, of course, a fox is waiting by the Bethesda Fountain. Jim Aylesworth has retold *The Gingerbread Man* with illustrations by Barbara McClintock and put the same story into a setting inspired by the nineteenth-century French illustrator Grandville.

GOOD MORNING, CHICK [92]

Written by Mirra Ginsburg
Illustrated by Byron Barton

Cloth: Greenwillow
Paper: Mulberry
Published: 1980

Young children like this barnyard story with its bright, simple full-color illustrations. A baby chick comes out of its little white house and explores the new world it has entered.

[93]

GOOD NIGHT, GORILLA [93]

Written and illustrated by Peggy Rathmann

Cloth: Putnam
Paper: Putnam
Published: 1994

It's bedtime and the little gorilla cleverly grabs the zookeeper's key chain and frees a parade of animals to follow the keeper home to bed. The keeper's wife returns them all to the zoo. Or does she? Bright, cartoony illustrations keep everyone laughing.

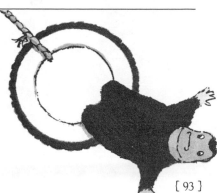

[93]

GOODBYE HOUSE   [94]

Written and illustrated by Frank Asch

Cloth: Prentice Hall
Paper: Aladdin
Published: 1986

A father helps his child bid farewell to the house after the moving van has emptied it. An upsetting situation handled in a thoughtful and soothing way.

GOODNIGHT MOON   [95]

Written by Margaret Wise Brown
Illustrated by Clement Hurd

Cloth: HarperCollins
Paper: Harper Trophy
Published: 1947

One of the most popular of all American books for the bedtime rituals of very young children. A small rabbit settles down for the night in that familiar but fantastic place "the great green room" and

[95]

[97]

says good night to all the things and creatures there. The illustrations, subtle and complex as well as droll, are perhaps even more soothing than the text.

GOOSE [96]

Written and illustrated by Molly Bang

Cloth: Scholastic
Paper: Scholastic
Published: 1996   **Prizes: Caldecott Honor**

Geese so often have unfortunate reputations; here's the emergence of a charming hero. The gosling hatches right on the cover and adventures ensue.

GRANDFATHER TWILIGHT [97]

Written and illustrated by Barbara Helen Berger

Cloth: Philomel
Paper: Paper Star
Published: 1984

A peaceful bedtime book with some gentle magic. Grandfather Twilight spreads dusk and mysterious shadows with his magic pearl, which, as darkness comes and he reaches the shore, is transformed into the rising moon. The full-color illustrations have a luminous quality that is captivating.

[96]

THE GUINEA PIG ABC   [98]

Written and illustrated by Kate Duke

Cloth: Dutton
Paper: Unicorn
Published: 1983

The letters in the sunny ABC are made by a troupe of appealing guinea pigs with unusual acrobatic skills. *Guinea Pigs Far and Near* features the same cast illustrating concepts such as behind, beside, and between.

HAPPY BIRTHDAY, MOON   [99]

Written and illustrated by Frank Asch

Cloth: Prentice Hall
Paper: Aladdin
Published: 1982

This is one of a series of simple stories about a little bear illustrated in a particularly appealing and rather childlike fashion with strong blocks of color that young children find very pleasing. Other favorites include *Good-Night, Horsey, Bear's Bargain,* and *Bread & Honey.*

HAROLD AND THE PURPLE CRAYON   [100]

Written and illustrated by Crockett Johnson

Cloth: HarperCollins
Paper: Harper Trophy
Published: 1955

[99]

One night when Harold can't sleep, he takes his purple crayon and draws himself a walk. He follows the moon, goes to a desert isle, climbs a stair, and ends up home and in bed. Simple and glorious, this book is especially loved by very young children. The related titles are *Harold's ABC, Harold's Circus,* and *Harold's Trip to the Sky.*

HARRY AND THE TERRIBLE WHATZIT [101]

Written and illustrated by Dick Gackenbach

Cloth: Clarion
Paper: Clarion
Published: 1978

Harry follows his mother down into the dark cellar to save her from the terrible two-headed Whatzit that amazingly shrinks when confronted by Harry's courage. Emboldened, Harry even sends it away. Reassuring to youngsters passing through a monster phase.

HARVEY POTTER'S BALLOON FARM

[102]

Written by Jerdine Nolen
Illustrated by March Buehner

Cloth: Lothrop, Lee & Shepard
Paper: Mulberry
Published: 1994

The narrator, a balloon farmer herself, remembers how government inspectors certified Harvey Potter's crop way back in 1920, when she was a girl. The illustrations, in intense balloon colors, imagine the balloon crop quite plausibly.

HAVE YOU SEEN MY DUCKLING? [103]

Written and illustrated by Nancy Tafuri

Cloth: Greenwillow
Paper: Mulberry
Published: 1984   **Prizes: Caldecott Honor**

In a series of stunning double-page illustrations executed in a bold but vaguely Oriental style, the mother duck looks for her eighth duckling, whom the reader can see in some visible but cleverly camouflaged corner. Great fun for very young children. *Early Morning in the Barn* is about three chicks who sing with other barnyard animals. *Snowy, Flowy, Blowy* is a counting book that goes through the seasons.

HELLO TOES! HELLO FEET! [104]

Written by Ann Whitford Paul
Illustrated by Nadine Bernard Westcott

Cloth: DK Ink
Published: 1998

A full day of adventures for one little girl and her feet. From first touching the floor to kicking the stairs, jumping from rock to rock, squishing in the mud, washing in the tub and then to bed—busy feet, busy girl. Exuberant verse, delightful watercolor illustrations.

A HOLE IS TO DIG: A FIRST BOOK OF DEFINITIONS [105]

Written by Ruth Krauss
Illustrated by Maurice Sendak

Cloth: HarperCollins
Paper: Harper Trophy
Published: 1952   **Prizes: New York Times Best Illustrated Book**

This little book fits perfectly into preschool- and kindergarten-size hands and is full of wonderful things to think about. The small line drawings capture wistful, funny, ordinary children in motion. The text sets out fine child-evolved definitions—arms are to hug. A favorite for decades.

THE HOLES IN YOUR NOSE [106]

Written and illustrated by Genichiro Yagyu

Cloth: Kane/Miller
Paper: Kane/Miller
Published: 1994

The topic holds endless fascination for small children and squeamish distaste for many adults, but the Japanese approach such sub-

jects with matter-of-fact practicality, as evidenced here and in other books about bodily functions such as *Everyone Poops*. The text is clear and frank, the illustrations crisp and bold.

[106]

HONEY, I LOVE AND OTHER LOVE POEMS   [107]

Written by Eloise Greenfield
Illustrated by Diane and Leo Dillon

Cloth: HarperCollins
Paper: Harper Trophy
Published: 1978

A collection of short poems about emotions and ordinary childhood experiences. The illustrations of black children are appealing.

HOORAY FOR SNAIL   [108]

Written and illustrated by John Stadler

Cloth: HarperCollins
Paper: Harper Trophy
Published: 1984

The idea of Snail hitting a home run, which means that Snail must circle the bases, is a joke everyone, even the young sports fan, can see coming and enjoy all the way around. *Snail Saves the Day* shifts the action to the football field. Beginning sports fans might make the effort to find these.

HORACE AND MORRIS BUT MOSTLY DOLORES   [109]

Written by James Howe
Illustrated by Amy Walrod

Cloth: Atheneum
Published: 1999

The adventures of three happy "now-and-forever" friends are halted when Horace and Morris form a boys' club, saying "A boy mouse must do what a boy mouse must do." Never fear; Dolores finds a way for fine friendship to win out. The collage-and-paint illustrations of the mice are droll and distinctive.

HUE BOY   [110]

Written by Rita Phillips Mitchell
Illustrated by Caroline Binch

Cloth: Dial
Published: 1993   **Prizes: New York Times Best Illustrated Book**

The setting is Caribbean, but the problem is universal: Hue Boy is small, too small. Everyone in the village has suggestions for how he can stretch, but when his daddy comes home from the sea and they walk through the village together, Hue Boy feels tall.

HURRAY FOR THE FOURTH OF JULY   [111]

Written and illustrated by Wendy Watson

Cloth: Clarion
Paper: Houghton Mifflin
Published: 1992

America's birthday is celebrated in a small town in a festive and appealing way. Traditional verses, rhymes, and jokes are set in boxes within full-page illustrations brimming with children, dogs, and merriment.

[109]

HURRY, HURRY, MARY DEAR   [112]

Written by N. M. Bodecker
Illustrated by Erik Blegvad

Cloth: Margaret K. McElderry
Published: 1998

Mary Dear is a New England farm wife of another era who is instructed to rush about her autumn chores in the verse that forms the text to this enchanting book. The watercolor illustrations capture the brisk, white-haired Mary and her black cat as they hurry through the apple picking, the butter churning, the canning, and so on as the leaves fall, the sky darkens, and winter comes on. There's a joke at the end, and much to talk about in the work and the weather the illustrations depict.

HUSH, LITTLE BABY [113]

Written and illustrated by Marla Frazee

Cloth: Harcourt Brace
Published: 1999

Look elsewhere for tender traditional settings of the old folk tune. This one, set in Appalachia on a dark night some time ago, features a squalling baby, a mischievous older sister set on finding all those things in the verses—the diamond ring, pony, etc. By dawn everyone is exhausted. If your taste is sweet, look for Caroline Cooney or Sylvia Long's recent versions. Long has a mother rabbit singing to her baby.

I AM A BUNNY [114]

Written by Ole Risom
Illustrated by Richard Scarry

Cloth: Golden/Western
Published: 1967

"I am a bunny. I live in a hollow tree." This tall, sturdy book with its very simple text and illustrations that capture the seasons in the life of a little rabbit wearing red overalls is a timeless favorite, especially with toddlers. There are companion stories: *I Am a Kitten, I Am a Puppy.*

I LOST MY BEAR [115]

Written and illustrated by Jules Feiffer

Cloth: Morrow Junior Books
Published: 1998   **Prizes: New York Times Best Illustrated Book**

The title says it all, but doesn't suggest what a complete psychological tale of terror is set out and resolved in the form of a picture book. The heroine is driven to distraction by her loss and the entire household is turned upside down before the bear is found. The details of family life are pitch perfect, the illustrations operatic in their echoing of the text.

I SAW ESAU: THE SCHOOLCHILD'S POCKET BOOK [116]

Written by Iona Opie and Peter Opie
Illustrated by Maurice Sendak

Cloth: Candlewick Press
Published: 1992

These are *not* the familiar Mother Goose verses, but rather a collection of the wicked, the sly, and the naughty, and they are delightful, as are the illustrations in Sendak's beloved "fat" style. The book is small to hold and a pleasure to touch.

[117]

I WANT TO BE AN ASTRONAUT

[117]

Written and illustrated by Byron Barton

Cloth: HarperCollins
Paper: Harper Trophy
Published: 1988   **Prizes: New York Times Best Illustrated Book**

There are only five short sentences in this giddy, imaginative "travel" book for small dreamers. Space is brilliantly blue, the astronauts look a lot like Lego figures, and the earth looks comforting and not so far away. The simplicity of the illustrations in which the figures are outlined with strong black lines is persuasive. There are a number of books on space for children in preschool and the lower grades, including *Zoom, Zoom, Zoom, Off to the Moon.*

I'LL SEE YOU WHEN THE MOON IS FULL [118]

Written by Susi Gregg Fowler
Illustrated by Jim Fowler

Cloth: Greenwillow
Published: 1994

Father is packing to leave on a business trip and explains to Abe that he will be home when the moon is full. There's more than lunar facts involved here; there's humor, love, details of family life, and an optimism that comes with the understanding that the moon will be full and Father will be home.

IF YOU GIVE A MOUSE A COOKIE [119]

Written by Laura Joffe Numeroff
Illustrated by Felicia Bond

Cloth: HarperCollins
Paper: Harper Trophy
Published: 1985

The logic to this wonderfully nonsensical book is perfectly sound, as it must be to lead the reader through such a caper about the consequences of greed. You see, if you give a mouse a cookie, well then, logically he'll ask for a glass of milk. Need one add that it's a chocolate chip cookie and the winsome mouse in overalls has a wonderfully pert nose? Or that there are many merchandise spin-offs and less successful sequels including *If You Give a Moose a Muffin* and *If You Give a Pig a Pancake.*

IKTOMI AND THE BERRIES [120]

Written and illustrated by Paul Goble

Cloth: Orchard Books
Paper: Orchard Books
Published: 1989

The Lakota Indians called their trickster character Iktomi, and in this story the foolish fellow doesn't understand that the buffalo berries he sees in the water are really reflections. In this and several other Iktomi tales (*Iktomi and the Boulder* and *Iktomi and the Ducks*), the format—with stylized illustrations and participant clues in the text—is designed to be read aloud with young children.

IN THE RAIN WITH BABY DUCK [121]

Written by Amy Hest
Illustrated by Jill Barton

Cloth: Candlewick Press
Published: 1995

In the first of the books about Baby Duck, her parents, and especially her wise grandfather, Baby Duck is miserable (and unducklike) about going out in the rain. Her grandpa finds a beautiful red umbrella and they go off together. Other life dramas are confronted in *Baby Duck and the Bad Eyeglasses, You're the Boss, Baby Duck,* and *Off to School, Baby Duck.*

[122]

IS THIS A HOUSE FOR HERMIT CRAB? [122]

Written by Megan McDonald
Illustrated by S. D. Schindler

Cloth: Orchard Books
Paper: Orchard Books
Published: 1990

The hermit crab must find a new home, and he trudges across the sand (even the pages are sandy-colored) trying out different domiciles just lying there on the beach—a rock, driftwood, a plastic pail—until the right place comes along. Text and illustrations are perfectly married, making this a delightful story as well as fine natural science for the very young.

JAMBO MEANS HELLO: SWAHILI ALPHABET BOOK [123]

Written by Muriel Feelings
Illustrated by Tom Feelings

Cloth: Dial
Paper: Dial
Published: 1974

A fine anthropological alphabet book that conveys a vision of tribal life in East Africa. A companion volume, *Moja Means One,* is a counting book. This is really for school-age children and adults.

[123]

JESSE BEAR, WHAT WILL YOU WEAR? [124]

Written by Nancy White Carlstrom
Illustrated by Bruce Degan

Cloth: Macmillan
Paper: Aladdin
Published: 1986

A lilting rhyme that begins as Jesse Bear wakes up and makes some decisions about his day. A happy book, with happy illustrations, for preschoolers who enjoy making the same kinds of decisions. The bears are endearing, and return in other titles, including *It's About Time, Jesse Bear, Better Not Get Wet, Jesse Bear, Happy Birthday, Jesse Bear*, and *Guess Who's Coming, Jesse Bear?*

JOSEPH HAD A LITTLE OVERCOAT [125]

Written and illustrated by Simms Taback

Cloth: Viking Press
Published: 1999   **Prizes: Caldecott Medal**

Joseph the tailor, in this adaptation of a Yiddish folktale, cleverly cuts and restitches his worn-out overcoat. It gets smaller and smaller, but die-cut holes in the page lead the story on to show how each successive garment is cleverly used until there is just a button. And when the button is lost . . . there is enough to make a story. Ebullient illustrations.

[127]

LATKES AND APPLESAUCE: A HANUKKAH STORY [126]

Written by Fran Manuskin
Illustrated by Robin Spowart

Cloth: Scholastic
Paper: Scholastic
Published: 1990

A blizzard has made it impossible to dig potatoes and gather apples for the traditional Hanukkah dinner of latkes and applesauce, and supplies are running low; nevertheless, the poor family takes in a stray kitten and dog. At the end of the storm, on the eighth night, the new pets reveal a modest miracle. An appealing holiday tale.

LENTIL [127]

Written and illustrated by Robert McCloskey

Cloth: Viking Press
Paper: Puffin
Published: 1940

Once upon a time in Alto, Ohio, a boy named Lentil and his harmonica saved the day when a grand celebration was planned. An enchanting old-time story.

THE LION'S WHISKERS: AN ETHIOPIAN FOLKTALE [128]

Written by Nancy Raines Day
Illustrated by Ann Grifalconi

Cloth: Scholastic
Published: 1995

The story of Fanaye's quest for her stepson's love is a traditional tale from a predominantly Christian tribe in Ethiopia, and the shrewd advice of the medicine man who teaches her the patience necessary by demanding three chin whiskers from a fierce old lion has been charmingly illustrated. For adults and children in new-formed families, it is a story with special dignity and warmth. There are several other versions of the story, but with less winning illustrations.

[128]

LITTLE CLAM [129]

Written and illustrated by Lynn Reiser

Cloth: Greenwillow
Published: 1998

Here's an enchanting bedtime book that doubles as a fine lesson in seashore science. In a moonlit cottage on the dunes, a mother tells her own little mollusk about the life cycle of a little clam "who lived in a shell at the edge of the sea." The simple and witty illustrations

show his cleverly designed shell, foot, and siphons; his allies and his enemies; and the tidal rhythm of his life. Just before sleep there's a clever little clam game to play at home.

LITTLE ELEPHANT   [130]

Written by Miela Ford
Illustrated by Tana Hoban

Cloth: Greenwillow
Paper: Mulberry
Published: 1994

Meet a baby elephant playing quietly in a pool on a sunny day. It's a very modest adventure story, beautifully photographed and simply told by a mother-daughter team. A book genuinely suitable for toddlers.

THE LITTLE ENGINE THAT COULD

[131]

Written by Watty Piper
Illustrated by George and Doris Hauman

Cloth: Platt & Munk
Published: 1930

One of the basic books of American childhood, this is the saga of the little engine that thought it could help deliver toys and fruits to the children living over the mountain. Avoid the gussied-up editions. The little engine need not pop up or go fast; it is, after all, just a little engine, like the young child who is listening to the chant: "I think I can, I think I can."

[133]

THE LITTLE FUR FAMILY   [132]

Written by Margaret Wise Brown
Illustrated by Garth Williams

Cloth: HarperCollins
Paper: Harper Trophy
Published: 1951

This is about a day in the life of a little fur child, ending with a bedtime song. The little fur family is "warm as toast, smaller than most." The cover is fuzzy fake fur.

LITTLE GORILLA   [133]

Written and illustrated by Ruth Bornstein

Cloth: Clarion
Paper: Clarion
Published: 1976

[129]

A very simple and appealing story about wide-eyed Little Gorilla, who grows and grows and grows and is still loved, even when he is a big gorilla. Very young children find it a soothing tale, perhaps because the small gorilla is so easy to identify with. A toddler favorite.

THE LITTLE HOUSE   [134]

Written and illustrated by Virginia Lee Burton

Cloth: Houghton Mifflin
Paper: Houghton Mifflin
Published: 1942   **Prizes: Caldecott Medal**

Here is the now-classic story of a little house that was built on a hill long ago, and how, as time passed, the city closed in upon it. Eventually the little house was rescued and brought back to rural peace and calm. With its windows, door, and stoop that together look like a smiling face, the little house is back where it belongs—on a country hilltop. Beneath the charm and sweetness there is a profound antiurbanism to both text and illustration, which adults can see clearly but may choose not to mention.

THE LITTLE RED HEN
(MAKES A PIZZA)   [135]

Written by Philemon Sturges
Illustrated by Amy Walrod

Cloth: Dutton
Published: 1999

[134]

Suppose, just suppose, that the Little Red Hen lived in the city, and instead of making a loaf of bread, she decides to make . . . a pizza. Her companions, the dunce dog, the hipster cat, and the silly duck, are uncooperative about helping, of course, but Hen shares, and they clean up. The witty collage illustrations, showing, for example, the contents of the refrigerator and the toppings on the pizza, are inspired.

LITTLE TIM AND THE BRAVE SEA CAPTAIN   [136]

Written and illustrated by Edward Ardizzone

Cloth: HarperCollins
Paper: Puffin
Published: 1936/2000

This beloved English picture book adventure, hard to find for far too long, tells how young Tim stows away on a steamship and nearly goes down with the captain. The watercolor illustrations capture the changing moods of the sea beautifully. A thrilling book with a happy ending. Other Tim books worth looking for include *Tim and Ginger, Tim and Charlotte,* and *Tim and Towser.*

THE LITTLEST DINOSAURS   [137]

Written and illustrated by Bernard Most

Cloth: Harcourt Brace
Paper: Voyager
Published: 1990

A book about the little guys—two dozen lesser, or at least smaller, dinosaurs. They are engagingly described, and brightly illustrated, often placed for reasons of scale, and narrative amusement, in contemporary settings.

MADELINE   [138]

Written and illustrated by Ludwig Bemelmans

Cloth: Viking Press
Paper: Puffin
Published: 1939   **Prizes: Caldecott Medal**

"In an old house in Paris that was covered with vines" begins the beloved story, and the singsong rhymed text carries the twelve little girls and their headmistress, dear Miss Clavel, through a series of madcap adventures. The brilliant, busy Gallic illustrations capture, and indeed encapsulate, a sense of Paris as so many people, children and adults, believe it once was. Other titles include *Madeline and the Bad Hat, Madeline and the Gypsies, Madeline in London,* and *Madeline's Rescue.* It is now being heavily merchandised.

[139]

THE MAESTRO PLAYS   [139]

Written by Bill Martin, Jr.
Illustrated by Vladimir Radunsky

Cloth: Henry Holt
Paper: Harcourt Brace
Published: 1994

[144]

The 1971 text, a wonderful catalog of adverbs, is reillustrated in exuberant paper cuts showing us a circus maestro who plays: loudly, proudly, ringingly, swingingly, leapingly, and so on, using fourteen different instruments. More of a wake-up than a bedtime book.

THE MAGGIE B   [140]

Written and illustrated by Irene Haas

Cloth: Margaret K. McElderry
Paper: Aladdin
Published: 1975

Margaret Barnstable has a very simple fantasy—she dreams of spending a perfect day aboard the sturdy little ship the *Maggie B,* with only her baby brother, James, for company. But because it is a fantasy, the enchanting vessel comes equipped with a top-deck farm and a peach tree, among other unusual amenities. It is very easy to substitute names of real siblings when reading the nicely cadenced text aloud.

MAKE WAY FOR DUCKLINGS   [141]

Written and illustrated by Robert McCloskey

Cloth: Viking Press
Paper: Puffin
Published: 1941   **Prizes: Caldecott Medal**

[138]

In Boston, where there is a higher order to things, a family of ducklings on their way to the Public Gardens can stop traffic. It doesn't matter a whit if these illustrations seem old-fashioned—they are endearing and firmly establish the park as an estimable place to raise a family. In fact, if you happen to visit, you might see them there today, in statue form.

MAMA DON'T ALLOW [142]

Written and illustrated by Thacher Hurd

Cloth: HarperCollins
Paper: Harper Trophy
Published: 1984

Noise, noise, noise! The Swamp Band plays loudly all night for the Alligator Ball. Lush, funny illustrations and an interesting setting for a familiar folk song. *The Pea Patch Jig* has a similar exuberance.

[142]

MAX'S FIRST WORD [143]

Written and illustrated by Rosemary Wells

Cloth: Dial
Paper: Dial
Published: 1979

Max, a lovable rabbit toddler who has a bossy and talkative older sister named Ruby, stars in an outstanding series of board books for very young children. Max is curious and quite independent. In addition to *Max's New Suit, Max's Ride,* and *Max's Toys: A Counting Book,* there is a series of four "Very First" titles covering bath, bedtime, birthday, and breakfast.

MAY I BRING A FRIEND? [144]

Written by Beatrice Schenk de Regniers
Illustrated by Beni Montresor

Cloth: Atheneum
Paper: Aladdin
Published: 1964   **Prizes: Caldecott Medal**

The king and queen keep inviting the little boy to visit, and each time, he brings along a remarkable assortment of animal friends whose manners are not what they should be.

[146]

[147]

MICE TWICE   [145]

Written and illustrated by Joseph Low

Cloth: Margaret K. McElderry
Paper: Aladdin
Published: 1980   **Prizes: Caldecott Honor**

Cat invites Mouse to dinner, planning to eat him. Mouse brings an unexpected companion, and a frenzy of competitiveness and surprises ensues, all illustrated with great wit.

MILLIONS OF CATS   [146]

Written and illustrated by Wanda Gag

Cloth: Coward
Paper: Paper Star
Published: 1928   **Prizes: Newbery Honor**

This is the story of the little old man who went to find a cat to please the little old woman and brought home hundreds of cats, thousands of cats, millions of cats. Eventually the cats fight, and only one scrawny, shy kitten is left to keep the old couple company. A classic picture book whose text can be recited by hundreds of people, thousands of people, millions and millions and millions of people. Timeless. Ageless. Always touching.

MINERVA LOUISE [147]

Written and illustrated by Janet Morgan Stoeke

Cloth: Dutton
Published: 1988

Minerva Louise is a curious, well-intentioned, very polite . . . chicken. She's also rather addled and with the best will in the world always misinterprets her surroundings. There are a quartet of books about her barnyard world, including *Minerva Louise at School, A Hat for Minerva Louise,* and *A Friend for Minerva Louise,* but the repeated joke of her misunderstanding what she sees stays fresh with her audience.

MOMMY DOESN'T KNOW MY NAME [148]

Written by Suzanne Williams
Illustrated by Andrew Shacht

Cloth: Houghton Mifflin
Paper: Houghton Mifflin
Published: 1990

Hannah's mommy's nicknames for her are meant to be sweet and affectionate. But as Hannah considers herself as a chicadee, a pumpkin, a funny monkey, and a mouse, she gets more and more worried. At the end of the day things are sweetly clarified. The illustrations capture Hannah's frustrations nicely. *But Not Billy,* an old but charming book, tells the same kind of a story about a baby.

[149]

MOMMY GO AWAY! [149]

Written by Lynne Jonell
Illustrated by Petra Mathers

Cloth: Putnam
Published: 1997

The first in a series of interesting, provocative stories. Turnabout may not be fair play in some households, but can be very helpful in others. In a rage, a little boy named Christopher shrinks his mommy and sets her adrift on a paper boat in the bathtub. In his newfound position of great power, he's rather kind, but it's a very different way

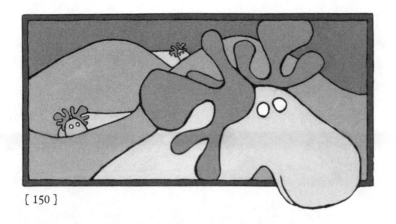

[150]

of looking at issues of temper. The illustrations are willfully child-like. The other titles are *I Need a Snake* and *It's My Birthday Too!*

MOOSES COME WALKING   [150]

Written by Arlo Guthrie
Illustrated by Alice M. Brock

Cloth: Chronicle
Paper: Chronicle
Published: 1995

The friendliest possible moose come walking up to a house and, having peered through the windows, amble away. The folksinger's text reassures the listener that the "mooses look into your window at night. . . . they think it's a zoo." Calm, silly, reassuring verse; calm, silly, reassuring illustrations—both plain and simple and very soothing.

MORE, MORE, MORE SAID THE BABY   [151]

Written and illustrated by Vera B. Williams

Cloth: Greenwillow
Paper: Mulberry
Published: 1990   **Prizes: Caldecott Honor**

Three delicious babies, the adults who adore them, and the special, tickling, tossing, teasing games they play. More, more, more. A perfect present for new grandparents as well as babies.

61

MOUSE PAINT [152]

Written and illustrated by Ellen Stoll Walsh

Cloth: Harcourt Brace
Paper: Harcourt Brace
Published: 1989

Three white mice discover three pots of paint—red, yellow, and blue—and dive in. Presto! This small book is a delightful exploration of color as the mice pitter-pat through puddles and marvel at the changes they make. The funny, cute illustrations are made from cut-paper collage. *Mouse Count* counts mice, natch.

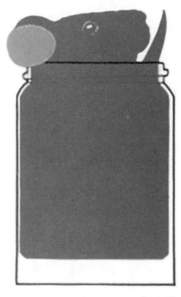

[152]

MR. AND MRS. PIG'S EVENING OUT

[153]

Written and illustrated by Mary Rayner

Cloth: Atheneum
Paper: Aladdin
Published: 1976

Mr. and Mrs. Pig don't take careful notice of the babysitter before they leave Mrs. Wolf in charge of their ten piglets. Her true nature emerges late in the evening, and she is about to make a meal of the youngest when she is routed and vanquished, only to reappear in *Garth Pig and The Ice-Cream Lady*. In *Mrs. Pig's Bulk Buy*, there is no wolf, but a lightly told moral lesson about what happens when the piglets have all they want of catsup, their favorite food, and more. There is also a collection of family stories, *Mrs. Pig Gets Cross*. These are increasingly difficult to find, but worth the effort for both the gentle humor of the stories and the charm of the watercolor illustrations.

MR. GUMPY'S OUTING [154]

Written and illustrated by John Burningham

Cloth: Henry Holt
Paper: Henry Holt
Published: 1971

Prizes: New York Times Best Illustrated Book

On a hot summer afternoon an ungainly assortment of children and animals pile into Mr. Gumpy's little boat, but of course they don't all fit—with predictable results. Another delightful book about the good fellow and his friends is *Mr. Gumpy's Motor Car*.

MR. RABBIT AND THE LOVELY PRESENT   [155]

Written by Charlotte Zolotow
Illustrated by Maurice Sendak

Cloth: HarperCollins
Paper: Harper Trophy
Published: 1962

Mr. Rabbit helps a gentle little girl gather the components of a truly lovely present for her mother. Part of the book's enduring charm is the generous context for giving in a world that has grown so very commercial even to the young.

MY GRANDSON LEW   [156]

Written by Charlotte Zolotow
Illustrated by William Pène du Bois

Cloth: HarperCollins
Paper: Harper Trophy
Published: 1974

Lew's grandfather died when he was quite small, but it turns out that Lew recalls him in vivid fragments while he and his mother talk about remembering.

[152]

MY LITTLE SISTER ATE ONE HARE
[157]

Written by Bill Grossman
Illustrated by Kevin Hawkes

Cloth: Crown
Paper: Random House
Published: 1996

Not all counting books are polite; this one is deliciously gross. That little sister just keeps eating, starting with a rabbit, until . . . you guessed it. Funny illustrations, too. Great for reading aloud with groups.

MY MAMA NEEDS ME   [158]

Written by Mildred Pitts Walter
Illustrated by Pat Cummings

Cloth: Lothrop, Lee & Shepard
Paper: Mulberry
Published: 1983

Jason wants to be a good big brother, but he is both excited and scared about the new baby coming home. Then it turns out she sleeps almost all the time, and Jason is relieved.

MY MOM TRAVELS A LOT   [159]

Written by Caroline Feller Bauer
Illustrated by Nancy Winslow Parker

Cloth: Frederick Warne
Paper: Puffin
Published: 1981   **Prizes: New York Times Best Illustrated Book**

This is a good news/bad news story familiar to all children with parents whose work requires them to travel. It is told in a bright, breezy way, because, after all, travel is a fact of life.

[162]

MY VERY FIRST MOTHER GOOSE

[160]

Written by Iona Opie
Illustrated by Rosemary Wells

Cloth: Candlewick Press
Published: 1996   **Prizes: New York Times Best Illustrated Book**

There are many fine editions of Mother Goose; this one, with just sixty-eight kindly, funny, or reassuring rhymes, is truly for the very young. Although the number of verses is modest, everything else is large and generous, including the size of the book—perfect to hold in a lap with a toddler and read aloud. The verses have been arranged to cover a day's activities from dawn to bedtime, which are acted out by an appealing and affectionate cast of people and animals. There is also *Here Comes Mother Goose.*

MYSTERIOUS THELONIOUS   [161]

Written and illustrated by Chris Raschka

Cloth: Orchard Books
Published: 1997   **Prizes: New York Times Best Illustrated Book**

A small book to hold, large in concept. The tones of the color wheel have been matched to the chromatic musical scale. Then the notes of one of the American jazz composer Thelonious Monk's most remarkable pieces, "Misterioso," have been translated into color, with watercolor illustrations of Monk himself sitting at his piano placed on top of the music, as it were. Remarkable fun, and surprisingly accessible to young children.

THE NATIVITY   [162]

Illustrated by Julie Vivas

Cloth: Harcourt Brace
Paper: Harcourt Brace
Published: 1988

Most illustrated versions of the Nativity aim for authenticity of illustration or are set in medieval or Gothic costume, reflecting the great art of those periods. In this gloriously realized, universally contemporary people's Nativity (using the King James text), the angel Gabriel wears boots and talks to the Virgin Mary over a cup

of coffee. She grows truly huge with child. And the baby, oh, the baby, he's plump and real and everything sweet the world ever saw. In these light, sandy-toned watercolors, the loose-limbed people have a slightly blurred and disheveled quality. This appealing retelling is especially accessible and plausible to very young children, but it would be difficult to outgrow its charms.

THE NIGHT BEFORE CHRISTMAS

[163]

Written by Clement C. Moore
Illustrated by Anita Lobel

Cloth: Knopf
Paper: Knopf
Published: 1984

The ultimate New York (or rather, Brooklyn, where Moore lived) edition of the Christmas verse, with illustrations set in an authentic and cozy Victorian brownstone house there with the Brooklyn Bridge in the background. There are many other editions available, from the 1912 version with illustrations by Jesse W. Smith to James Marshall's (cartoonish) and Wendy Watson and Ruth Sanderson's (country).

NIGHT DRIVING   [164]

Written by John Coy
Illustrated by Peter McCarty

Cloth: Henry Holt
Published: 1996

Although told in the present tense, this is a memory story about a drive a boy and his father took to get to the mountains in the days, or actually nights, before the interstate highway system was built. It's an ordinary night with baseball on the radio and deer in the wood. Subtle black-and-white illustrations. Peaceful and spare.

[167]

NO, DAVID! [165]

Written and illustrated by David Shannon

Cloth: Scholastic
Published: 1998   **Prizes: New York Times Best Illustrated Book**

Just how many things can David do wrong today? Let us count the
ways. The catalog of misbehavior is extensive, the demonic little
boy in stick-like drawings is having a wonderful time, the repri-
manding text says "No, David," "I said no, David!" and "That's
enough, David," but most important, at the end of the day, the
mother assures him that she loves David. *David Goes to School*
continues the mayhem.

NO NAP [166]

Written by Eve Bunting
Illustrated by Susan Meddaugh

Cloth: Clarion
Paper: Clarion
Published: 1990

Instead of taking her nap, Susie exhausts her daddy. When Mommy
comes home, the house is a mess, and guess who is asleep? A cautionary tale with winning illustrations. The demonic look in Susie's
eye when she is the center of the domestic hurricane may be familiar.

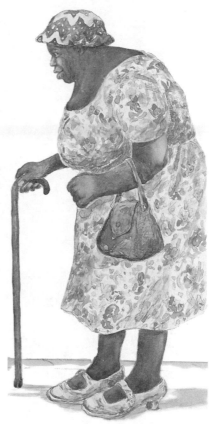

[167]

NOT SO FAST, SONGOLOLO [167]

Written and illustrated by Nicki Daly

Cloth: Margaret K. McElderry
Paper: Puffin
Published: 1986

Cheerful, detailed watercolor illustrations accompany the story of
little Malusi and his trip to the city with his granny to buy what in
South Africa are called tackies and what American children know
as sneakers. The simple everyday quality of the expedition is part of
the book's charm.

NOTHING EVER HAPPENS ON MY BLOCK   [168]

Written and illustrated by Ellen Raskin

Cloth: Atheneum
Paper: Aladdin
Published: 1966   **Prizes: New York Times Best Illustrated Book**

A jewel-like example of ironic storytelling with droll illustrations. Chester Filbert sits on his stoop complaining that nothing ever happens on his block, while all around him there is mystery, excitement, and adventure—witches, fires, robbery, mayhem. All ages find it fresh and funny. The trick in reading it aloud is "reading" everything that is happening as well as the text.

[169]

NUTSHELL LIBRARY   [169]

Written and illustrated by Maurice Sendak

Cloth: HarperCollins
Published: 1962

These four little books—*Alligators All Around: An Alphabet; Chicken Soup with Rice: A Book of Months; One Was Johnny: A Counting Book;* and *Pierre: A Cautionary Tale in Five Chapters and a Prologue*—come in a small box, fit in small hands, and are memorable both separately and together. In addition, they are the source of the lyrics to many of the best, catchiest songs in *Really Rosie,* the TV special/video/play, with music by Carole King. Everyone can sing along. Avoid the new large-size edition.

OLD BLACK FLY   [170]

Written by Jim Aylesworth
Illustrated by Stephen Gammell

Cloth: Henry Holt
Published: 1992

Inside the text to this meditation on just how much chaos a black fly can cause in the summer are highlighted capital letters that spell out the alphabet. That's all fine, but it's much more fun to search for the red-eyed fly in the funny illustrations.

OLD MOTHER HUBBARD   [171]

Written and illustrated by David A. Johnson

Cloth: Margaret K. McElderry
Published: 1998

In this version of the traditional rhyme about the doting dog owner, Old Mother Hubbard is a roly-poly Victorian lady and he's a flop-eared mutt. It's all very delicate but funny. Other editions include *Old Mother Hubbard and Her Wonderful Dog,* illustrated by James Marshall, and *The Comic Adventures of Old Mother Hubbard and Her Dog,* illustrated by Tomie di Paola.

ON MARKET STREET   [172]

Written by Arnold Lobel
Illustrated by Anita Lobel

Cloth: Greenwillow
Paper: Mulberry
Published: 1981   **Prizes: New York Times Best Illustrated Book**

In this unusual and lavish alphabet book, a boy goes down Market Street buying presents for a friend, beginning with each letter of the alphabet. The letters are figures made of apples, quilts, wigs, and so on.

ONCE A MOUSE...   [173]

Written and illustrated by Marcia Brown

Cloth: Scribner
Paper: Aladdin
Published: 1961   **Prizes: Caldecott Medal**

A reconsideration of magic in a successful picture book. The story comes from an Indian folktale and tells how a hermit transforms a mouse successively into a cat, a dog, a tiger. But the tiger is so proud the hermit pauses. Hmmm. Woodcut illustrations.

[165]

ONE FINE DAY [174]

Written and illustrated by Nonny Hogrogian

Cloth: Macmillan
Paper: Aladdin
Published: 1971   **Prizes: Caldecott Medal**

In this wittily illustrated Armenian folktale, a sly fox steals milk from an old woman. She gets her revenge on his tail, and he must do elaborate penance before she will sew it on again.

ONE FISH TWO FISH RED FISH BLUE FISH [175]

Written and illustrated by Dr. Seuss

Cloth: Random House (Beginner Books)
Published: 1960

Designed as an early reader using rhyme and very limited vocabulary, this collection of verses about Seussian creatures at play and rest is wildly successful with toddlers and younger children, and remains endurable to the reading adults who recite it night after night.

[175]

ONE GORILLA: A COUNTING BOOK [176]

Written and illustrated by Atsuko Morozumi

Cloth: Farrar, Straus & Giroux
Paper: Sunburst
Published: 1990   **Prizes: New York Times Best Illustrated Book**

A smiling gorilla wanders through house, garden, jungle, woods, storm, and sea, blissfully counting and being counted till the numbers equal ten. The illustrations are delicate and filled with detail. *My Friend Gorilla* isn't a sequel, but rather a companion volume about the same sweet ape.

[175]

ONE MONDAY MORNING [177]

Written and illustrated by Uri Shulevitz

Cloth: Scribner
Paper: Aladdin
Published: 1967

In this fine urban fantasy, a little boy who lives in an old apartment building in a downtown somewhere imagines that the king and queen are coming to visit him. But since he's very busy, he misses them on each return visit. Meanwhile their retinue grows, so that while the text remains disarmingly simple, the illustrations grow increasingly complex.

OUR ANIMAL FRIENDS AT MAPLE HILL FARM [178]

Written and illustrated by Alice and Martin Provensen

Cloth: Random House
Published: 1974

The animals who live at the authors' Maple Hill Farm in New York State—the cats, dogs, sheep, goats, horses, children, and others—all have whimsical names (the cats are Eggnog, Willow, and Gooseberry) but the owners are matter-of-fact about their behavior and witty about their foibles. This splendid book, which is very appealing to toddlers and preschoolers for all the information it contains as well as the beguiling illustrations, was out of print for a while. A 1992 reissue is worth finding.

OUR GRANNY [179]

Written by Margaret Wild
Illustrated by Julie Vivas

Cloth: Ticknor & Fields
Paper: Clarion
Published: 1994

Two preschoolers tell about their beloved granny, who has a wobbly bottom, wears a funny bathing suit, marches in political demonstrations, and best of all, lives with them. There's a generosity of discussion here about "some grannies"—where they live, what they do, what they are like—that includes many possibilities. The funny, fuzzy watercolor illustrations are wonderfully affectionate. Good for starting conversations.

OVER THE MOON [180]

Written by Rachel Vail
Illustrated by Scott Nash

Cloth: Orchard Books
Published: 1998

This is quite literally a play on the nursery rhyme, a backstage drama of personality and conflict, and an explication of prepositions. In her first three tries, the Mother Goose cow jumps under, next to, and through the moon. The monkey writer-director, Hiram Diddle Diddle, is very possessive of his theatrical property. Other members of the cast and crew include a cat with a Stradivarius, a dachshund, and, of course, a dish and spoon. *Moonstruck: The True Story of the Cow Who Jumped Over the Moon* is another funny interpretation of the basic rhyme.

OVER THE MOON: AN ADOPTION TALE [181]

Written and illustrated by Karen Katz

Cloth: Henry Holt
Published: 1997

A bedtime story told by an adoring adoptive mother to a beloved child: Not so long ago, she says, the parents traveled to meet a new baby in a faraway place. The collage, gouache, and pencil illustrations are detailed and brightly colored. The message is one of renewed delight.

[184]

OWLY [182]

Written by Mike Thaler
Illustrated by David Wiesner

Cloth: HarperCollins/Walker
Paper: Walker
Published: 1982

One of the classic stories about children trying to define maternal devotion and the structure of the universe. Owly keeps asking his mother questions about the nature and shape of the world, and she wisely suggests that he seek answers for himself. The illustrations are in the pale colors of predawn, which is, after all, Owly's bedtime. Parental love is enabling, not possessive, in this very quiet bedtime story.

PAT THE BUNNY [183]

Written and illustrated by Dorothy Kunhardt

Cloth: Golden/Western
Published: 1940

The original baby's activity book—pat the bunny, feel Daddy's scratchy face, look in the mirror, put your finger through Mummy's ring. Some babies love it and eat several copies before they have even learned to walk. Be reassured that others could care less, and it is not a litmus test of future taste either way.

PETE'S A PIZZA [184]

Written and illustrated by William Steig

Cloth: HarperCollins
Published: 1998

The best recipe for curing a sulk might just well be turning the sulker, in this case a boy named Pete, into a pizza, using the kitchen table, some talcum powder flour, and red checker tomatoes, then baking on the couch till good humor is restored. This book is a cousin to Steig's other therapeutic masterwork, *Spinky Sulks*.

POLAR BEAR, POLAR BEAR, WHAT DO YOU HEAR? [185]

Written by Bill Martin, Jr.
Illustrated by Eric Carle

Cloth: Henry Holt
Published: 1991

The illustrations are dazzling collages of zoo animals and the text is a variation on *Brown Bear, Brown Bear;* all those noises—snorts, hoots, roars—just wait to be shouted out.

POOKINS GETS HER WAY [186]

Written by Helen Lester
Illustrated by Lynn Munsinger

Cloth: Houghton Mifflin
Paper: Houghton Mifflin
Published: 1987

Pookins is spoiled rotten, and by golly, today she wants to be a flower. She gets her way, but learns a lesson about cooperation. The author and illustrator have produced a group of funny/wise picture books that make small but important lessons lightly. Other titles include *A Porcupine Named Fluffy* and *It Wasn't My Fault. Tacky the Penguin* is also fine.

POSSUM COME A-KNOCKIN' [187]

Written by Nancy Van Laan
Illustrated by George Booth

Cloth: Knopf
Paper: Knopf
Published: 1990

The folks are inside doing more or less ordinary things and then this possum in a top hat and vest comes to the back door. The reader is somewhere outside looking at the mayhem that ensues as the cat and dog rouse the household. Manic illustrations. The cumulative rhyme is in an easy-to-read dialect.

[188]

RACHEL FISTER'S BLISTER [188]

Written by Amy McDonald
Illustrated by Marjorie Priceman

Cloth: Houghton Mifflin
Paper: Houghton Mifflin
Published: 1990

If you are going to start with a silly rhyme—say, one that begins "Rachel Fister found a blister on her little left-hand toe"—it needs to get sillier and sillier till Queen Alice decrees, in advice "quite precise," the proper cure: a mother's kiss. The illustrations are properly ebullient.

THE RAINBOW FISH [189]

Written and illustrated by Marcus Pfister

Cloth: North-South
Paper: North-South
Published: 1992

This story of the most beautiful fish in the sea learning that beauty is not the key to friendship, with its distinctive pastel sparkling cover, is popular around the world. It comes in many editions and forms, including a board book.

RAINY MORNING [190]

Written by Daniel Pinkwater
Illustrated by Jill Pinkwater

Cloth: Atheneum
Published: 1999

There's nothing quite as funny as an old joke told well. Mr. and Mrs. Submarine are sitting at the breakfast table one wet morning when a soaking cat appears at the window. They offer a corn muffin and a place by the fire, little knowing that soon a dog, a horse, crows, lots more animals, even Ludwig van Beethoven and the United States Marine Band will squeeze into the kitchen to dry off. Hilarious.

[194]

READ-ALOUD RHYMES FOR THE VERY YOUNG [191]

Written by Jack Prelutsky
Illustrated by Marc Brown

Cloth: Knopf
Published: 1986

A fine, brightly illustrated collection of more than 200 rhymes, mostly familiar, ideal for reading aloud to young children. An introduction by Jim Trelease emphasizes the importance of reading aloud.

THE RED BALLOON [192]

Written and illustrated by Albert Lamorisse

Cloth: Doubleday
Paper: Zephyr
Published: 1957   **Prizes: New York Times Best Illustrated Book**

It's Paris just a shiver of time back in the past. This book, like the film on which it is based, captures the adventures of a little boy and his best friend, a glorious red balloon that follows him everywhere. An enduring favorite, illustrated with color photographs from the film.

RED-EYED TREE FROG [193]

Written by Joy Cowley
Illustrated by Nic Bishop

Cloth: Scholastic
Published: 1999

The red-eyed tree frog who hunts for food in the Central American rain forests is nocturnal, so the day begins at dusk and ends at dawn. Stunning, close-up photographs (the more startling for having been taken at night) make this an unusually interesting science book for readers of all ages.

THE RELATIVES CAME [194]

Written by Cynthia Rylant
Illustrated by Stephen Gammell

Cloth: Bradbury
Paper: Aladdin
Published: 1985

**Prizes: Caldecott Honor
New York Times Best Illustrated Book**

One summer, a whole slew of relatives gets up before dawn to come on down and visit. They crowd the house, create the happiest kind of chaos and commotion, but eventually have to leave. The spiky illustrations capture the homey confusion and delight of a childhood event that memory does not blur. A real charmer.

RICHARD SCARRY'S BEST WORD BOOK EVER [195]

Written and illustrated by Richard Scarry

Cloth: Golden/Western
Published: 1963

Most adults find this book unappealing. The pages are crowded with details, jumbles of jokes, and anthropomorphized creatures like Lowly Worm involved in running gags. But they are adults. Children, especially toddlers and preschoolers, consider it almost

[187]

endlessly interesting, full of things to label, activities to imagine, and jokes to savor again and again on a scale that seems somehow intelligible. If you remember it from your own childhood and think the present edition is slimmer, you are right—it has been abridged. There are dozens of books about Lowly and Huck and the other characters learning about and how to do all sorts of things.

RICHARD SCARRY'S WHAT DO PEOPLE DO ALL DAY? [196]

Written and illustrated by Richard Scarry

Cloth: Random House
Published: 1968

Well, what *do* people do? Here, in typical Scarry fashion (i.e., very busy pictures featuring many of his regular cast of animals), is a series of stories about building houses, baking bread, laying roads, going on a train or a boat, and more. Preschoolers can pore over the pages for hours, and many's the adult who has been intrigued at the clarity of the explanations. The present edition is abridged, alas.

ROAR AND MORE [197]

Written and illustrated by Karla Kuskin

Cloth: HarperCollins
Paper: Harper Trophy
Published: 1956; reissued 1990

The full-color edition of this delightful standard title for the very young is increasingly difficult to find, but worthwhile. The short, funny verses about animals are enhanced by the amusing typographical representation of their sounds.

THE ROOSTER'S GIFT [198]

Written by Pam Conrad
Illustrated by Eric Beddows

Cloth: HarperCollins
Published: 1995

Young rooster feels that he has the gift of making the sun rise every morning. But then one day he oversleeps and the sun comes up anyway. His youngest sister is his consolation, and ultimately he learns that heralding the sun and doing it well is a gift, too. Plump, jolly illustrations. Another hyperactive rooster in a beautifully illustrated book is *That Kookory!* by Margaret Walden Froehlich.

ROSIE'S WALK [199]

Written and illustrated by Pat Hutchins

Cloth: Macmillan
Paper: Aladdin
Published: 1968

Rosie the hen goes for a stroll around the barnyard, oblivious to the fox, who keeps botching his attempts to catch her. If the jokes are all telegraphed to the adult eye, that doesn't make them a whit less funny to toddlers and preschoolers. Fine stylized illustrations.

[200]

ROTTEN RALPH [200]

Written by Jack Gantos
Illustrated by Nicole Rubel

Cloth: Houghton Mifflin
Paper: Houghton Mifflin
Published: 1976

This is the first of a series of books about a very naughty cat named Ralph. Sarah, his owner, can never believe how badly he behaves, but oh, the reader can. The illustrations are distinctive and offbeat, featuring strong lines and bright colors. Ralph's name shows up in all the other titles.

[198]

RUBY [201]

Written and illustrated by Michael Emberley

Cloth: Little, Brown
Published: 1990

Just because *Little Red Riding Hood* is conventionally set in a deep wood doesn't mean it has to be so. In this big city version, Ruby is a little mouse with a red cloak who sets off across Boston to deliver some triple-cheese pies to her granny. On her way to Beacon Hill she encounters an unsavory reptilian street type and a suspicious cat. Very clever in every way. Wonderful to read aloud.

THE RUNAWAY BUNNY [202]

Written by Margaret Wise Brown
Illustrated by Clement Hurd

Cloth: HarperCollins
Paper: Harper Trophy
Published: 1972

The little bunny plays a pretend game of hide-and-seek and is comforted to realize that his mother will always know how to find him wherever he hides. The illustrations are lovely and lush; young children love spotting the bunny in the garden, on the mountain, at the circus. Some grown-ups think the mother's absolute authority is smothering and prefer other, more reassuring measurements of how much a mother loves her child.

[203]

SHEEP IN A JEEP [203]

Written by Nancy Shaw
Illustrated by Margot Apple

Cloth: Houghton Mifflin
Paper: Houghton Mifflin
Published: 1986

What a ride! On a bright, sunny day a flock of sheep set off for a ride in a jeep. The short (83 words), chantable text is great fun for toddlers and preschoolers in particular. The equally delightful, but definitely difficult to speak, series includes *Sheep on a Ship* and *Sheep in a Shop* and on to *Sheep Out to Eat* and *Sheep Take a Hike*.

[201]

SHY CHARLES   [204]

Written and illustrated by Rosemary Wells

Cloth: Dial
Paper: Pied Piper
Published: 1988

It happens that Charles is perfectly happy playing by himself, and social contacts are an endless ordeal. The little mouse can't or won't say thank you in public places, can't or won't cope with dancing lessons or football. But when the babysitter falls down the stairs, Charles is able to comfort her and call for help on the telephone before resuming his shy silence. A nicely told fable as helpful for their parents as for shy children in need of respect. *Edward the Unready* is another fellow who just isn't ready for deep water, overnights, or school, and is therefore a reassuring friend indeed.

SNOW   [205]

Written by Uri Shulevitz

Cloth: Farrar, Straus & Giroux
Published: 1998   **Prizes: Caldecott Honor**

On a gray day in a dreary town perhaps long ago, only a boy and his dog believe that it's really going to snow. But it does, and it's a magical snowfall, bringing wonder and, surprisingly, wit, when some real magic springs from a bookstore. The book is a companion to other snow stories, of course, but also to Shulevitz's other meditation on the magic in nature, *Dawn*.

SNOW BEAR   [206]

Written by Jean Craighead George
Illustrated by Wendell Minor

Cloth: Hyperion
Published: 1999

A child and a bear go out to play—not one morning in Maine, but one rosy day in the frozen Arctic. The youngsters, whose guardians keep their watchful distance, have a wonderful time. There is a looming threat when a giant polar bear appears, but nothing happens, so it is a perfect, peaceful adventure.

THE SNOWY DAY   [207]

Written and illustrated by Ezra Jack Keats

Cloth: Viking Press
Paper: Puffin
Published: 1962   **Prizes: Caldecott Medal**

One snowy day a little black boy named Peter puts on his red snowsuit and explores his city neighborhood. The brightly colored collage illustrations have an undiminished freshness . . . like new-fallen snow itself. Peter also appears in *Goggles, A Letter to Amy, Peter's Chair,* and the delightful *Whistle for Willie.*

[210]

SO SAY THE LITTLE MONKEYS   [208]

Written by Nancy Van Laan
Illustrated by Yumi Heo

Cloth: Atheneum
Published: 1998

A fine read-aloud story about the tiny blackmouth monkeys who live along the Rio Negro river in Brazil, jabbering away all day long. "Jibba jibba jabba," they say, and never get around to making a dry nest or taking care of themselves in any other way, so when the rain comes, "plinka plinka," or the wind or the jaguar, they huddle together high in the trees.

SPLASH!   [209]

Written and illustrated by Ann Jonas

Cloth: Greenwillow
Paper: Mulberry
Published: 1995

What looks like an amusing summer storybook is, in truth, addition and subtraction for preschoolers disguised as pure entertainment. The narrator has a backyard pond with turtles, catfish, frogs, and goldfish. Her cat and dog squabble and various creatures fall in and jump out. Everyone gets wet. Keep counting.

STELLA & ROY   [210]

Written and illustrated by Ashley Wolff

Cloth: Dutton
Published: 1993

Stella has almost outgrown her blue-wheeled tricycle, and she zooms ahead while little Roy just coasts along on his small four-

wheeler. Who reaches the popcorn stand first? Remember the tortoise and the hare, then guess. *Stella & Roy Go Camping* is another small adventure. The woodcut illustrations are bright and cheery as are the children.

STELLALUNA [211]

Written and illustrated by Janell Cannon

Cloth: Harcourt Brace
Paper: Harcourt Brace
Published: 1993

The adventures of the little baby bat who finds herself in a bird's nest are endearing, and children identify with the pale upside-down creature. The book comes in several editions and there are toy products available as well.

THE STORY OF LITTLE BABAJI [212]

Written by Helen Bannerman
Illustrated by Fred Marcellino

Cloth: HarperCollins
Published: 1996

An Englishwoman living in India wrote *The Story of Little Black Sambo* in 1898 to amuse her children. It was published soon after and was a worldwide success until it was charged with racism and

[212]

went out of print. This enchanting version, firmly setting the story of a little boy, his finery, a greedy tiger, and a supper of 169 pancakes and butter, in India, is small to hold and echoes the pace of the Bannerman original. Julius Lester transplanted the story to the American South, and his version, *Sam and the Tigers,* was lavishly illustrated by Jerry Pinkney.

WAKE UP, SUN! [213]

Written by David L. Harrison
Illustrated by Hans Wilhelm

Cloth: Random House
Published: 1986

[214]

This entertaining early reader is about a silly dog who wakes up in the middle of the night, can't find the sun, and then wakes up his friends to help him find it.

SWIMMY [214]

Written and illustrated by Leo Lionni

Cloth: Pantheon
Paper: Knopf
Published: 1963   **Prizes: New York Times Best Illustrated Book**

Little Swimmy is alone in the sea. The rest of his school was swallowed by a tuna, but he figures out a camouflage plan for survival. It is a delightful tale of ingenuity and leadership told with minimal text and elegant collage illustrations.

THE TALE OF PETER RABBIT [215]

Written and illustrated by Beatrix Potter

Cloth: Frederick Warne
Paper: Frederick Warne
Published: 1902

Flopsy, Mopsy, and Cottontail are good little bunnies, but Peter disobeys and goes to Mr. MacGregor's garden, with nearly disastrous consequences. One of the best-known and best-loved stories for children, *Peter Rabbit* is dramatic, exciting, and complete all on a very small scale. The watercolor illustrations are exquisite. The original Warne editions, with their smooth paper and trim green

[211]

binding, small enough to hold in the hand, were rephotographed and reissued in 1987 and are as readily available and inexpensive as, and far nicer than, any others. But others abound. There are all sorts of auxiliary books and merchandise as well: coloring books, cutout versions, pop-up books, etc. Some are well done, others sloppy and exploitative; choose carefully among them. Peter's immediate relative is, of course, *The Tale of Benjamin Bunny*, but some of the other books in the canon are *The Tale of Squirrel Nutkin*, *The Tale of Mrs. Tiggy-Winkle*, *The Tale of Tom Kitten*, and *The Tale of Jemima Puddle-Duck*.

THE TEENY-TINY WOMAN: A GHOST STORY [216]

Written and illustrated by Paul Galdone

Cloth: Houghton Mifflin
Paper: Clarion
Published: 1984

The teeny-tiny woman hides the teeny-tiny bone she finds in the teeny-tiny churchyard. A slightly scary and mostly funny old English ghost story, retold with enthusiasm. Other versions have been illustrated by Tomie dePaola and Jane O'Conner.

TELL ME AGAIN ABOUT THE NIGHT I WAS BORN [217]

Written by Jamie Lee Curtis
Illustrated by Laura Cornell

Cloth: HarperCollins
Paper: Harper Trophy
Published: 1996

Tell me, tell me, and with no coaching at all our narrator breathlessly tells her parents the whole story she knows so well of her birth and adoption, about how they went to where she was born and brought her back. Every nugget of information begins with her asking them to tell her. Charming illustrations. The narrator bears a close resemblance to the narrator in the same collaborators' book *When I Was Little: A Four-Year-Old's Memoir of Her Youth*.

[215]

TEN LITTLE RABBITS   [218]

Written by Virginia Grossman
Illustrated by Sylvia Long

Cloth: Chronicle
Published: 1991

The rabbits who inhabit this imaginative counting book illustrate, in their garb and in their behavior, cultural aspects of Native American tribes, including the Sioux, Tewa, Blackfoot, and Nez Percé. The illustrator's distinctive style extends to other animals and is charmingly displayed in *Sylvia Long's Mother Goose*.

TEN, NINE, EIGHT   [219]

Written and illustrated by Molly Bang

Cloth: Greenwillow
Paper: Tupelo Books
Published: 1983   **Prizes: Caldecott Honor**

This is both a bedtime and a counting book. The story, told in lush and soothing illustrations, is about the bedtime rituals of one little girl and her father, and comes in various editions, including a board book.

[218]

TERRIBLE TERESA AND OTHER VERY SHORT STORIES   [220]

Written and illustrated by Mittie Cuetara

Cloth: Dutton
Published: 1997

A sharply imagined collection of fourteen four-line rhyming anecdotes whose funny titles convey the plots, such as they are: "Baby Light-Fingers" "The keys are gone—oh please/Won't you tell us where they are?" or the title verse "Did you make the baby wail?/Did you leave a sticky trail?/Did you pull the kitty's tail?" A companion volume of sorts is *Crazy Crawler Crane: And Other Very Short Truck Stories.*

[220]

THERE WAS AN OLD LADY WHO SWALLOWED A FLY   [221]

Written and illustrated by Simms Taback

Cloth: Viking Press
Paper: Puffin
Published: 1997

**Prizes: Caldecott Honor
New York Times Best Illustrated Book**

A particularly clever and brightly illustrated setting of the folk song about that silly old woman who kept on swallowing larger and larger things until eventually she swallowed a horse. She died, of course. This version has die-cut holes in the illustrations allowing you to see through to the fly, spider, bird, and so on as she gulps, looking one way, and flipping back, to see the accumulating creatures. Glen Rounds has done a manic alternative version, almost scary for the very youngest, irresistible to school-age and older readers. It features a demonic and possibly demented fly that gets larger and loonier with each turning page. Nadine Bernard Wescott has illustrated a more charming version.

[220]

Woody's cowboy band, Pampa, Texas

[224]

THERE'S A DRAGON IN MY SLEEPING BAG   [222]

Written by James Howe
Illustrated by David S. Rose

Cloth: Atheneum
Paper: Aladdin
Published: 1994

Simon explains to his little brother, Alex, that Dexter, a dragon, is in his sleeping bag, so Alex better sleep somewhere else. Not to be done out of fun or companionship, Alex soon finds an imaginary friend, too, a camel. Wonderfully solemn illustrations capture the well-told sibling rivalry.

THIS IS BETSY   [223]

Written and illustrated by Gunilla Wolde

Cloth: Random House
Published: 1982

Small, bright books about an engaging preschooler's ordinary experiences. Titles in the series include *Betsy's Baby Brother, Betsy's First Day at Nursery School, Betsy and the Doctor,* as well as *Betsy's First Day at Day Care* and *Betsy and the Chicken Pox.* The illustrations are simple and appealing. Check with a library for titles in paperback.

[221]

THIS LAND IS YOUR LAND [224]

Written by Woody Guthrie
Illustrated by Kathy Jakobsen

Cloth: Little, Brown
Published: 1998

The music and all the verses to the song everyone knows are set out in a kind of picture album that tells the story of Woody Guthrie and the country he saw while hitchhiking around America in 1940. The complex illustrations—miniature panoramas including those deserts, redwood forests, and the New York skyline—reward close examination, and the song goes on forever.

THREE COOL KIDS [225]

Written and illustrated by Rebecca Emberley

Cloth: Little, Brown
Paper: Little, Brown
Published: 1995

The Billy Goats Gruff have moved to town, and in the inner city a sewer rat blocks their passage to the grassy green lot across the street. The paper collage illustrations are delightful—Little, the smallest goat, has red sneakers with purple laces. Another variation on the story is *Hey, Pipsqueak!* by Kate McMullen, in which a troll is blocking Jack from getting to a party.

THE THREE LITTLE PIGS [226]

Written and illustrated by Margot Zemach

Cloth: Farrar, Straus & Giroux
Paper: Aladdin
Published: 1988

[225]

In this pretty and amusing version of the familiar story, the wolf wears a frock coat while the pigs are downright ragtag. There are, of course, many other editions, including an exuberant one by Paul Galdone, a roisterous slapstick one by James Marshall, and one by William G. Hooks, in which the clever pig is a female. The deconstructed truth has been revealed in *The True Story of the Three Little Pigs* and in *The Three Little Wolves and the Big Bad Pig.*

THROUGH MOON AND STARS AND NIGHT SKIES [227]

Written by Ann Warren Turner
Illustrated by James Graham Hale

Cloth: HarperCollins
Paper: Harper Trophy
Published: 1990

[228]

Every child loves his or her birth or arrival story. The family of this adopted Asian child retell the story of his arrival on a huge plane that came through the night sky. He found parents, house, red dog, and quilt waiting. The prose is lyric, the tone universally reassuring.

THY FRIEND OBADIAH [228]

Written and illustrated by Brinton Turkle

Cloth: Viking Press
Paper: Puffin
Published: 1969   **Prizes: Caldecott Honor**

One of a number of books about the Starbuck family of Nantucket, nineteenth-century Quakers, featuring Obadiah and his sister, Rachel. The illustrations are full of period detail that are easy to discuss. The others are *Rachel and Obadiah, Obadiah the Bold,* and *The Adventures of Obadiah.*

TIKKI TIKKI TEMBO [229]

Written by Arlene Mosel
Illustrated by Blair Lent

Cloth: Henry Holt
Paper: Henry Holt
Published: 1968

This story about how Chinese children came to have short names has been chanted by generations of nursery-school children. Help can be summoned for brother Chang, but for Tikki Tikki Tembo, it's more problematic. Teenagers and adults, too, remember and find themselves absently mumbling that wonderful rolling name: "Tikki Tikki Tembo No Sa Rembo Chari Bari Ruchi Pip Peri Pembo."

TIME FOR BED   [230]

Written by Mem Fox
Illustrated by Jane Dyer

Cloth: Harcourt Brace
Paper: Harcourt Brace
Published: 1993

Charming bedtime verses, perfect for reading aloud, set on pages of lush, complex illustrations of various mothers and children including mice, cats, cows, sheep, deer, dogs, birds, and geese—even honeybees.

TIME TO SLEEP   [231]

Written and illustrated by Denise Fleming

Cloth: Henry Holt
Published: 1997

Bear sniffs the air and smells winter, but before going to sleep, he tells Snail. The word is passed from one creature to another as animals and insects settle down to hibernate . . . snail to skunk to turtle to woodchuck to ladybug, who wakes Bear to remind him to go to sleep. The mottled autumnal illustrations darken gently.

[234]

TODAY I FEEL SILLY: & OTHER MOODS THAT MAKE MY DAY [232]

Written by Jamie Lee Curtis
Illustrated by Laura Cornell

Cloth: HarperCollins
Paper: Harper Trophy
Published: 1998

[233]

The narrator races through a total of thirteen of her moods, but the reader suspects there may be many more. She's breathless and busy and quite engaging, and there's a mood wheel at the end for youngsters to plot some of their own mood swings. Engaging watercolor illustrations.

TOWN MOUSE, COUNTRY MOUSE

[233]

Written and illustrated by Jan Brett

Cloth: Putnam
Published: 1994

The best-known story of trading places is lushly depicted in this pretty, old-fashioned edition. The artist uses borders and side panels (her signature style) to give a humorous commentary on the mice's enemies, a cat and an owl. Lap listeners love the combined effect. Other pretty versions include those illustrated by Helen Craig, Janet Stevens, Lorinda Bryan Cauley, and Paul Galdone. *Milly and Tilly: The Story of a Town Mouse and a Country Mouse*, illustrated by Kate Summers, is another variation.

TUESDAY [234]

Written and illustrated by David Wiesner

Cloth: Clarion
Published: 1991   **Prizes: Caldecott Medal**

It's as though the author caught the fragment of a weird dream of floating frogs, and on waking followed his dream with elegant draftsmanship. Then the story was born: one Tuesday evening at moonrise, myriad amphibians perched on lily pads rise out of the swamp and fly into an ordinary suburban neighborhood.

THE TWELVE DAYS OF CHRISTMAS

[235]

Written and illustrated by Jan Brett

Cloth: Putnam
Paper: Paper Star
Published: 1986

This version of the Christmas carol is bright and gay, with jewel-like, detailed illustrations embellished with the artist's characteristic style of folk-art borders and embroidery-like patterns. There are other editions, including a mysteriously romantic one by Louise Brierley, Robert Sabuda's amazing pop-up version, and *Emma's Christmas,* which is an amusing variation.

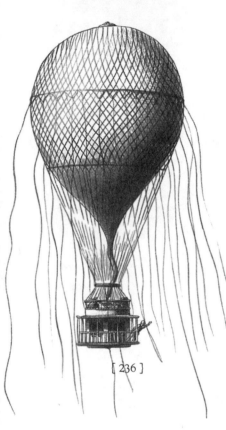

[236]

THE TWENTY-ONE BALLOONS   [236]

Written and illustrated by William Pène du Bois

Cloth: Viking Press
Paper: Puffin
Published: 1947   **Prizes: Newbery Medal**

Here is a wonderfully illustrated account of what happens when Professor William Waterman Sherman is found in the middle of the ocean with what is left of twenty-one balloons. This delightful fantasy continues to appeal.

TWO WAYS TO COUNT TO TEN: A LIBERIAN FOLKTALE   [237]

Written by Ruby Dee
Illustrated by Susan Meddaugh

Cloth: Henry Holt
Paper: Henry Holt
Published: 1988

In this African folktale, the jungle beasts learn to count, all right, but more important, they learn, once again, that being strong is not the same as being smart. Witty illustrations.

VERA'S FIRST DAY OF SCHOOL [238]

Written and illustrated by Vera Rosenberry

Cloth: Henry Holt
Published: 1999

Vera is *so* excited about going to school she wakes up before anyone else, but somehow, when her older sisters run off and leave her
alone on the playground, she panics and runs home. Her mother
finds her and everything ends well, of course. Vera is also the star
of *When Vera Was Sick,* another small drama.

THE VERY HUNGRY CATERPILLAR

[239]

Written and illustrated by Eric Carle

Cloth: Philomel
Paper: Philomel
Published: 1969

The very hungry caterpillar eats his way through his life cycle and
the cutout pages of this classic picture book until he becomes a butterfly. If you are going to buy it, this is a book to have in the original hardback edition, with its large format and stiff pages, because
little fingers need to poke through the holes in the apple, pear,
strawberry, and other edibles. The miniature paperback edition just
isn't strong enough or large enough. *The Very Busy Spider* is suited
to seeing-impaired children.

VOYAGE TO THE BUNNY PLANET [240]

Written and illustrated by Rosemary Wells

Cloth: Dial
Paper: Dial
Published: 1992

[240]

If it's been just an awful day, what you really need is a trip to the
Bunny Planet where you can have "the day that should have been."
There are three books in the series (and a boxed-set edition), and the
titles give a clue to the solace that is to be found in the delightful
fantasy: *First Tomato, Island Light,* and *Moss Pillow.*

WASHDAY ON NOAH'S ARK   [241]

Written and illustrated by Glen Rounds

Cloth: Holiday House
Paper: Holiday House
Published: 1985

If you stop to think about it, the question of how they did the washing on Noah's Ark is a reasonable one. The answer proposed here, which involves a living laundry line, is hilarious, as are the illustrations.

WATCH WILLIAM WALK   [242]

Written and illustrated by Ann Jonas

Cloth: Greenwillow
Published: 1997

Every word in this alliterative story begins with W: the boy, William; his friend Wilma; the dog, Wally; the duck, Wanda. They walk, waddle, and wade, and what is more, their adventures are seen from directly above, as though from the perspective of, say, a giant. Great fun.

[245]

WAVING: A COUNTING BOOK   [243]

Written and illustrated by Peter Sis

Cloth: Greenwillow
Published: 1988

There is so much friendly activity in this delightful urban counting book. The action begins as Mary and her mother wave at "1 taxi." Then "2 bicyclists waved back at her" and "3 boys walking dogs waved at the bicyclists." Soon the streets are full of people, not to mention the interesting neighborhood buildings and things to look at and talk about in addition to the accumulating numbers. In *Beach Ball,* Mary runs off after a striped ball and her mother follows her through illustrations that convey concepts including number, alphabet, size. There's even a maze.

[244]

WE WERE TIRED OF LIVING IN A HOUSE [244]

Written by Liesel Moak Skorpen
Illustrated by Joe Cepeda

Cloth: Putnam
Published: 1999

Three children, two little boys and their older sister, are "tired of living in a house" so they pack up what they need—sweaters, socks, mittens—and set off. They try out delightful locations—a tree a pond, a cave, the seaside—and enjoy the special pleasures of each, collecting treasures along the way. Eventually, this being an entirely happy fantasy, they go back to live in the house. The jaunty illustrations of the intrepid children parading around with their accumulating baggage are very cute.

WE'RE GOING ON A BEAR HUNT [245]

Written by Michael Rosen
Illustrated by Helen Oxenbury

Cloth: Margaret K. McElderry
Paper: Scott Foresman & Co.
Published: 1989

The whole family sets out, but catching a bear isn't like going to the corner for a quart of milk. Oh, no! Slog through grass, mud, snow, forest, river, on to the cave, and then—whoops!—rush back home again.

[245]

THE WEDDING PROCESSION OF THE RAG DOLL AND THE BROOM HANDLE AND WHO WAS IN IT [246]

Written by Carl Sandburg
Illustrated by Harriet Pincus

Cloth: Harcourt Brace
Paper: Voyager
Published: 1967

A glorious setting for an excerpt from the Rootabaga Stories about a fine procession that includes Spoon Lickers, Dirty Bibs, Musical Soup Eaters, and others. The angular illustrations are eccentric and funny. Perfect for bedtime reading aloud together.

WENDY WATSON'S MOTHER GOOSE [247]

Written and illustrated by Wendy Watson

Cloth: Lothrop, Lee & Shepard
Published: 1990

The verses are so familiar, an artist has great freedom in organizing a setting for the rhymes we call Mother Goose. This selection is placed in cozy New England: pretty towns, pleasant woods, chubby folks in comfortable houses. Lots of snow.

WHATEVER HAPPENED TO THE DINOSAURS? [248]

Written and illustrated by Bernard Most

Cloth: Harcourt Brace
Paper: Voyager
Published: 1978

Some possible, and some impossible, answers to a very commonly asked question. The illustrations, which put the great lizards in improbable settings—like pirate ships and large cities—are bright and amusing. The companion title is *If the Dinosaurs Come Back*.

[250]

THE WHEELS ON THE BUS [249]

Illustrated by Paul O. Zelinsky

Cloth: Dutton
Published: 1990

Okay, let's just all sing together as we turn the pages and follow the folks on and off as the bus goes on its rounds. It's not as though we don't know the song, is it?

[252]

WHEN SOPHIE GETS ANGRY— REALLY, REALLY ANGRY . . . [250]

Written and illustrated by Molly Bang

Cloth: Scholastic
Published: 1999   **Prizes: Caldecott Honor**

Ever met a toddler with a temper? When Sophie loses it, she roars a scarlet roar. It's visible—indeed, it practically quivers on the page, she slams the door, and runs into a forest—till, ultimately, she calms down. Quite a diva, Sophie is; how perfectly the illustrations capture the rage and frustration she feels. Like Hiawyn Oram's *Angry Arthur,* it's a fine book that is also an opportunity for conversation about temper.

WHEN THE NEW BABY COMES I'M MOVING OUT [251]

Written and illustrated by Martha Alexander

Cloth: Dial
Paper: Pied Piper
Published: 1971

Oliver's problem is pretty clear, but he learns to cope. There is a related title, also low-key and comic: *Nobody Asked Me If I Wanted a Baby Sister.* Other books about boys and their baby sisters include: *Baby Talk* by Fred Hiatt, *Talk, Baby!* by Harriet Ziefert, and *Oonga Boonga* by Frieda Wishinsky.

WHEN THE WIND STOPS [252]

Written by Charlotte Zolotow
Illustrated by Stefano Vitale

Cloth: HarperCollins
Paper: Harper Trophy
Published: 1995

The little boy is sorry to see the beautiful day end. His mother explains that it doesn't end; it merely starts in another place. The serene text—has science ever been so reassuring?—is set against glowing illustrations.

WHEN WILL THE SNOW TREES GROW? [253]

Written and illustrated by Ben Shecter

Cloth: HarperCollins
Published: 1993

Who better than a friendly bear to explain to a curious little boy the way the seasons work? They carry on a conversation about the gradual change as the autumnal illustrations shift colors. At the end the mittened boy waves goodbye to the bear, who hears the call of the snow trees and must begin his long winter sleep.

WHERE ARE YOU GOING, LITTLE MOUSE? [254]

Written by Robert Kraus
Illustrated by Jose Aruego and Ariane Dewey

Cloth: Greenwillow
Paper: Mulberry
Published: 1986

Having decided that no one loves him, Little Mouse sees nothing left to do but run away from home. He gets to the nearest phone booth, and his parents come to the rescue. Of course this was before cell phones and beepers. Even so, it's endearing and more about misery than electronics. Earlier books *Whose Mouse Are You?* and *Come Out and Play, Little Mouse* complete the trilogy.

[256]

WHERE THE WILD THINGS ARE   [255]

Written and illustrated by Maurice Sendak

Cloth: HarperCollins
Paper: Harper Trophy
Published: 1963

**Prizes: Caldecott Medal
New York Times Best Illustrated Book**

[255]

This is the story of the night Max wore his wolf suit and was sent to bed supperless, only to dream a strange, wild, violent, glorious dream and then return to where he is loved best of all. It is perhaps the greatest picture book of permission for young children, acknowledging and allowing the terrible temper and urge for independence that they feel but cannot fully act upon. The illustrations remain fresh and funny/scary; only time passes.

WHERE'S OUR MAMA?   [256]

Written and illustrated by Diane Goode

Cloth: Dutton
Published: 1991

Holding the baby in her arms, Mama runs after her hat in a French train station, telling the two older children to wait for her. A friendly police officer tries to help them find her, but their descriptions are not quite precise enough. The pretty, stylized illustrations suggest Paris in the belle epoque. Never fear, Mama returns. Indeed, there's also *Mama's Perfect Present*.

WHERE'S SPOT?   [257]

Written and illustrated by Eric Hill

Cloth: Putnam
Published: 1980

Mother dog Sally cannot find her puppy, Spot, and goes searching, and behind the flap on each double-page illustration is something silly—there's a striped snake in the clock, a funny lion under the stairs. Perfectly wonderful nonsense, satisfying to children of most early ages. This is the first and the best in a large and generally suc-

[256]

cessful series. Other good titles include *Spot's First Walk, Spot's First Christmas,* and *Spot Goes to School.*

WHERE'S THE BABY?   [258]

Written and illustrated by Pat Hutchins

Cloth: Greenwillow
Published: 1988

This humorously hideous family first seen in *The Very First Monster* is back, and this time, little Hazel helps her mother and grandmother follow the baby monster's muddy tracks as he wreaks havoc through the entire house. Very pleasing to preschoolers with younger siblings.

[257]

WHERE'S THE BEAR?   [259]

Written by Charlotte Pomerantz
Illustrated by Byron Barton

Cloth: Greenwillow
Paper: Mulberry
Published: 1984

This story of how a bear is sighted in the forest and how the villagers respond is brilliantly told in just seven words of text. The bold illustrations capture a breathless, exciting chase. Great fun to read aloud with the very young.

WHO SAID RED?   [260]

Written by Mary Serfozo
Illustrated by Keiko Narahashi

Cloth: Margaret K. McElderry
Paper: Aladdin
Published: 1988

The simple text here is a happy rhyming chat between two children, siblings perhaps, about color, very specific colors such as "cherry, berry, very red" and "slicker yellow" and "green bean green," and the happy, mysterious rainbow illustrations have an airy charm. In

Who Wants One? they continue their conversation and discuss numbers: "One butterfly, one raisin bun/One rainbow coming with the sun."

[266]

WHO SANK THE BOAT?   [261]

Written and illustrated by Pamela Allen

Cloth: Coward
Paper: Paper Star
Published: 1983

A cow, a donkey, a sheep, a pig, and a mouse decide to go out rowing in a boat that is, however, very small. The joke is unmistakable, even to very small children.

WHO'S WHOSE   [262]

Written and illustrated by Jan Ormerod

Cloth: Lothrop, Lee & Shepard
Published: 1998

In an urban neighborhood with relaxed adults and lots of children of companionable ages, the permutations of who is where, doing what and with whom, and just what is whose are delightful. For starters there are four parents, one granny, a total of eight children, a dog, and a guinea pig. There is also a very independent cat. A lot to count and talk about.

WILL I HAVE A FRIEND?   [263]

Written by Miriam Cohen
Illustrated by Lillian Hoban

Cloth: Macmillan
Paper: Aladdin
Published: 1967

[260]

The first of three books dealing with some perfectly reasonable fears and anxieties about kindergarten. The answer to the title question, happily, is yes. Paul makes friends with Jim on the very first day. In *The New Teacher,* they cope with a midyear replacement, and in *Best Friends,* they cope with an emergency.

WILLIAM'S DOLL [264]

Written by Charlotte Zolotow
Illustrated by William Pène du Bois

Cloth: HarperCollins
Paper: Harper Trophy
Published: 1972

It was shocking, years ago, that William wanted a doll to play with. Certainly, his father and his brother objected. But William got his doll and, in playing with him, imagined how he would one day be a father. Time has passed since this book was published, and what we read today seems modest and wry, but of considerable comfort to some children.

[264]

WILLY WHYNER,
CLOUD DESIGNER [265]

Written by Michael and Esther Lustig
Illustrated by Michael Lustig

Cloth: Four Winds
Published: 1994

Willy is a dreamer with very serious, very uninteresting parents. Left to his own resources, the boy takes up cloud design with astonishing results. A book for dreamers, with a guide to common cloud formations on the jacket flap for when it is time to return to ordinary fantasy.

[268]

WINDOW MUSIC [266]

Written by Anastasia Suen
Illustrated by Wade Zahares

Cloth: Viking Press
Published: 1998   **Prizes: New York Times Best Illustrated Book**

The title refers to a late nineteenth-century slang phrase for passing scenery, and the text concentrates of what a toddler sees looking out the window, with easy rhymes and repetitions: "Train on the track, clickety clack." The colors are intense and almost as hypnotic as the words. *Delivery* is about how things get where they are going.

THE WINTER BEAR [267]

Written by Ruth Croft
Illustrated by Erik Blegvad

Cloth: Margaret K. McElderry
Paper: Aladdin
Published: 1975

Three children take a walk in the country on a cold, snowy day and, of course, find a bear. The illustrations have a delicacy that reflects thin winter light.

THE WINTER WREN [268]

Written and illustrated by Brock Cole

Cloth: Farrar, Straus & Giroux
Paper: Sunburst
Published: 1984

Simon, a simple boy, and his little sister, Meg, hear that Spring is asleep at Winter's farm. When they get there and Meg disappears, a winter wren intercedes. The story has the tone and richness of a fable, and the watercolor illustrations catch winter's dark grayness and the sweet tones of spring.

[262]

WOMBAT DIVINE [269]

Written by Mem Fox
Illustrated by Kerry Argent

Cloth: Harcourt Brace
Paper: Voyager
Published: 1997

Christmas in Australia, and all the animals are auditioning for the Nativity play. Poor old Wombat tries out for everything but is wrong for the parts that go to Emu, Bilby, Numbat, and the Kangaroos. But when they find the right part . . . Wombat is divine. The illustrations are affectionate and hilarious, and theirs is certainly one of the best Nativity plays ever.

YONDER [270]

Written by Tony Johnston
Illustrated by Lloyd Bloom

Cloth: Dial
Paper: Dutton
Published: 1988

Some time in the last century, somewhere in the wilderness, a young farmer brings a new wife home. The couple plant a plum tree, say a prayer, then set about being fruitful and multiplying. A tree is planted for each child, and by the time the old farmer dies and a tree is planted to mark that event, too, there is a large orchard. The rhythmic text is simple, returning to the phrase "Yonder," meaning "there, just over there." The oil-painting illustrations, especially the five double-page spreads capturing the seasons and the growth of the plum tree, are perfectly lovely.

[269]

Story Books

Here are books with ample, sometimes lavish illustrations and strong stories, often with complex vocabularies as well. Younger children can frequently listen to the text and then "read" the books for themselves with pleasure, but they are best suited for children in the early grades. Precocious readers have not graduated from the pleasures of story books either, and they find special satisfaction in the combination of pictures and text. There are many fine examples of books about history, biography, and science in this section.

A WAVE IN HER POCKET   [271]

Written by Lynn Joseph
Illustrated by Brian Pinkney

Cloth: Clarion
Published: 1991

In Trinidad a tantie is an older woman, often an aunt or great-aunt who helps raise children and often tells them meaningful stories. Here are six typical tantie tales; pay close attention, there are morals. There is a second collection called *The Mermaid's Twin Sister: More Stories from Trinidad.*

THE ACCIDENT   [272]

Written by Carol Carrick
Illustrated by Donald Carrick

Cloth: Clarion
Paper: Clarion
Published: 1976

This is the pivotal book in a series of three about a boy named Christopher and his dog, Bodger. In *Lost in the Storm*, the boy must wait out a storm before searching for his dog. In *The Accident*, the dog is hit by a truck and killed, and Christopher must grieve. In *The Foundling*, Christopher concludes his mourning. The stories are all sensitively and thoughtfully done, worthwhile if read separately or serially. The illustrations are low-key and unobtrusive.

THE ADVENTURES OF TAXI DOG   [273]

Written by Debra Baracca
Illustrated by Marc Buehner

Cloth: Dial
Published: 1990

Maxi was once a street mutt, but Jim rescued him, and now he rides around New York City all day in Jim's taxi. He sticks his head out the window or turns around and entertains passengers—like Sadie, the showgirl with whom Max sings a duet. The first in an entertaining series that includes *Maxi the Hero* and *Maxi the Star.*

AESOP & COMPANY: SCENES FROM HIS LEGENDARY LIFE   [274]

Written by Barbara Bader
Illustrated by Arthur Geisert

Cloth: Houghton Mifflin
Paper: Houghton Mifflin
Published: 1991

Here is a collection of nineteen concisely written fables, each followed by its pithy moral in boldface type and presented with an etching showing a real, unadorned, animal on the facing page. Austere, elegant, and engrossing. There's also an interesting essay about the way the tales have traveled. By contrast, Barbara McClintock's *Animal Fables from Aesop* are depicted dressed in eighteenth- or nineteenth-century costumes and on stage sets.

ALEXANDER AND THE TERRIBLE, HORRIBLE, NO GOOD, VERY BAD DAY   [275]

Written by Judith Viorst
Illustrated by Ray Cruz

Cloth: Atheneum
Paper: Aladdin
Published: 1972

It is somehow soothing for readers of all ages—i.e., children and their parents—to know that there *are* just those terrible, horrible

[273]

110

rotten days that are miserable from beginning to end, no matter what. Everything that can go wrong does, and Alexander is simply furious. The two-color illustrations fairly quiver with the boy's mounting frustrations. Positively a modern classic for good cause. Other books about Alexander and his brothers are *I'll Fix Anthony, Alexander, Who Used to be Rich Last Sunday, Alexander, Who's Not (Do You Hear Me? I Mean It!) Going to Move,* and *Absolutely Positively Alexander.* The collected crisis stories are *Absolutely Positively Alexander.*

ALL ABOUT ALFIE [276]

Written and illustrated by Shirley Hughes

Cloth: Lothrop, Lee & Shepard
Paper: Mulberry
Published: 1984

Alfie is the quintessential four-year-old—kind, well-meaning, but not quite as brave as he would like to be. His adventures are small and perfectly told. The deft full-color illustrations sweetly capture characters, as well as the domestic settings, in a comfortable, slightly run-down urban neighborhood. Other titles in the series include *Alfie Gets in First, An Evening at Alfie's, Alfie and the Birthday Surprise,* and *The Alfie Collection.* His little sister, Annie Rose, stars in books for younger children: *Bathwater's Hot* and *All Sizes and Shapes.* There is also a large-format *Alfie and Annie Rose Storybook.*

ALWAYS ROOM FOR ONE MORE [277]

Written by Sorche Nic Leodhas
Illustrated by Nonny Hogrogian

Cloth: Henry Holt
Paper: Henry Holt
Published: 1965   **Prizes: Caldecott Medal**

In this retelling of a story that occurs in many cultures, it is given as a Highlands tale about Lachie MacLachlan, whose hospitality extends to every traveler who passes by until the walls of his house burst. The three-color illustrations have a misty quality of mountain air.

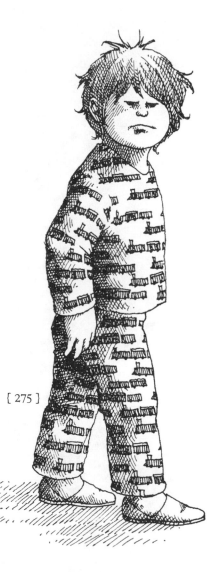

[275]

THE AMAZING BONE [278]

Written and illustrated by William Steig

Cloth: Farrar, Straus & Giroux
Paper: Sunburst
Published: 1976   **Prizes: Caldecott Honor**

Steig stories are always different, always identifiable by their wit and loony reasonableness. The heroine is Pearl, who happens to be a piglet, finds a talking bone that has fallen out of a witch's basket.

AMAZING GRACE [279]

Written by Mary Hoffman
Illustrated by Caroline Binch

Cloth: Dial
Published: 1991

Raj and the other schoolchildren tell Grace that she won't get the part of Peter Pan in the class play, but she's determined, and when her Nana takes her to the ballet and she sees a beautiful brown-skinned ballerina, she has a role model. She practices and practices . . . and guess what? She gets the part. It's the winning illustrations that everyone studies and remembers. Such a smile. *Such* a smile. In *Boundless Grace,* our heroine goes to visit her father in Africa.

[279]

AMERICAN FOLK SONGS FOR CHILDREN [280]

Written by Ruth Crawford Seeger
Illustrated by Barbara Cooney

Cloth: Doubleday
Paper: Zephyr
Published: 1970

A collection of ninety songs you probably know but you can't remember all the words to anymore. This standard collection has user-friendly suggestions about adapting songs for play and dancing, and altering the words for your family.

AMERICAN TALL TALES [281]

Written by Mary Pope Osborne
Illustrated by Michael McCurdy

Cloth: Knopf
Published: 1991

A collection of traditional stories from all over the country, well told. The black-and-white woodcut illustrations are apt, and the tall slim format is appealing.

[279]

AN AMISH CHRISTMAS [282]

Written by Richard Ammon
Illustrated by Pamela Patrick

Cloth: Atheneum
Published: 1996

A handsomely illustrated account of the plain and joyful days of holiday celebration in an Amish community is the first of a series about contemporary Amish life. The other titles are *An Amish Wedding* and *An Amish Year*.

ANANSI THE SPIDER: A TALE FROM THE ASHANTI [283]

Written and illustrated by Gerald McDermott

Cloth: Henry Holt
Paper: Henry Holt
Published: 1973   **Prizes: Caldecott Honor**

In this witty illustrated story about Anansi, the West African spider-hero, he has six sons who combine their talents to save their father.

THE ANIMAL FAMILY [284]

Written by Randall Jarrell
Illustrated by Maurice Sendak

Cloth: Pantheon
Paper: Harper Trophy
Published: 1965   **Prizes: Newbery Honor**

This is a facsimile of the handsome original edition of the distin-guished American poet's memorable fantasy about a solitary hunter

who miraculously acquires a family, including a mermaid, a bear, a lynx, and finally, a boy. Extraordinary writing and fine, restrained decorations. Splendid for reading aloud again and again.

ANNA BANANA AND ME   [285]

Written by Lenore Blegvad
Illustrated by Erik Blegvad

Cloth: Margaret K. McElderry
Paper: Aladdin
Published: 1985

The boy who tells this story is afraid of a lot of things, unlike his utterly brave friend Anna Banana. They are playing in New York's Central Park at a socially benign time. The illustrations capture Anna's daring and the narrator's anxieties and eventual triumph.

ANNIE AND THE OLD ONE   [286]

Written by Miska Miles
Illustrated by Peter Parnell

Cloth: Little, Brown
Paper: Little, Brown
Published: 1971   **Prizes: Newbery Honor**

A little Indian girl recognizes that her grandmother is going to die and learns to accept the cycle of life and death. The story is told with delicacy and caring, and the fine illustrations are a perfect complement.

ANNIE AND THE WILD ANIMALS

[287]

Written and illustrated by Jan Brett

Cloth: Houghton Mifflin
Paper: Houghton Mifflin
Published: 1985

It's midwinter somewhere in the north country when Annie's cat, Taffy, disappears. The story of what is really happening is told in the borders. In the meantime, at the center of each double page, Annie tries to make friends with a series of wild animals who emerge from the woods as winter fades into damp, mossy spring. At the end, Taffy reappears with her kittens. The illustrations are exquisitely detailed and have a folkloric and Scandinavian quality. In *The Mitten,* the motifs are Ukranian and a white mitten is lost in the snow. Other books similarly illustrated include *Berlioz the Bear, The First Dog, Fritz and the Beautiful Horses,* and *Christmas Trolls.*

ART DOG   [288]

Written and illustrated by Thacher Hurd

Cloth: HarperCollins
Paper: Harper Trophy
Published: 1996

By day, Arthur Dog is a quiet security guard at the Dogopolis Museum of Art. But when the moon is full, he is transformed by night into Art Dog. Then the *Mona Woofa* is stolen one night and Art Dog is arrested. Lots of visual jokes about famous paintings and museums, and a slam-bang-funny fight scene.

ARTHUR'S NOSE   [289]

Written and illustrated by Marc Brown

Cloth: Little, Brown
Paper: Little, Brown
Published: 1976

This is the first of a popular series of gently comic books that appeal to children in the early grades, and their younger siblings as well. The tone was set way before Arthur moved to television. Arthur is a young aardvark who deals with life's daily issues in an appealing way. Here he learns to accept his most distinctive features. Other titles include *Arthur's Eyes* (about getting glasses), *Arthur's Tooth* (about losing the first one), and *Arthur's Halloween* (about not being so frightened). There are also books about Arthur's kid sister, D.W.

[289]

ASHANTI TO ZULU: AFRICAN TRADITIONS   [290]

Written by Margaret Musgrove
Illustrated by Leo Dillon

Cloth: Dial
Paper: Pied Piper
Published: 1976

Prizes: Caldecott Medal
New York Times Best Illustrated Book

A remarkable alphabet book that also describes and brilliantly illustrates aspects of African culture. The captions are small gems of anthropological reporting. Among the tribes described are the Dogon, the Fanta, and the Kung. This is a picture book definitely for older children and adults. The library may have it shelved with large-format and travel books, but keep looking; it's worth it.

AUNT ELAINE DOES THE DANCE FROM SPAIN   [291]

Written by Leah Komaiko
Illustrated by Petra Mathers

Cloth: Doubleday
Published: 1992

Stories about eccentric family members are both entertaining and reassuring. Katie's Aunt Elaine, born and raised in Maine, is also a Spanish dancer. Katie goes with her and has a chance to perform. There are several other wonderful aunts with artistic aspirations and enthusiasms, including *When Aunt Lena Did the Rumba* by Eileen Kurtis Kleinman and *Pamela's First Musical* by Wendy Wasserstein.

[292]

AUTHOR: A TRUE STORY [292]

Written and illustrated by Helen Lester

Cloth: Houghton Mifflin
Published: 1997

This lighthearted account of "my life and times" goes from toddler-to-teen-scribbling to prose, on to the author's alternative careers and success writing children's books. The solid model is on every page: discipline, practice, editing, false starts, failed ideas, all told with wit and goodwill. Both reassuring and encouraging to beginning authors faced with writing assignments.

BABA YAGA: A RUSSIAN FOLKTALE [293]

Written and illustrated by Katya Arnold

Cloth: North-South
Published: 1993

This is just one of many of the stories about the archetypal Russian witch and comes from a nineteenth-century collection by Aleksandr Afanasev. It's about a childless couple whose wish is magically fulfilled by the arrival of a son they call Tishka. He is caught by Baba Yaga, and of course eventually escapes. The illustrations here are inspired by traditional Russian lubok pictures, a kind of hand-colored wood engraving. Patricia Polacco has done *Babushka Baba Yaga* in her familiar collage style, and Mariana Mayer did a lavish *Baba Yaga and Vasilisa the Brave,* a Cinderella variation. There are many other editions as well.

BABUSHKA: AN OLD RUSSIAN FOLKTALE [294]

Written and illustrated by Charles Mikolaycak

Cloth: Holiday House
Paper: Holiday House
Published: 1984   **Prizes: New York Times Best Illustrated Book**

An affecting retelling of a traditional Russian tale about an old woman who was too busy to go when she was invited to visit the baby Jesus and now searches endlessly for him. The darkly lit illustrations are dramatic.

THE BAKER'S DOZEN: A COLONIAL AMERICAN TALE [295]

Written by Heather Forest
Illustrated by Susan Gaber

Cloth: Harcourt Brace
Paper: Harcourt Brace
Published: 1988

In Albany, New York, in colonial times, a baker named Van Amsterdam grew greedy and cheated on his St. Nicholas cookies. Soon his fortunes failed. However, when he learned the value of generosity both in his measurements and his attitude and gave thirteen cookies to the dozen, he prospered. Snowy illustrations capture the wintry feeling of December days long ago.

THE BALANCING GIRL [296]

Written by Bernice Rabe
Illustrated by Lillian Hoban

Cloth: Dutton
Paper: Unicorn
Published: 1981

This remarkable book is about Margaret, who is in a wheelchair and has developed her own special skill at balancing things. She uses her talent to benefit her whole school in an imaginative way. Thus, a book about a physically disabled child conveys a message about social tolerance that is accessible for a preschool child. *Margaret's Moves,* for older readers, takes up the story a few years later, as Margaret deals with new problems and especially her brother, Rusty. Margaret is a determined, optimistic, yet believable character.

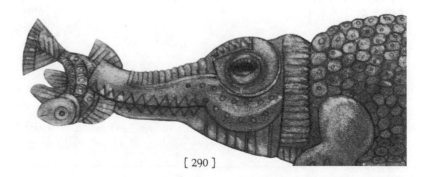

[290]

BAND OF ANGELS:
A STORY INSPIRED BY
THE JUBILEE SINGERS   [297]

Written by Deborah Hopkinson
Illustrated by Raul Colón

Cloth: Atheneum
Published: 1999

The story is based on the life of Ella Sheppard Moore, born a slave in 1851, who arrived at the Fisk School in Nashville in 1868 with $6. She became the pianist for a group of students who went out on tour to raise money for the school. The group became the Jubilee Singers, known then and now for their arrangements of spirituals and traditional music, and the school became Fisk University. There are sketches of the other singers on the endpapers.

BASEBALL SAVED US   [298]

Written by Ken Mochizuki
Illustrated by Dom Lee

Cloth: Lee & Low
Paper: Lee & Low
Published: 1993

It's 1942 and Shorty and his family are in the Japanese internment camp in Nevada and everyone is frustrated and anxious. Shorty's dad and others improvise a playing field, and soon there are teams and even uniforms. Baseball proves to be far more than a diversion, and Shorty turns out to be a fine player. Obviously there is a lot going on in this story that needs discussion, and children of different ages will understand it differently.

THE BAT-POET   [299]

Written by Randall Jarrell
Illustrated by Maurice Sendak

Cloth: Macmillan
Paper: Harper Trophy
Published: 1964   **Prizes: New York Times Best Illustrated Book**

A little brown bat-poet cannot sleep during the day—he keeps waking up and looking at the world. His lyric descriptions of the ani-

mals and things he sees are filled with wonder. This collaboration between a fine poet and a fine artist is properly considered a classic.

THE BATTLE OF LUKE AND LONGNOSE [300]

Written and illustrated by Barbara McClintock

Cloth: Houghton Mifflin
Published: 1994

In a splendidly costumed dream fantasy, Luke wakes up and find that the toy stage he was playing with has come to life. Whipping out a cloak he keeps under his bed, Luke joins the fray, dueling with the villainous Longnose. Lavish illustrations. Another of McClintock's charming books is *The Heartaches of a French Cat*.

BEA AND MR. JONES [301]

Written and illustrated by Amy Schwartz

Cloth: Bradbury
Paper: Aladdin
Published: 1982

Bea is tired of kindergarten and her father, Mr. Jones, is tired of being an advertising executive, so they swap jobs. The results are very satisfying. The distinctive line drawings, old-fashioned and somewhat cartoonish, are very amusing, especially Bea and Mr. Jones, with their smug, fat faces.

THE BEAST OF MONSIEUR RACINE [302]

Written and illustrated by Tomi Ungerer

Cloth: Farrar, Straus & Giroux
Paper: Sunburst
Published: 1971

[300]

A retired tax collector finds a strange, friendly, rather squooshy creature in his garden. Approaching it scientifically, Monsieur Racine takes it to the Academy of Sciences in Paris, where it breaks apart, revealing the two children from next door. The quirky fable suggests a Gallic worldliness in its inimitable style.

[301]

BEST FRIENDS   [303]

Written and illustrated by Steven Kellogg

Cloth: Dial
Paper: Aladdin
Published: 1985

Kathy and Louise are best friends. While Louise is away for the summer, Kathy meets a new neighbor whose dog is expecting puppies, with some unforeseen and poignant results. Detailed and imaginative full-color illustrations add depth and humor.

THE BEST TOWN IN THE WORLD   [304]

Written by Byrd Baylor
Illustrated by Ronald Himler

Cloth: Scribner
Paper: Aladdin
Published: 1983

A prose poem that celebrates a place in the American Southwest where all the wildflowers had "butterflies to match" and "of course you knew everyone's name and everyone knew yours." The full-color sun-dappled illustrations are romantic.

BIG SISTER AND LITTLE SISTER   [305]

Written by Charlotte Zolotow
Illustrated by Martha Alexander

Cloth: HarperCollins
Paper: Harper Trophy
Published: 1966

Sometimes you just have to run away from your bossy big sister to find out how she really feels about you.

BIRD TALK [306]

Written and illustrated by Ann Jonas

Cloth: Greenwillow
Published: 1999

The text of this inspired story consists of overheard "memory phrases"—what bird watchers call the sounds different birds make. The plot consists of scenes from a day in the life of a mockingbird, who acts as a kind of master of ceremonies and repeats key phrases. From the sooty tern calling "Wide-a-wake" at dawn to the great horned owl calling "Who's awake? Me too!" it's a delight. Also handy to keep near a window when you hear a familiar call.

BLACK WHITENESS: ADMIRAL BYRD ALONE IN THE ANTARCTIC [307]

Written by Robert Burleigh
Illustrated by Walter Lyon Krudop

Cloth: Atheneum
Published: 1997

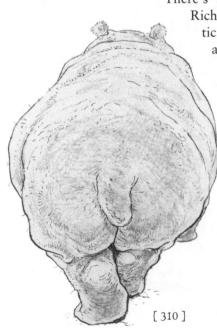

There's a fine line between bravery and madness. Admiral Richard E. Byrd, who led several expeditions to the Antarctic, set out in 1934 to spend a solo winter there. This account, drawn from his diaries, chronicling the preparations of a bunker beneath the snow, the approach of the polar darkness, the terrible cold, his life-threatening illness, increasing claustrophobia, disorientation, and panic, and final rescue. It's an extraordinary account well matched by dark, mysterious illustrations. *Trapped by the Ice!* tells of Sir Ernest Shackleton's 1914 expedition to cross the polar ice cap and the fate of his ship, the *Endurance*.

[310]

THE BOOK OF PIGERICKS: PIG LIMERICKS   [308]

Written and illustrated by Arnold Lobel

Cloth: HarperCollins
Paper: Harper Trophy
Published: 1983

A piggy feast: thirty-eight original limericks (very hard to accomplish; try writing some) illustrated with glowing good humor. The cast of Lobelian porkers is splendidly costumed.

THE BOOK OF TENS   [309]

Written and illustrated by Mark Podwal

Cloth: Greenwillow
Paper: Mulberry
Published: 1994

Of interest to Jewish and non-Jewish readers, this slender, elegantly illustrated book sets out some of the mysterious properties of the number 10 in Jewish faith and practice. For starters there's the ten commandments, the ten men needed for the minyan, or communal prayer. But wait, what about the ten blessings, the ten plagues, the ten spies who lied to Moses. Wonderfully provocative for bedtime reading aloud.

THE BOY WHO WAS FOLLOWED HOME   [310]

Written by Margaret Mahy
Illustrated by Steven Kellogg

Cloth: Dial
Paper: Pied Piper
Published: 1975

This is an inspired shaggy hippopotamus story. One day an amiable hippo follows a proper little boy home from school. Then there is another. The hippos multiply daily until there are forty-three of them. The story has a compelling logic, a ridiculous witch, some magic, and an unexpected and funny final twist. The illustrations are hilarious. This is the only Mahy picture book currently available in the United States in which the illustrations are the equal of the text.

[310]

BRATS [311]

Written by X. J. Kennedy
Illustrated by James Watts

Cloth: Margaret K. McElderry
Paper: Aladdin
Published: 1986

A bright collection of forty-two short original poems about an assortment of brats—obnoxious, rude, noisy, and various other combinations of familiar and unpleasant. The illustrations are apt and amusing. There is also *Drat Those Brats!* and *Fresh Brats,* another forty-one bits of mischief.

BRAVE IRENE [312]

Written and illustrated by William Steig

Cloth: Farrar, Straus & Giroux
Paper: Sunburst
Published: 1986   **Prizes: New York Times Best Illustrated Book**

Irene Bobbin, the dressmaker's daughter, volunteers to deliver the duchess's new ball gown and sets off in a fierce snowstorm. The wicked wind blows the dress out of the box, Irene soldiers on, and there is a happy ending. This is vintage Steig. As with his other storybooks, lap listeners are almost as interested as children who can read the story for themselves.

[312]

BREAD AND JAM FOR FRANCES [313]

Written by Russell Hoban
Illustrated by Lillian Hoban

Cloth: HarperCollins
Paper: Harper Trophy
Published: 1960

Frances is a bright, willful, whimsical little badger who often makes up songs about aspects of her days—bedtime, sibling rivalry, friendship, candy. Her adventures in this and the other books in the series reflect the small and specific concerns of children in preschool and the early grades but transcend bibliotherapy. *A Baby Sister for Frances, Best Friends for Frances, A Birthday for Frances,* and *Egg Thoughts and Other Frances Songs* are all delightful, although not all are in print anymore. Whenever you hear people talk about a Chompo bar, they have been reading Frances. The Frances books have more text than pictures, but because they read aloud so well, they appeal to children of a wide age range—roughly from toddlers to third grade.

[313]

BUGS [314]

Written by Nancy Winslow Parker and Joan Richards Wright
Illustrated by Nancy Winslow Parker

Cloth: Greenwillow
Paper: Mulberry
Published: 1987

Humorous verses introduce sixteen common insects, including fleas, flies, and mosquitoes, which make this first book of entomology an engaging browsing book. It is a good early independent reading book for young scientists, as is the fascinating *Frogs, Toads, Lizards, and Salamanders,* by the same team. The illustrations are clear, precise but cartoonish, enough to allow the phobic a chance to enjoy the subject.

CALEB AND KATE [315]

Written and illustrated by William Steig

Cloth: Farrar, Straus & Giroux
Paper: Sunburst
Published: 1978

After yet another spat, Caleb goes into the forest to get away from Kate. A witch casts a spell, and he's turned into a dog. Caleb returns to Kate, who accepts him as a pet until the day when thieves arrive. . . . Impossible, of course. Wonderful, too—especially for children in the early grades.

CATWINGS [316]

Written by Ursula K. Le Guin
Illustrated by S. D. Schindler

Cloth: Orchard Books
Paper: Scholastic
Published: 1988

Mrs. Jane Tabby's four new little kittens seem to have, er, um, wings. They live in an unsafe urban area and their harassed mother does her best, but ultimately sends them to the country alone. The laconic, matter-of-fact prose is utterly believable. The delicate ink-and-watercolor illustrations are faintly Victorian and thoroughly enchanting and suited to the small, palm-size shape of the book. The series continues with *Catwings Return, Wonderful Alexander and the Catwings,* and *Jane on Her Own: A Catwings Tale.*

A CHAIR FOR MY MOTHER [317]

Written and illustrated by Vera B. Williams

Cloth: Greenwillow
Paper: Mulberry
Published: 1982

Prizes: Caldecott Honor

This is the first of three stories about Rosa, her mother, who works in the Blue Tile Diner, and her grandmother. Burned out of their home, they relocate and start saving for a comfortable chair. The chair, lush and pink and covered with roses, is, like the book, unusual and fine. The illustrations, with their distinctive borders and themes, are wry rather than whimsical. The two other equally enchanting titles are *Something Special for Me* and *Music, Music Everywhere.*

[316]

126

THE CHALK DOLL [318]

Written by Charlotte Pomerantz
Illustrated by Frané Lessac

Cloth: HarperCollins
Paper: Harper Trophy
Published: 1989

Rose is home in bed with a cold and her mother is settling her for a nap, telling her about when she was a little girl in Jamaica. They were too poor for store-bought dolls, but she made a fine rag doll, who even had high-heeled shoes. You don't need to be sick, or even at home, to remember the story.

A CHILD'S TREASURY OF POEMS [319]

Edited by Mark Daniel

Cloth: Dial
Published: 1986

A charming collection of familiar English poems, mostly by nineteenth-century authors—Tennyson, Stevenson, Wordsworth, Rossetti. The lavish period illustrations of appropriate paintings and engravings are reproductions from works in museums and private collections. Many of the illustrations are unfamiliar but seem especially apt. This is a presentation gift/read-aloud collection for all ages.

EL CHINO [320]

Written and illustrated by Allen Say

Cloth: Houghton Mifflin
Paper: Houghton Mifflin
Published: 1990

The American dream—of unlimited possibility, and finding your true self somehow, somewhere—is told quietly and powerfully in this almost cinematic account of Bong Way, who became Billy Wong. A Chinese-American athlete "too short for basketball," he found his sport, and goal, in the bull ring in Spain. In becoming a matador he also reclaimed his Chinese heritage. It is a stunning story book with beautiful, spare illustrations that burst into brilliant

color when Billy Wong sees the bull ring. It can be read at many levels, even by young children, but is perhaps most rewarding for middle graders, who are grappling with questions of identity.

CHITA'S CHRISTMAS TREE [321]

Written by Elizabeth Fitzgerald Howard
Illustrated by Floyd Cooper

Cloth: Bradbury
Paper: Aladdin
Published: 1989

This description of a Christmas in Baltimore at the end of the nineteenth century has been drawn from the family recollections of Elizabeth McCard Shipley, the real Chita and the only child of one of the first African American doctors in the city. The illustrations are full of rich domestic detail, but it is the beguiling Chita who is the star. There's also *Papa Tells Chita a Story* and *Aunt Flossie's Hat and Crab Cakes Later*.

CHRISTINA KATERINA AND THE TIME SHE QUIT THE FAMILY [322]

Written by Patricia Lee Gauch
Illustrated by Elsie Primavera

Cloth: Putnam
Paper: Paper Star
Published: 1987

Family life sometimes gets to be too much. One morning when it does, Christina Katerina just up and quits the family. "Call me Agnes," she says, and spends the next days doing just what she wants. Her savvy mother handles the situation neatly. Our heroine also appears in *Christina Katerina and the Box*, *Christina Katerina and Fats and the Great Neighborhood War* and *Christina Katerina and the First Annual Grand Ballet*.

THE CHRISTMAS ALPHABET [323]

Written and illustrated by Robert Sabuda

Cloth: Orchard Books
Published: 1994

There's a real question about whether this elegant pop-up book, showing leaping angels, ringing bells, a star surrounded by doves, even a Yule log, all in un-Christmassy hues, is actually a book for children. Certainly it is not for little ones who couldn't reliably manipulate the delicately engineered, dancing illustrations. For those who are old enough, on through adults, it is a consistent, ingenious delight. As is the glorious, pure white rendition of *The Twelve Days of Christmas*.

THE CHRISTMAS MIRACLE OF JONATHAN TOOMEY [324]

Written by Susan Wojciechowski
Illustrated by P. J. Lynch

Cloth: Candlewick Press
Published: 1995

Loss and redemption. Jonathan Toomey is the lonely widowed wood-carver townfolks called Mr. Gloomy. The widow McDowell and her son, Thomas, move to town, and she asks Toomey to carve Christmas figures to replace a set they have lost. If the plot is obvious, the text is sweetly rhythmic and the watercolor illustrations are affecting.

CINDERELLA [325]

Written by Charles Perrault
Illustrated by Marcia Brown

Cloth: Scribner
Paper: Aladdin
Published: 1954   **Prizes: Caldecott Medal**

A fine translation in an appealingly illustrated edition of the familiar story about the dutiful daughter and the glass slipper. There are also unusual editions illustrated by Susan Jeffers and James Mar-

shall, and many set in other cultures, including a collection written and illustrated by Shirley Climo: *The Egyptian Cinderella, The Irish Cinderlad, The Korean Cinderella,* and *The Persian Cinderella. Cendrillon,* a Creole version, is by Robert San Souci and illustrated by Brian Pinkney.

THE CLOWN OF GOD: AN OLD STORY [326]

Written and illustrated by Tomie dePaola

Cloth: Harcourt Brace
Paper: Voyager
Published: 1978

This lovely retelling of a French folktale about a juggler's gift to the Christ Child has appealing, stylized illustrations recalling Pierrot.

COME A TIDE [327]

Written by George Ella Lyon
Illustrated by Stephen Gammell

Cloth: Orchard Books
Paper: Orchard Books
Published: 1990

Grandma, who is old, wise, and lives at the top of the hill someplace in the Appalachians, knows that after a four-day spring rain, "It'll come a tide." Because of the lighthearted, almost lyric text and the exuberant, funny illustrations, what happens during a recurring natural disaster—flooding—becomes a great adventurous romp.

[328]

D'AULAIRES' BOOK OF GREEK MYTHS [328]

Written and illustrated by Ingri and Edgar Parin d'Aulaire

Cloth: Doubleday
Paper: Picture Yearling
Published: 1962

Rightfully, the best-known modern book of the Greek myths adapted for children. The stories are organized around Zeus and his

[328]

family, minor gods, and mortal descendants. The complex illustrations, full of symbols and evoking the classical tradition, are distinguished. The stories are, of course, thrilling. There are dozens of storybooks of individual myths, of varying quality. For night-after-night bedtime reading, the large collection is recommended. The *d'Aulaires' Norse Gods and Giants,* now out of print, is worth finding; it's an excellent introduction to another family of myths.

DAKOTA DUGOUT [329]

Written by Ann Turner
Illustrated by Ronald Himler

Cloth: Simon & Schuster
Paper: Aladdin
Published: 1985

A memoir of the life of a young bride living in a sod house on the Dakota prairie in the late nineteenth century. The black-and-white illustrations set off the text with distinction.

DEAR BENJAMIN BANNEKER [330]

Written by Andrea Davis Pinkney
Illustrated by Brian Pinkney

Cloth: Harcourt Brace
Paper: Harcourt Brace
Published: 1994

Banneker (1731–1806), a free black man, was a Maryland tobacco farmer, a publisher, and a self-taught mathematician and astronomer. He is remembered for his accomplishments and also because

[332]

he corresponded with Thomas Jefferson. There is also a story book biography of his grandmother, *Mary Banakee,* a remarkable woman settler in Virginia who married a freed man.

THE DESERT IS THEIRS [331]

Written by Byrd Baylor
Illustrated by Peter Parnall

Cloth: Scribner
Paper: Aladdin
Published: 1975

For readers who live in or near the desert, or in other parts of the world and wonder, this is a lyrical introduction to many of the creatures who live there. There is an ecological message about species' adaptation to climate. The illustrations are fine line drawings.

THE DEVIL'S STORYBOOK [332]

Written and illustrated by Natalie Babbitt

Cloth: Farrar, Straus & Giroux
Paper: Sunburst
Published: 1974

The devil seen in these ten stories is a clever joker who, when restless, comes to earth and plays dirty tricks on unsuspecting types. He returns, spry and inventive as ever, in *The Devil's Other Storybook.* There is interesting moral fiction hidden in the supple prose.

DINOSAUR BOB AND HIS ADVENTURES WITH THE FAMILY LAZARDO   [333]

Written and illustrated by William Joyce

Cloth: HarperCollins
Paper: HarperCollins
Published: 1988

The Lazardo family acquired the little dinosaur that resembled Uncle Bob when they were off on safari. They brought it home to Pimlico Hills and it joined the local baseball team, the Pimlico Pirates. Honest. Just look at those wonderfully plausible pictures of Bob and the rest of the team. Glorious fantasy for sports fans and pint-sized paleontologists.

DINOSAURS, BEWARE! A SAFETY GUIDE   [334]

Written by Stephen Krensky
Illustrated by Marc Brown

Cloth: Little, Brown
Paper: Little, Brown
Published: 1982

A basic guide to household safety—everything from playing with fire to telephone manners—but the households pictured are those of ridiculously entertaining dinosaurs, who set some truly bad examples to avoid. Basic means that many modern technological terrors—VCRs and computers, cell phones and microwaves—are not included.

DINOSAURS DIVORCE: A GUIDE FOR CHANGING FAMILIES   [335]

Written by Marc Brown and Laurene Krasny Brown
Illustrated by Marc Brown

Cloth: Little, Brown
Paper: Little, Brown
Published: 1986

Set in a cartoon world with a cast of dinosaurs, this story book for children of all ages deals with the trauma of divorce. The text is

straightforward, and although silly and funny, the illustrations are also sophisticated enough to allow older children to return to the book for its sound and reassuring advice without feeling embarrassed.

DOCTOR DE SOTO [336]

Written and illustrated by William Steig

Cloth: Farrar, Straus & Giroux
Paper: Sunburst
Published: 1982

Prizes: Newbery Honor

Doctor De Soto, a mouse, has a dental practice on a busy city street. As a rule, he does not accept patients threatening to his species, but he makes an exception for a fox with an emergency, and outsmarts the fox, whose gratitude is ultimately questionable. A glorious book with matchlessly witty full-color illustrations. *Doctor De Soto Goes to Africa* is fun but not as inspired.

[338]

134

DON'T YOU KNOW THERE'S A WAR ON? [337]

Written and illustrated by James Stevenson

Cloth: Greenwillow
Published: 1992

In slim storybooks with spare watercolor illustrations, the prolific *New Yorker* artist and illustrator has composed a moving autobiographical series about growing up in the 1930s and '40s. Only this title remains in print, but the others are worth finding: *When I Was Nine, Higher on the Door,* and *July.* A lovely link to a fading past.

[336]

THE DRAGONS ARE SINGING TONIGHT [338]

Written by Jack Prelutsky
Illustrated by Peter Sis

Cloth: Greenwillow
Paper: Mulberry
Published: 1993

The first of a series of delightful poetry collections that are also inspired collaborations between poet and artist. The verses are witty and imaginative, perfect for reading aloud, and the illustrations of scaly creatures, often with winsome smiles, are a perfect match. Other titles include *Monday's Troll* and *The Gargoyle on the Roof.*

DUFFY AND THE DEVIL [339]

Written by Harve Zemach
Illustrated by Margot Zemach

Cloth: Farrar, Straus & Giroux
Paper: Sunburst
Published: 1973   **Prizes: Caldecott Medal**

This is a wry Cornish version of Rumpelstiltskin. Duffy is the servant girl Squire Lovel believes can spin and knit so well. But then the devil takes back the clothes he made, much to the squire's embarrassment. Bright, cheerful full-color illustrations. *The Judges* is also a witty tale of justice.

DUKE ELLINGTON: THE PIANO PRINCE AND THE ORCHESTRA [340]

Written by Andrea Davis Pinkney
Illustrated by Brian Pinkney

Cloth: Hyperion
Published: 1998   **Prizes: Caldecott Honor**

A brief life of the stylish, sophisticated composer and conductor. The text skillfully explains a number of jazz terms and conventions without appearing didactic. The illustrations could be set to music.

EDWARD AND THE PIRATES [341]

Written and illustrated by David McPhail

Cloth: Little, Brown
Published: 1997

An adventure story that happens to be about reading, this book introduces Edward, a bespectacled little fellow who is reading in bed one night when the pirates of the tale burst into his room. What with one thing and another, he not only vanquishes the dastardly fellows, he ends up teaching them to read.

[342]

ELOISE [342]

Written by Kay Thompson
Illustrated by Hilary Knight

Cloth: Simon & Schuster
Published: 1955

You remember me, Eloise. I'm six and rawther adorable and I live in the Plaza Hotel in New York City. I have lots of fun there: I order from room service and ride the elevators and check out what's happening all over the hotel. I'm terribly clever. A timeless favorite about a terrorizing child, now available everywhere. Additional titles include *Eloise in Paris, Eloise in Moscow,* and several cut-and-paste books of advice that are really for grown-ups.

THE EMPEROR'S
NEW CLOTHES   [343]

Written by Hans Christian Andersen
Illustrated by Angela Barrett

Cloth: Candlewick Press
Published: 1997

The illustrations in this elegant edition of the familiar story of sheer vanity place the tale in some pre–World War I luxe kingdom filled with fancy cars and dogs and lavish furnishings, and make it one that older children might grapple with. Dorothea Duntze has also done an elegant version. In contrast, the version with illustrations by Anne Rockwell, now difficult to find, is much more appropriate for young children—light bright illustrations of a very pink, very silly emperor.

THE ENORMOUS EGG   [344]

Written by Oliver Butterworth
Illustrated by Louis Darling

Cloth: Little, Brown
Paper: Dell Yearling
Published: 1956

Life was just going along until one of Nate Twitchell's hens laid an egg the size of a melon and then hatched a . . . think prehistoric favorite. Great fun to read aloud.

EVERETT ANDERSON'S
GOODBYE   [345]

Written by Lucille Clifton
Illustrated by Ann Grifalconi

Cloth: Henry Holt
Paper: Henry Holt
Published: 1983

Everett Anderson, a little black boy, must deal with his father's death. His feelings are eloquently evoked in simple poems and underscored in gentle pencil illustrations. Two other Everett Anderson books have been reissued: *Some of the Days of Everett Anderson* and *Everett Anderson's Nine Month Long.*

[342]

EVERYBODY COOKS RICE [346]

Written by Norah Dooley
Illustrated by Peter J. Thornton

Cloth: Carolrhoda
Published: 1990

Carrie tours the neighborhood looking for her little brother and, just incidentally, checking out what's cooking—rice everywhere, and from everywhere. The children end up at home with *risi e bisi*, a dish from their Italian great-grandmother. Carrie has already tasted rice dishes (recipes included at the end) from Barbados, Puerto Rico, Vietnam, India, China, and Haiti. Nifty neighborhood.

EVERYBODY NEEDS A ROCK [347]

Written by Byrd Baylor
Illustrated by Peter Parnall

Cloth: Scribner
Paper: Aladdin
Published: 1974

Here is a guide to finding your own special rock, a bit of the earth to have and hold. Incidentally, the search for a special talisman teaches a good deal about the universe. The dramatic line drawings are engrossing in this seamless and persuasive collaboration between author and illustrator.

EVERYONE KNOWS WHAT A DRAGON LOOKS LIKE [348]

Written by Jay Williams
Illustrated by Mercer Mayer

Cloth: Four Winds
Paper: Aladdin
Published: 1976   **Prizes: New York Times Best Illustrated Book**

Of course, the truth is that everyone doesn't know what a dragon looks like, even in the Chinese kingdom wittily portrayed in this traditional tale. The story skillfully pokes fun at people's presumptions and prejudices.

FABLES [349]

Written and illustrated by Arnold Lobel

Cloth: HarperCollins
Paper: Harper Trophy
Published: 1980   **Prizes: Caldecott Medal**

These are short original fables with unexpected and definitely contemporary morals—pleasing to adult readers as well as children for their gentle wit and full-color illustrations.

FAIRY TALES OF EASTERN EUROPE [350]

Written by Neil Philip
Illustrated by Larry Wilkes

Cloth: Clarion
Published: 1992

This selection of twenty-two well-annotated and amusingly illustrated traditional stories from Eastern European countries begins with a creation tale from Serbia in which mankind is born from a drop of sweat from God's brow and includes stories about fools, maidens with golden hair, and magical flying ships from Romania, Russia, Hungary, Poland, and elsewhere.

THE FAROLITOS OF CHRISTMAS [351]

Written by Rudolfo Anaya
Illustrated by Edward Gonzales

Cloth: Hyperion
Paper: Hyperion
Published: 1995

World War II has ended, but Father has not come home yet, and Grandfather is ill and in the hospital, so it falls to Luz to find a way to light the farolitos—the candles placed in paper bags weighted with sand—that mark the path for pilgrims. Of course she does. The family story continues in *Farolitos for Abuelo,* which deals with the death of Luz's beloved grandfather.

FOLLOW THE DREAM: THE STORY OF CHRISTOPHER COLUMBUS [352]

Written and illustrated by Peter Sis

Cloth: Knopf
Paper: Dragonfly
Published: 1991

In telling the story of Christopher Columbus, the Czech-born artist also manages to convey the essential nature of the Middle Ages in Europe, the enclosed lives and societies, and the smallness of man in the vastness of exploration. The exquisite, detailed illustrations are worth hours of study.

THE FOOL OF THE WORLD AND THE FLYING SHIP [353]

Written by Arthur Ransome
Illustrated by Uri Shulevitz

Cloth: Farrar, Straus & Giroux
Paper: Sunburst
Published: 1968

Prizes: Caldecott Medal

The Fool of the World is a peasant who wins the hand of the czar's daughter by paying close attention to good advice and taking advantage of the skills of the Listener, the Swift-goer, the Drinker, and others. The old folktale is illustrated with great charm and wit.

FRANCIS: THE POOR MAN OF ASSISI [354]

Written and illustrated by Tomie dePaola

Cloth: Holiday House
Paper: Holiday House
Published: 1982

An episodic life of the well-loved saint, illustrated in a characteristic, stylized fashion by an artist with a folkloric touch.

[358]

THE FROG PRINCE CONTINUED [355]

Written by Jon Scieszka
Illustrated by Steve Johnson

Cloth: Viking Press
Published: 1991

So they got married, and then what happened? Well, it wasn't easy for a princess to be married to a former frog. He kept hopping around the furniture and occasionally flicking his tongue. This thoroughly logical sequel picks up the story when the prince goes off into the deep dark woods to find a witch who can leave her duties in other stories and help him. The clever story is matched by brilliantly stylish illustrations. Another clever variation on the story is *The Prog Frince: A Mixed-Up Tale* by C. Drew Lamm.

[356]

GALIMOTO [356]

Written by Karen Lynn Williams
Illustrated by Catherine Stock

Cloth: Lothrop, Lee & Shepard
Paper: Mulberry
Published: 1990

Kondi lives in a village on the shores of Lake Malawi. An imaginative and energetic boy, he spends an entire day collecting the bits of scrap he needs to build his very own galimoto. The word in Kondi's language, Chichewa, means both car and a kind of push toy. The text is precise and pleasing; the illustrations are delightfully rich and detailed. Watching Kondi collect his wires and snippets may inspire other young inventors.

[358]

THE GARDEN OF ABDUL GASAZI [357]

Written and illustrated by Chris Van Allsburg

Cloth: Houghton Mifflin
Published: 1979

A cautionary tale about a boy who lets the dog he is supposed to be caring for wander into the garden of a magician who specifically warns strangers not to enter. The first of a dazzling series of sophis-

ticated story books by an artist whose drawings are technically unparalleled but whose vision, particularly in the early books, is often chilly. Still, it's a cautionary tale.

[359]

THE GARDENER [358]

Written by Sarah Stewart
Illustrated by David Small

Cloth: Farrar, Straus & Giroux
Published: 1997   **Prizes: Caldecott Honor**

Hard times force the family to send Lydia Grace Finch from the family home on the farm to live with her uncle Jim in the city. Here the text is but an outline; the richness and depth of the story is in the wonderful illustrations that convey the family relationships, the meaning of hard times, and the true talents of a gardener.

GEORGE AND MARTHA [359]

Written and illustrated by James Marshall

Cloth: Houghton Mifflin
Paper: Houghton Mifflin
Published: 1972   **Prizes: New York Times Best Illustrated Book**

The first in a hilarious series of stories about two dear friends (who happen to be large, awkward hippos) with prominent buckteeth and a knack for finding themselves in farcical situations. Other titles include *George and Martha Back in Town, George and Martha One Fine Day, George and Martha Tons of Fun, George and Martha Rise and Shine, George and Martha Round and Round,* and the treasury entitled *George and Martha: The Complete Stories of Two Best Friends.*

THE GIFT OF THE SACRED DOG [360]

Written and illustrated by Paul Goble

Cloth: Simon & Schuster
Paper: Aladdin
Published: 1978

The beautifully illustrated legend tells about the arrival of the sacred dog, the horse, which totally changed the buffalo-hunting ways of the Plains Indians. The brilliant colors and stylized design make the horses especially vivid.

THE GIRL WHO DREAMED ONLY GEESE: AND OTHER TALES OF THE FAR NORTH [361]

Written by Howard Norman
Illustrated by Leo and Diane Dillon

Cloth: Harcourt Brace
Published: 1997 **Prizes: New York Times Best Illustrated Book**

[359]

A collection of ten stories of the ancient Arctic, culled from many spoken versions, engagingly told and handsomely illustrated. Some stories are nearly universal—for example, the one here called "Noah and the Woolly Mammoths." *The Dancing Fox* by John Bierhorst is another accessible collection of northern tales that wears its scholarship lightly.

THE GIRL WHO LOVED WILD HORSES [362]

Written and illustrated by Paul Goble

Cloth: Bradbury
Paper: Aladdin
Published: 1978 **Prizes: Caldecott Medal**

The romantic and compelling Plains Indian legend of a girl who so identifies with the wild horses that eventually she goes and joins them is beautifully illustrated in this prizewinning book. The artist's style abstracts traditional Indian design motifs.

[361]

143

THE GLORIOUS FLIGHT: ACROSS THE CHANNEL WITH LOUIS BLÉRIOT [363]

Written and illustrated by Alice Provensen

Cloth: Viking Press
Paper: Puffin
Published: 1983

Prizes: Caldecott Medal

In this spectacular book, history and art are in winning combination. It is the story of Louis Blériot, a Frenchman, and the flying machine he built to cross the English Channel. The illustrations convey both science and social period.

GOLDIE THE DOLLMAKER [364]

Written and illustrated by M. B. Goffstein

Cloth: Farrar, Straus & Giroux
Paper: Sunburst
Published: 1969

Goldie the dollmaker, who appears in delicate, careful drawings, is an artist who lives alone and makes dolls. She chooses the wood, carves the dolls carefully, then paints them with precision. It is an unusually satisfying story about love and work.

[368]

THE GOOD GIANTS AND THE BAD PUKWUDGIES [365]

Written by Jean Fritz
Illustrated by Tomie dePaola

Cloth: Putnam
Paper: Sandcastle
Published: 1982

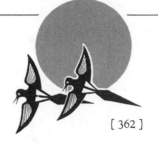

[362]

A folkloric account, drawn from Indian legends, about the formation of Cape Cod. The giant Mauship, his wife, Quant, and their five sons coexist with creatures called the pukwudgies, who sometimes appear as mosquitoes or fireflies. The author is a distinguished historian for children, the artist a prizewinner. Once the geography lesson is pointed out, the map of the Cape comes clear.

GORKY RISES [366]

Written and illustrated by William Steig

Cloth: Farrar, Straus & Giroux
Paper: Sunburst
Published: 1980   **Prizes: New York Times Best Illustrated Book**

Another zany Steig fable, this one about Gorky, a young frog, who fools around in the kitchen one summer morning when his parents are out. He makes a potion that, wondrously, later causes him to rise and fly through the soft afternoon.

GRANDFATHER TANG'S STORY [367]

Written by Ann Tompert
Illustrated by Robert Andrew Parker

Cloth: Crown
Published: 1990

Tangrams, the ancient Chinese puzzles in which a square is divided into five triangles, a square, and a rhomboid, are commonly used in teaching mathematical concepts throughout elementary school. Their storytelling properties should not be underestimated. Grandfather Tang and Little Soo sit under a tree and make up a story they illustrate with tangram pieces. First they make two foxes, then a rabbit, then a dog . . .

[362]

GRANDFATHER'S JOURNEY [368]

Written and illustrated by Allen Say

Cloth: Houghton Mifflin
Paper: Houghton Mifflin
Published: 1993   **Prizes: New York Times Best Illustrated Book**

This is the story of two journeys of discovery—the grandfather, who left Japan as a young man and moved to the United States, then went back to Japan, and the author/narrator, who was raised in Japan and moved to the United States. The portrait illustrations, calm and elegant, have a startling intensity. *Tea with Milk* is the story of the person in the middle, the author's mother, who also appears in *Tree of Cranes*.

GRANDMOTHER'S PIGEON [369]

Written by Louise Erdrich
Illustrated by Jim LaMarche

Cloth: Hyperion
Paper: Hyperion
Published: 1996

A story of modest magic. Without warning, Grandmother interrupts her annual visit to hop a porpoise to Greenland. A year later, the family find a nest of three eggs that hatch and, it turns out, belong to an extinct species, the passenger pigeon. The prose is lyric and illustrations capture the delicate magic of the nest and the children's wonder and determination to see that right is done.

GRANDPA TAKES ME TO THE MOON [370]

Written by Timothy R. Gaffney
Illustrated by Barry Root

Cloth: Tambourine
Published: 1996

At bedtime, Grandpa tells about his trip to the moon on an Apollo spacecraft. The illustrations show the mission; however, the crew has had some amendments. It consists of grandfather as he is today, wrinkled and leathery, his youthful grandson, and another astronaut. It's a surprisingly affecting book, recalling the thrill of those journeys. There are several other story books with solid information about the

Apollo missions and the problems and excitement of manned space travel, including *Man on the Moon* by Anastasia Suen, *Here in Space* by David Milgrim, and *Floating Home* by David Getz.

A GREAT BIG UGLY MAN CAME UP AND TIED HIS HORSE TO ME [371]

Written and illustrated by Wallace Tripp

Cloth: Little, Brown
Paper: Little, Brown
Published: 1973

A collection of hilarious poems and nonsense, illustrated in deadpan fashion by an artist who challenges the reader's attention by inserting famous people, past and present, in improbable settings. Great fun to read with children, but they happily read it alone. *Grandpa Griggs* is another great collection.

A HANDFUL OF BEANS: SIX FAIRY TALES [372]

Written by William Steig
Illustrated by Jeanne Steig

Cloth: HarperCollins
Published: 1998   **Prizes: New York Times Best Illustrated Book**

Traditional tales, including "Hansel and Gretel," "Jack and the Beanstalk," and "Little Red Riding Hood," amusingly told (each ends with a rhyme) and charmingly illustrated. A small book, nice to hold in the hand and read to a lap listener who might or might not already know when to laugh or be worried.

HANSEL AND GRETEL [373]

Written by Rika Lesser
Illustrated by Paul O. Zelinsky

Cloth: Dodd, Mead/Putnam
Paper: Paper Star
Published: 1984   **Prizes: Caldecott Honor**

This lush version of the most familiar of the Grimm stories is based on the first transcription of the tale. The oil paintings that illustrate

it are in the style of eighteenth-century European landscape painting. There are, of course, many other editions of the story, including those illustrated by Susan Jeffers, who favors large, wide-eyed faces; Lisbeth Zwerger, whose style is very delicate and subtle; Paul Galdone, who uses broad, cartoonish lines; and Margot Tomes, whose quirky pen-and-ink characters have psychological weight. James Marshall's version has a slapstick quality, and Jane Ray's is ornate.

HARLEM [374]

Written by Walter Dean Myers
Illustrated by Christopher Myers

Cloth: Scholastic
Published: 1997

The verse rides on the A train, and the vibrant collage illustrations bring the New York City neighborhood that is also a state of mind and a historic reference into sharp focus. Good for talking about.

THE HATMAKER'S SIGN: A STORY OF BENJAMIN FRANKLIN [375]

Written by Candace Fleming
Illustrated by Robert Andrew Parker

Cloth: Orchard Books
Published: 1998

A twofer: an amusing story about interesting historical figures that relates directly to a problem every young writer (every writer!) faces—revision. During the drafting of the Declaration of Independence in July 1776, Benjamin Franklin is said to have consoled Thomas Jefferson, who was frustrated by delegates' changes to his prose, with the story of a Boston hatmaker and the sign he wanted for his shop.

[378]

HATTIE AND THE WILD WAVES: A STORY FROM BROOKLYN [376]

Written and illustrated by Barbara Cooney

Cloth: Viking Press
Paper: Puffin
Published: 1990

The daughter of well-to-do German Americans in Brooklyn at the turn of the century, Hattie wants to be a painter. As the large household progresses pleasantly bemused by her through the seasons and years, Hattie remains determined, and eventually she succeeds in enrolling in the art institute. The illustrations and text capture the affectionate family and their comfortable days with such charm and nuances of insight it is not surprising to learn that Hattie, who really did become a painter, is based on the author's mother.

HAVING A WONDERFUL TIME [377]

Written and illustrated by Tom Pohrt

Cloth: Farrar, Straus & Giroux
Published: 1999

Ah, what a trip. Eva and her cat, Sam, catch a zeppelin and find themselves someplace with deserts and oases, palm trees and crocodiles. In these delicate line and watercolor illustrations the place looks quite wonderful and glamorous, rather like French North Africa half a century or more in the past. The tone is calm, as though this sort of adventure might just happen any day to you and your pet.

HAWK, I'M YOUR BROTHER [378]

Written by Byrd Baylor
Illustrated by Peter Parnall

Cloth: Scribner's
Paper: Aladdin
Published: 1976

In the Southwest, a bare land of mountains and wide sky, a boy named Rudy dreams of flying like a hawk over Santos Mountain. He captures a young hawk and eventually sets it free. The adults are wise and understanding. A very affecting book that is thrilling to read out loud, with spare evocative illustrations.

HER MAJESTY, AUNT ESSIE   [379]

Written and illustrated by Amy Schwartz

Cloth: Bradbury
Paper: Penguin
Published: 1984

The little girl who narrates this story can just tell that her aunt Essie, who has moved into her family's apartment (located in an inner-city neighborhood in perhaps the 1940s), used to be a queen. Aunt Essie's style, habits, and gentleman caller make it clear—and believable. It is an affectionate look at eccentricity in family life.

HEROES   [380]

Written by Ken Mochizuki
Illustrated by Dom Lee

Cloth: Lee & Low
Paper: Lee & Low
Published: 1995

In the 1960s Donnie Okada took a lot of razzing from the other boys in the neighborhood; they insisted that he had to be the enemy in their war games because he looked like the enemy, and they did not believe his father and uncle had served in the American military. Dad and Uncle Yosh give those boys a dignified and effective lesson.

HERSHEL AND THE HANUKKAH GOBLINS   [381]

Written by Eric Kimmel
Illustrated by Trina Schart Hyman

Cloth: Holiday House
Paper: Holiday House
Published: 1989

Prizes: Caldecott Honor

The setting is an Eastern European village, and the plot borders on Halloween Hanukkah. It seems that goblins are occupying the synagogue on the hill. Along comes plucky Hershel of Ostropol, and he cleverly outwits the definitely spooky demons on the successive nights of Hanukkah.

HEY, AL [382]

Written by Arthur Yorinks
Illustrated by Richard Egielski

Cloth: Farrar, Straus & Giroux
Paper: Sunburst
Published: 1986   **Prizes: Caldecott Medal**

Al, a janitor, and Edie, his dog, live together in a small room on the West Side of Manhattan. When they are offered a chance to go to a paradisiacal island, they discover that the life of luxury, lush as it may be, has too high a price. They manage to escape and are grateful to return home. The brilliant full-color illustrations—from the cramped apartment to the tropical island—are just right.

HILDILID'S NIGHT [383]

Written by Cheli Duran Ryan
Illustrated by Arnold Lobel

Cloth: Macmillan
Paper: Aladdin
Published: 1971   **Prizes: Caldecott Honor**

Hildilid is an old woman who is determined to put off the night. Among other things, she tries to sweep it out, tie it up, burn it. She fails, of course, but a sleep-resisting child enjoys the effort.

HOME RUN: THE STORY OF BABE RUTH [384]

Written by Robert Burleigh
Illustrated by Mike Wimmer

Cloth: Harcourt Brace
Published: 1998

The story of the mighty baseball legend is told in lushly romantic illustrations and data-filled, old-style bubble-gum baseball cards. His record of sixty home runs stood for thirty-four years, and his legend lasts.

HOMES IN THE WILDERNESS: A PILGRIM'S JOURNAL OF THE PLYMOUTH PLANTATION IN 1620 BY WILLIAM BRADFORD AND OTHERS OF THE MAYFLOWER COMPANY [385]

Written and illustrated by Margaret Wise Brown

Cloth: Linnet Books/Shoestring Press
Paper: Linnet Books/Shoestring Press
Published: 1939

This simply written adaptation of the actual Pilgrim diaries, reissued in 1988, has a thrilling immediacy. The clear drawings and maps help the modern reader to understand the geography and scale of the community.

HORTON HATCHES THE EGG [386]

Written and illustrated by Dr. Seuss

Cloth: Random House
Published: 1940

To be truly successful, nonsense has to be unrelenting and, by its own lights, logical, and in his early books Dr. Seuss was a master of the genre. Horton the elephant agrees to hatch an egg, and he sticks to his promise through a year of hilarious trials and outrageous tribulations. Then his kindness and devotion are truly rewarded.

THE HOSPITAL BOOK [387]

Written by James Howe
Illustrated by Mal Warshaw

Cloth: Crown
Paper: Beech Tree Books
Published: 1981

Here is a detailed introduction to both routine and unusual hospital procedures for older children. It is illustrated with black-and-white photographs showing everything from the insertion of intravenous tubes to special oxygen tanks. The text is straightforward and very informative.

HOW MANY DAYS TO AMERICA? A THANKSGIVING STORY [388]

Written by Eve Bunting
Illustrated by Beth Peck

Cloth: Clarion
Paper: Clarion
Published: 1988

At the end of this account of the recent arrival on U.S. shores of an open boat filled with refugees from an unnamed island, a welcoming soul offers two children heaping dinner plates and an explanation: "Long ago, unhappy people came here to start new lives. . . . They celebrated by giving thanks." It's a good thing to remember.

HOW MANY SPOTS DOES A LEOPARD HAVE? AND OTHER TALES [389]

Written by Julius Lester
Illustrated by David Shannon

Cloth: Scholastic
Published: 1989

A surprisingly vivid and effective collection of African and Jewish folktales, told with colloquial verve and illustrated with lush full-page color paintings. Easy and satisfying to read aloud.

HOW MUCH IS A MILLION? [390]

Written by David M. Schwartz
Illustrated by Steven Kellogg

Cloth: Lothrop, Lee & Shepard
Paper: Mulberry
Published: 1985

A series of lighthearted conceptualizations and visualizations of really big numbers, such as how big a bowl you would need to hold, say, a million goldfish. The giddy full-color illustrations hold up under intense scrutiny. *If You Made a Million* goes at that big idea another way, but the illustrator is the same.

HOW MY PARENTS LEARNED TO EAT [391]

Written by Ina Friedman
Illustrated by Allen Say

Cloth: Houghton Mifflin
Paper: Puffin
Published: 1984

A little girl describes her parents' courtship ritual, which was caring and thoughtful, as her father was an American sailor stationed in Japan and her mother was a proper young Japanese lady. The illustrations are subtly reminiscent of nineteenth-century Japanese woodcuts.

HOW SANTA GOT HIS JOB [392]

Written by Stephen Krensky
Illustrated by S. D. Schindler

Cloth: Simon & Schuster
Published: 1998

So what did Santa do before he got the job at the North Pole? Here's an amusing resume of sorts, visually set in the 1950s in urban America, about a fine fellow too much of a perfectionist to hold jobs for very long. But a little chimney cleaning, a little cooking, a little zoo work, and well, one thing leads to another. Quite charming and fun for believers and cynics alike.

HOW THE GRINCH STOLE CHRISTMAS [393]

Written and illustrated by Dr. Seuss

Cloth: Random House
Published: 1957

[393]

Dr. Seuss's sermon on the true meaning of Christmas features one of the best Scrooges of the twentieth century, that wretched, selfish Grinch. The animated version is shown on television regularly but, like "The Night Before Christmas," it's more fun to read aloud than watch.

HOW YOU WERE BORN   [394]

Written by Joanna Cole
Illustrated by Margaret Miller

Cloth: Morrow Junior Books
Paper: Mulberry
Published: 1984

When the appropriate time comes, this is a fine book to read with young children who want to know how babies grow inside the mother and are born. The text is clear and accurate; the photographs are beautiful, rather than alarming, for readers from toddler to middle grade level.

THE HUCKABUCK FAMILY AND HOW THEY RAISED POPCORN IN NEBRASKA AND QUIT AND CAME BACK   [395]

Written by Carl Sandburg
Illustrated by David Small

Cloth: Farrar, Straus & Giroux
Published: 1999

[393]

One of the more enduring of the Rootabaga Stories has been gloriously illustrated. After a fire popped their entire popcorn harvest, the Huckabucks and their daughter Pony Pony traveled around the Midwest for three years of adventures. The illustrations set the tale during the Depression and include some splendid barnyard animals and industrial scenes.

I, CROCODILE   [396]

Written and illustrated by Fred Marcellino

Cloth: HarperCollins
Published: 1999   **Prizes: New York Times Best Illustrated Book**

Loosely based on the fact that Napoleon Bonaparte imported an Egyptian crocodile and it was the talk of Paris, here is the story, elaborated and narrated by same creature. The illustrations are rich and droll; the vocabulary may be a bit too rich and droll for younger readers.

I HEAR AMERICA SINGING [397]

Written by Walt Whitman
Illustrated by Robert Sabuda

Cloth: Philomel
Published: 1991

The celebratory hymn to diversity and strength is illustrated in this edition with linoleum-cut prints in pastel hues. The full text of the poem is included at the end. Another great nineteenth-century text, similarly illustrated, is *The Gettysburg Address,* with woodcuts by Michael McCurdy.

I KNOW A LADY [398]

Written by Charlotte Zolotow
Illustrated by James Stevenson

Cloth: Greenwillow
Paper: Mulberry
Published: 1984

In this collaboration between author and artist, a child describes the old lady in her small-town neighborhood who offers perfect friendship to the children as well as small seasonal gifts like homemade cookies or lemonade. The illustrations evoke New England and a nostalgic sense of a social order—of the way things ought to be.

I LIKE THE MUSIC [399]

Written by Leah Komaiko
Illustrated by Barbara Westman

Cloth: HarperCollins
Paper: Harper Trophy
Published: 1987

The girl who tells this story likes urban street music; she's hip and cool. Her grandmother, who is pretty hip herself, takes the child to her first outdoor symphony concert, with happy results. The full-color illustrations are festive.

[400]

I ONCE WAS A MONKEY: STORIES BUDDHA TOLD [400]

Written and illustrated by Jeanne M. Lee

Cloth: Farrar, Straus & Giroux
Published: 1999

A collection of six jatakas, the fables that the Buddha told his disciples, featuring enlightened animals whose form the Buddha took at one time or another: a forest sprite, a dove, a monkey. They can be read separately or together with children of a wide range of ages, and provide a great deal to talk about.

IF YOU ARE A HUNTER OF FOSSILS [401]

Written by Byrd Baylor
Illustrated by Peter Parnall

[400]

Cloth: Scribner
Paper: Aladdin
Published: 1980

Here is a splendid introduction to paleontology, with spare, poetic prose and pictures showing how rocks reveal secrets of past life.

IN COAL COUNTRY [402]

Written by Judith Hendershot
Illustrated by Thomas Allen

Cloth: Knopf
Paper: Knopf
Published: 1987

Papa returns from the coal mine blue-eyed, of course, but black-faced from coal dust, grinning at his daughter, who has come to meet him and is seen, in an evocative illustration, reflected in the glass of his head lamp. The text, which recalls growing up in a coal-mining town in the 1950s, is unsentimental and proud; the rich illustrations seem properly smudged with the omnipresent dust.

[402]

IN THE NIGHT KITCHEN [403]

Written and illustrated by Maurice Sendak

Cloth: HarperCollins
Paper: Harper Trophy
Published: 1970

Prizes: Caldecott Honor
New York Times Best Illustrated Book

Mickey's dream adventure carries him into the night kitchen, where the bakers are making cake for the morning. The brilliant illustrations are also about movies and New York City in the 1930s. Some adults have found the story—not to mention Mickey's frontal nudity—alarming, but children, especially boys, adore the nocturnal adventure.

IN THE TIME OF THE DRUMS [404]

Written by Kim L. Siegelson
Illustrated by Brian Pinkney

Cloth: Hyperion
Published: 1999

The setting is the Sea Islands off the coast of Georgia. Grandmother Twi tells Mentu of the slaves who walked into the water. It's a haunting and subversive tale of defiance, eloquently told, handsomely illustrated.

THE INCREDIBLE PAINTING OF FELIX CLOUSSEAU [405]

Written and illustrated by Jon Agee

Cloth: Farrar, Straus & Giroux
Paper: Sunburst
Published: 1988

At a grown-up level, the story of Felix Clousseau and the literal triumph of his paintings, which come to life and leave the salon in Paris, is about art and the establishment. From a young child's perspective it's purely funny, and the droll pictures make more of shades of gray than anyone might reasonably imagine. Older children may find a lot to think about behind the jokes.

[405]

THE INK DRINKER [406]

Written by Eric Sanvoisin
Illustrated by Martin Matje

Cloth: Delacorte
Published: 1998

The son of a used- and rare-book dealer, Odilon is a little boy with a taste for tales . . . and he sucks ink from the printed page with a straw, savoring the flavor of each story. The adventure continues in *A Straw for Two*. These little books are translated from the French by George Moroz, but retain a Gallic sophistication that will appeal to older children and adults.

IRA SLEEPS OVER [407]

Written and illustrated by Bernard Waber

Cloth: Houghton Mifflin
Paper: Houghton Mifflin
Published: 1972

A first sleepover, even if it is at the house of a close friend like Reggie, who lives right next door to Ira, is a big event. Here it is handled tenderly, and the story is told almost entirely in pricelessly accurate dialogue. The important question is whether a boy takes his teddy bear along. *Ira Says Goodbye* takes place a few years later, when Reggie's family decides to move, and deals as sensitively with a different problem of separation.

ISLAND BOY   [408]

Written and illustrated by Barbara Cooney

Cloth: Viking Press
Paper: Puffin
Published: 1988

Consider the life of Matthais Tibbetts, who lived a full, rich one mostly on a small island off the coast of Maine. His parents and eleven siblings all abandoned the island for easier places, but Matthais returned from a career at sea and settled in. The brilliantly spare New England voice telling the story is calm and controlled. The haunting illustrations are washed with the blues of sea and sky. It is a companion, in its way, to *Miss Rumphius.*

[412]

IT COULD ALWAYS BE WORSE   [409]

Written and illustrated by Margot Zemach

Cloth: Farrar, Straus & Giroux
Paper: Sunburst
Published: 1977

Prizes: Caldecott Honor
New York Times Best Illustrated Book

A poor man thinks his overflowing household in an Eastern European town is so intolerably crowded that he goes to the rabbi to ask for advice. Amazingly, amusingly, astonishingly, his life gets worse, and the man learns to count his blessings. A familiar folktale, told and illustrated with charm. Another version of the same story is *Too Much Noise* by Anne McGovern.

JOAN OF ARC   [410]

Written and illustrated by Diane Stanley

Cloth: Morrow Junior Books
Published: 1998

This handsome storybook account of the life of Joan of Arc comes with a lot of support for the young reader in the text, maps, even a pronunciation guide. The detailed illustrations are also worth studying. Another storybook by Josephine Poole also covers the same material handsomely, and *Young Joan,* a novel for middle to upper grade readers by Barbara Dana, is a good next step for an interested reader.

JOHN HENRY [411]

Written by Julius Lester
Illustrated by Jerry Pinkney

Cloth: Dial
Paper: Puffin
Published: 1994

It's not really clear if there was a real John Henry, but a former slave of that name may have worked on the Big Bend Tunnel of the Chesapeake & Ohio Railroad that was built in the Allegheny Mountains between 1870 and 1873. This skillful account gives details and speculations about a legend lost in song. The large format illustrations are dignified and absorbing.

JOHNNY APPLESEED [412]

Written by Reeve Lindbergh
Illustrated by Kathy Jakobsen

Cloth: Little, Brown
Published: 1990

The primitive-style illustrations, with details of quilt motifs in the borders, carry a narrative poem about John Chapman along briskly. The endpapers show a map, decorated with blooming apple trees, in which the states he walked through—from Massachusetts to Indiana—are outlined in fruit.

JULIUS, THE BABY OF THE WORLD [413]

Written and illustrated by Kevin Henkes

Cloth: Greenwillow
Paper: Mulberry
Published: 1990

This is big-time sibling rivalry, even if it takes place in a family of mice. In word and gesture, Lilly makes it clear just how affronted she is by the thing they are all cooing over and praising to the skies. The parents are caught in shrewd characterizations as well, and the final spin—Lilly defending baby Julius from cousin Garland—is utterly believable. Life for Lilly gets better when she has her own book (*Lilly's Purple Plastic Purse*).

[412]

161

[414]

JUMANJI   [414]

Written and illustrated by Chris Van Allsburg

Cloth: Houghton Mifflin
Published: 1981

Prizes: Caldecott Medal
New York Times Best Illustrated Book

Two restless, cranky children find a board game in the park. They take it home and somehow unleash jungle creatures in the house. Complex, haunting pencil illustrations create a real sense of threat and excitement before a safe return to reality. Ignore the movie.

KASHTANKA   [415]

Written by Anton Chekhov
Illustrated by Gennady Spirin

Cloth: Harcourt Brace
Paper: Harcourt Brace
Published: 1995

Prizes: New York Times Best Illustrated Book

The story of the faithful dog who gets lost, ends up in a small circus, and then is spotted by her master and his family, who are in the audience one night, is beautifully captured by the Russian artist whose style is unmistakably lavish and detailed.

[415]

KING ISLAND CHRISTMAS [416]

Written by Jean Rogers
Illustrated by Rie Munoz

Cloth: Greenwillow
Paper: Mulberry
Published: 1985

The Eskimo community of King Island has to rescue its new priest and get him from his stranded ship in the Bering Sea to the village in time for Christmas. An unusual story with glorious illustrations in the myriad blues of the north.

KING MIDAS AND
THE GOLDEN TOUCH [417]

Written by Charlotte Craft
Illustrated by K. Y. Craft

Cloth: Morrow Junior Books
Published: 1999

This version of the familiar tale of the king who wished for a golden touch is set in a lavish, rather Victorian court, and is altogether sumptuous and grand. Another contemporary telling, *The Midas Touch* by Jan Mark sets the story in ancient Greece and has an introduction that explains the pagan premise to the tale, while *King Midas* by John Warren Stewig is a kind of sitcom telling of the tale with lavish but joky illustrations.

LASSIE COME-HOME [418]

Written by Rosemary Wells
Illustrated by Susan Jeffers

Cloth: Henry Holt
Published: 1995

The original 1938 story of the noble collie, by Eric Knight, is out of print. This large format storybook handsomely captures the essence of the tale. The devoted dog travels from her new home in Scotland

all the way back to the poor Yorkshire boy who raised her. Not to be confused with the 1950s television series set in the American West.

LEON AND BOB   [419]

Written and illustrated by Simon James

Cloth: Candlewick Press
Published: 1997   **Prizes: New York Times Best Illustrated Book**

Leon is new in town, and Bob is the imaginary friend he confides in during this stressful time. Leon makes breakfast for Bob, goes to school with him, and wants to take him to meet the new boy who has moved in next door. But at a crucial moment, Bob disappears. Or does he?

LIKE JAKE AND ME   [420]

Written by Mavis Jukes
Illustrated by Lloyd Bloom

Cloth: Knopf
Paper: Knopf
Published: 1984   **Prizes: Newbery Honor**

Alex, who is quiet and rather shy, probably like his father, is trying to cope with his stepfather, Jake, a brash cowboy. The turning point comes when Alex rescues Jake from a wolf spider. This well-written story about the formation of new families carries special conviction. The illustrations are insightful.

[421]

LILLY'S PURPLE PLASTIC PURSE   [421]

Written and illustrated by Kevin Henkes

Cloth: Greenwillow
Paper: Mulberry
Published: 1996

Lilly, who goes to school wearing red cowboy boots and carrying her purple plastic purse that plays a tune when it is opened, runs into trouble with her beloved teacher Mr. Slinger because she is disrupting the class. The story of their crisis and reconciliation is glorious, not least because it rings so true. Lilly appears in *Julius, the Baby of the World* and *Chester's Way,* but here she is truly a star.

LINNEA IN MONET'S GARDEN   [422]

Written by Christina Bjork
Illustrated by Lena Anderson

Cloth: R & S
Published: 1987

One of the first and most popular of the many books about children interacting with artists. It features an enchanting blond child with freckles and the best-known Impressionist garden and gardener of all. It has proven enduringly popular, abetted by *Linnea's Almanac* and *Linnea's Windowsill Garden.*

[421]

THE LITTLE CAT AND THE GREEDY OLD WOMAN [423]

Written and illustrated by Joan Rankin

Cloth: Margaret K. McElderry
Published: 1995

A cautionary tale that is both entertaining and wise. The greedy old woman ignores her orange striped cat as she prepares a very special dinner just for herself. He asks politely, implores, and finally tries to snatch just a bit. The old woman throws him out in the rain, where, fueled by his anger, he grows into tiger size. When all's well and he's treated with respect, they again live harmoniously. Lovely watercolor illustrations.

THE LITTLE RED LIGHTHOUSE AND THE GREAT GRAY BRIDGE [424]

Written by Hildegarde Hoyt Swift
Illustrated by Lynd Ward

Cloth: Harcourt Brace
Paper: Voyager
Published: 1942

There really is a little red lighthouse that sits in the shadow of the George Washington Bridge, which spans the Hudson River at the northern edge of New York City. This has been a picture-book favorite for generations.

LITTLE RED RIDING HOOD [425]

Written by the Brothers Grimm
Illustrated by Trina Schart Hyman

Cloth: Holiday House
Paper: Holiday House
Published: 1983   **Prizes: Caldecott Honor**

The illustrator of this version of the classic tale has a distinctive style—lush, romantic, anxious, and at the same time tense—that suits the story well. There are many other editions, including cartoonish ones illustrated by Paul Galdone, James Marshall, and Harriet Pincus, and a very provocative one illustrated with photographs by Sarah Moon. Consider the age of the reader when choosing—younger children find the lighter, more cartoonish versions easier to handle.

THE LITTLE SHIPS: THE HEROIC RESCUE AT DUNKIRK IN WORLD WAR II [426]

Written by Louise Borden
Illustrated by Michael Foreman

Cloth: Margaret K. McElderry
Published: 1997

The story of the rescue of more than 300,000 Allied troops from the French beaches in 800 ships of all types and sizes, told through the eyes of a young British girl whose family's fishing boat took part. Powerful watercolor illustrations. It's a story book in form, with its brief text and extensive illustrations, but in terms of subject matter it is for middle grade readers grappling with history.

[423]

LITTLE SISTER AND THE MONTH BROTHERS [427]

Written by Beatrice Schenk de Regniers
Illustrated by Margot Tomes

Cloth: Clarion
Paper: Mulberry
Published: 1976

In this bright retelling of the Russian fairy tale about how the Month Brothers help Little Sister meet the seasonally impossible demands of her greedy stepmother, the illustrations are witty and washed with moody grays. There are other versions of the story, but this one is worth finding.

LON PO PO: A RED RIDING HOOD STORY FROM CHINA [428]

Written and illustrated by Ed Young

Cloth: Philomel
Paper: Paper Star
Published: 1989   **Prizes: Caldecott Medal**

Mysterious watercolor illustrations make this story of the three Chinese sisters who mistake the wolf for Po Po, their grandmother, very appealing. They realize their mistake, and the next day they cleverly lure the predator up into the ginkgo tree.

LORD OF THE DANCE: AN AFRICAN RETELLING [429]

Written and illustrated by Veronique Tadjo

Cloth: HarperCollins
Published: 1990

The Senufo people who live in the Ivory Coast have always worshiped spirits represented by sacred masks. The text is a transposition of the traditional hymn "Lord of the Dance," which is retold as the mask's song and which conveys the beliefs that guide Senufo tradition and modern life. The brilliantly colored illustrations are spare and the symbolism is accessible to young readers.

[428]

[430]

LOTTIE'S NEW BEACH TOWEL [430]

Written and illustrated by Petra Mathers

Cloth: Atheneum
Published: 1998

Aunt Mattie's note that comes with the red and white polka-dot beach towel suggests that Lottie the chicken might find her gift handy this summer. She certainly does. She and her friend Herbie the duck set to sea one fine beach day and . . . well, it's an adventure. In *Lottie's New Friend,* Herbie suffers from severe jealousy—needlessly, it turns out. The stylish faux-primitive illustrations are done in luminous pastel colors.

LOUIS THE FISH [431]

Written by Arthur Yorinks
Illustrated by Richard Egielski

Cloth: Farrar, Straus & Giroux
Paper: Sunburst
Published: 1980

A perfectly executed, scaly fantasy in which Louis, a respectable, aproned butcher, turns into a large fish—a salmon, actually. And he looks really ridiculous lying in bed under the covers, wearing striped pajamas over his fins. It's the kind of zany story that often appeals to parents as much as to children.

LOVE AS STRONG AS GINGER [432]

Written by Lenore Look
Illustrated by Stephen T. Johnson

Cloth: Atheneum
Published: 1999

The author's Chinese immigrant grandmother worked in a Seattle cannery cracking crabs in the 1960s and '70s. This loving anecdotal tale about going with her to the factory, about her labors and her heavenly cooking, about the hot bath needed to wash the chiubungbung—the very bad crab smell—from hair and skin has been delicately illustrated in pastel and watercolor.

LYLE, LYLE, CROCODILE [433]

Written and illustrated by Bernard Waber

Cloth: Houghton Mifflin
Paper: Houghton Mifflin
Published: 1965

The crocodile who first moved in with the Primm family in *The House on East 88th Street* now wants to make friends with Loretta the cat. The family copes, of course. Other titles in the series include *Lovable Lyle, Lyle and the Birthday Party,* and *Lyle Finds His Mother.*

[434]

THE MAGIC SCHOOL BUS AT THE WATERWORKS [434]

Written by Joanna Cole
Illustrated by Bruce Degen

Cloth: Scholastic
Paper: Scholastic
Published: 1986

With her outlandish outfits and diffident manner, Mrs. Frizzle may be the strangest teacher in the school, but the trip she takes her class on—going into the reservoir system and through the waterworks and back to school—is magical. Everyone—even Arnold, the anxious whiner—has a wonderful time and helps tell part of the tale. The straight scientific information is delivered in sidebar notes. The book is a model of witty, imaginative, and accurate science writing, with equally amusing and clever illustrations. The series includes

The Magic School Bus: Inside the Earth; The Magic School Bus: Inside the Human Body; and *The Magic School Bus: Lost in the Solar System.*

MAILING MAY [435]

Written by Michael O. Tunnell
Illustrated by Ted Rand

Cloth: Greenwillow
Published: 1998

Based on the true story of how, in 1914, five-year-old Charlotte May Pierstorff was sent by train across the Idaho mountains to visit her grandmother. May was sent as an under-fifty-pound package, labeled "baby chick." It's improbable, and while it could be frightening, terrifying even, it's told as a charming anecdote about goodwill, cooperation, and adventure, and comes complete with a photograph of the real May.

[433]

MAMA, DO YOU LOVE ME? [436]

Written and illustrated by Barbara M. Joosse

Cloth: Chronicle
Published: 1991

Children everywhere tease and test their mothers, and this little girl in Alaska is no exception. The naughtiness she imagines—"What if I put salmon in your parka, ermine in your mittens, and lemmings in your mukluks?"—is charmingly illustrated, and does not daunt Mama.

THE MAN WHOSE MOTHER WAS A PIRATE [437]

Written by Margaret Mahy
Illustrated by Margaret Chamberlin

Cloth: Viking Press
Paper: Puffin
Published: 1986

He's an office-worker wimp, his mother was a pirate, and now she wants to go home to the sea. So, with only a wheelbarrow and a

kite, Sam takes her. The illustrations to this grand story are broad and funny; the text, however, is far better still, and includes lyrical praise of the sea. This book is worth reading aloud again and again just for the pleasure of the language.

MANY MOONS   [438]

Written by James Thurber
Illustrated by Louis Slobodkin

Cloth: Harcourt Brace
Paper: Voyager
Published: 1943   **Prizes: Caldecott Medal**

There was once a little princess who wanted the moon—and she got it. A classic story with pale, subtle, haunting illustrations. There is also a newer edition, with illustrations by Marc Simont.

MARGUERITE, GO WASH YOUR FEET!   [439]

Written and illustrated by Wallace Tripp

Cloth: Houghton Mifflin
Paper: Houghton Mifflin
Published: 1985   **Prizes: New York Times Best Illustrated Book**

A collection of funny verse from Shakespeare to Spike Milligan, with subtly sharp illustrations, many of which contain cartoonish renditions of famous people.

MARTHA SPEAKS   [440]

Written and illustrated by Susan Meddaugh

Cloth: Houghton Mifflin
Paper: Houghton Mifflin   **Prizes: Caldecott Honor**
Published: 1992   **New York Times Best Illustrated Book**

The letters in the alphabet soup Martha ate went to her brain, not her stomach, and lo, the dog could speak. Her first thought is, of course, where her dinner is. Her conversations with her family are deadpan and hilarious, as are the illustrations. The sequels are *Martha Calling* and *Martha Blah Blah*.

MARTIN LUTHER KING, JR. [441]

Written by Rosemary L. Bray
Illustrated by Malcah Zeldis

Cloth: Greenwillow
Paper: Mulberry
Published: 1994

Vivid full-page paintings in a folk-art style give special strength to a straightforward biography for young readers of the civil rights leader.

MARVEN OF THE GREAT NORTH WOODS [442]

Written by Kathryn Lasky
Illustrated by Kevin Hawkes

Cloth: Harcourt Brace
Published: 1997

[436]

The author's grandfather was sent from his family's home in Duluth, Minnesota, during the influenza epidemic of 1918 to spend the winter at a logging camp in the Great North Woods. It is both a modest and an enormous adventure. He traveled alone and lived among giants, doing the work of a man, and then went home. Appealing illustrations.

MATH CURSE [443]

Written by Jon Scieszka
Illustrated by Lane Smith

Cloth: Viking Press
Paper: Puffin
Published: 1995

This is a sharp-tongued send-up of those cheerful math workbooks that drive children everywhere wild, complete with zany typography, breakneck speed, and what might best be called genial nihilism. The twenty-four hours of living math presented here isn't very serious, but it's a lot of fun.

MAZEL AND SHLIMAZEL [444]

Written by Isaac Bashevis Singer
Illustrated by Margot Zemach

Cloth: Farrar, Straus & Giroux
Paper: Sunburst
Published: 1967

This story, told in the manner of an Eastern European folktale, is about the contest between good and evil, which take the forms of the happy and good Mazel and the wicked old Shlimazel. The illustrations perfectly complement the fable.

A MEDIEVAL FEAST [445]

Written and illustrated by Aliki

Cloth: HarperCollins
Paper: Harper Trophy
Published: 1983

What happens when the king announces that he and his attendants plan to visit the lord of the manor? In this remarkably accomplished historical storybook, the detailed illustrations, in the medieval style, show both the structure of manor life and the elaborate preparations that must take place before the king arrives—how the food is prepared and served, the entertainment organized, and so on. Joe Lasker's *Merry Ever After* and *A Tournament of Knights* are fine companion titles.

[446]

MERRY EVER AFTER: THE STORY OF TWO MEDIEVAL WEDDINGS [446]

Written and illustrated by Joe Lasker

Cloth: Viking Press
Paper: Puffin
Published: 1976   **Prizes: New York Times Best Illustrated Book**

The celebration of two weddings offers a fine explanation of class and custom in the Middle Ages. The illustrations are detailed and high-spirited. *A Tournament of Knights* by the same author is another good story book about medieval life, as is *A Medieval Feast* by Aliki.

MIKE MULLIGAN AND
HIS STEAM SHOVEL   [447]

Written and illustrated by Virginia Lee Burton

Cloth: Houghton Mifflin
Paper: Houghton Mifflin
Published: 1939

A classic picture book with a message that has pleased generations
of young readers. Mike Mulligan and his steam shovel, Mary Anne,
are being declared obsolete, but fiercely determined, they find one
last job in a small town. They dig their way to a new career and a
happy ending.

MING LO MOVES
THE MOUNTAIN   [448]

Written and illustrated by Arnold Lobel

Cloth: Scholastic
Paper: Mulberry
Published: 1982

Ming Lo asks the wise man's help in moving the mountain away
from his house because of the falling debris that annoys his
cranky wife. The wise man puffs away on his water pipe and
eventually comes up with the perfect solution that convinces
Ming Lo and, more important, his wife that indeed the mountain
has moved.

MINN OF THE MISSISSIPPI   [449]

Written and illustrated by Holling C. Holling

Cloth: Houghton Mifflin
Paper: Houghton Mifflin
Published: 1951

A classic book about the great river. The margins are filled with
detailed illustrations of flora and fauna, and the text remains
engrossing, although the waterway has changed dramatically over
the half century since the book was originally published.

[446]

MIRANDY AND BROTHER WIND [450]

Written by Patricia C. McKissick
Illustrated by Jerry Pinkney

Cloth: Knopf
Paper: Dragonfly
Published: 1988   **Prizes: Caldecott Honor**

The cakewalk contest is coming and Mirandy, who plans on winning, needs a special partner. She decides on Brother Wind, but he's unreliable, and she ends up with Ezel, who adores her, instead. The story, inspired by a photograph of the author's grandparents taken in 1906, when, as teenagers, they won a similar contest, is wise and humorous. It captures the spirit of small-town festivals and the voices of older folks giving advice. The illustrations fairly dance.

MIRETTE ON THE HIGH WIRE [451]

Written and illustrated by Emily Arnold McCully

Cloth: Putnam
Paper: Puffin   **Prizes: Caldecott Medal**
Published: 1992   **New York Times Best Illustrated Book**

The setting is Paris in the late nineteenth century, and Mirette is a spunky heroine if ever there was. Her widowed mother runs a boardinghouse for traveling theatrical players. The great Bellini, a world-famous aerialist now beset with fear, arrives. Mirette secretly practices on the wire in the courtyard till she persuades Bellini to teach her. Lovely lush illustrations, and telling details of Parisian daily life and work.

MISS NELSON IS MISSING! [452]

Written by Harry Allard
Illustrated by James Marshall

Cloth: Houghton Mifflin
Paper: Houghton Mifflin
Published: 1977

The first in a trio of raucous books about the students in Room 207, their dear teacher, Miss Nelson, and her mean, hideous, lunatic sub-

[447]

stitute, Miss Viola Swamp. Other titles are *Miss Nelson Has a Field Day* and *Miss Nelson Is Back.*

MISS RUMPHIUS [453]

Written and illustrated by Barbara Cooney

Cloth: Viking Press
Paper: Puffin
Published: 1982

Miss Rumphius was told as a child that she must do something to make the world more beautiful. She traveled, had adventures, and found her calling as the Lupine Lady, sowing the seed of the blue and purple flowers by the seacoast where she lives. She is very old now, and quite magical. A small, jewel-like picture book that carries its moral imperative lightly. It is a kind of companion to *Island Boy.*

[453]

MOLLY'S PILGRIM [454]

Written by Barbara Cohen
Illustrated by Michael J. Deraney

Cloth: Lothrop, Lee & Shepard
Paper: Yearling
Published: 1983

The Pilgrim doll that Molly makes for her third-grade Thanksgiving class assignment reflects her experiences as a recent immigrant and the only Jewish child in the class. An unusual and provocative story, it was made into an award-winning short film. A companion book is *Make a Wish, Molly,* about Passover.

THE MORNING CHAIR [455]

Written by Barbara M. Joosee
Illustrated by Marcia Sewall

Cloth: Clarion
Paper: Clarion
Published: 1995

Bram and his family come to New York just after World War II and the little Dutch boy is quite baffled by the tumult of the move. Everything is different and strange and he especially misses the chair

in which he and Mama sat securely every morning. Many details of the voyage and new life and a happy resolution, of course.

MOSS GOWN [456]

Written by William H. Hooks
Illustrated by Donald Carrick

Cloth: Clarion
Paper: Clarion
Published: 1987

This story, drawn from Carolina folklore and set in the antebellum South, mixes elements of *King Lear* and *Cinderella.* Candace is rejected by her father for loving him "as much as meat loves salt." Magically transformed to Moss Gown, she becomes the mistress of a great plantation and years later is reconciled with her father. The language is rich and the illustrations are mysterious.

MOUNTAIN WEDDING [457]

Written by Faye Gibbons
Illustrated by Ted Rand

Cloth: Morrow Junior Books
Published: 1996

Mama has five children, including Mandy, who tells us the story, and now Mama is about to marry Mr. Long, who has seven children of his own. Everyone is appropriately anxious. There's a scuffle at the wedding, which takes place in the preacher's dusty yard, and by the end there's something for everyone to laugh about.

[451]

THE MOUNTAINS OF TIBET [458]

Written and illustrated by Mordicai Gerstein

Cloth: HarperCollins
Paper: Harper Trophy
Published: 1987   **Prizes: New York Times Best Illustrated Book**

The life cycle of a boy who grows up to become a woodcutter in a valley in Tibet is told in a brilliant storybook adaptation of the

Tibetan Book of the Dead. At his death, the woodcutter has the choice of becoming part of heaven or living another life. The illustrations help carry the story from that faraway valley into the cosmos itself and back to the valley. It is an awesomely accomplished book that can be read repeatedly by both children and adults.

[460]

THE MOUSE OF AMHERST   [459]

Written by Elizabeth Spires
Illustrated by Claire A. Nivola

Cloth: Farrar, Straus & Giroux
Published: 1999

Emmaline is a mouse with excellent taste in poetry. She lives in a house in Amherst, Massachusetts, and not only recognizes the genius of the reclusive Emily Dickinson, who lives there as well, but writes seven poems of her own to propel the plot of this elegant introduction to Dickinson and her work. Skillfully written and delicately illustrated with line drawings of Emmaline. In *Emily* by Michael Bedard, another story book about Dickinson for younger readers, a neighbor child befriends the poet.

THE MOUSEHOLE CAT   [460]

Written by Antonia Barber
Illustrated by Nicola Bayley

Cloth: Macmillan
Paper: Aladdin
Published: 1990

The story comes from a Cornish legend about a fishing village called Mousehole, meaning a safe cove. Mowser, the sleek, striped cat who is the hero of the tale, lives with old Tom the fisherman, who treats him very well. This telling has lyrically beautiful illustrations that evoke sea and storm and especially the Great Storm-Cat, which threatens the town in myriad shades of blue. And the fish—oh, so many gleaming fish!

MR. LUNCH TAKES A PLANE RIDE [461]

Written by J. Otto Seibold and Vivian Walsh
Illustrated by J. Otto Siebold

Cloth: Viking Press
Paper: Puffin
Published: 1993

Mr. Lunch is the computer-generated hound whose high altitude and high-tech adventures are amusing to adults as often as children. In this first book, he rides in the luggage hold of a plane in order to appear on a late-night television show. The other titles are *Mr. Lunch Borrows a Canoe* and *Free Lunch*.

MR. SEMOLINA-SEMOLINUS: A GREEK FOLKTALE [462]

Written by Anthony L. Manna and Christodula Mitakidou
Illustrated by Giselle Potter

Cloth: Atheneum
Published: 1997

In this wittily illustrated folktale, clever Areti ends up baking her own husband, making him from the finest almonds, sugar, and semolina. Not surprisingly he turns out to be both beautiful and kind. The story twists a bit, deliciously.

[462]

MRS. MOSKOWITZ AND THE SABBATH CANDLESTICKS [463]

[462]

Written and illustrated by Amy Schwartz

Cloth: Jewish Publication Society
Published: 1984

Mrs. Moskowitz and her cat, Fred, have moved to a new apartment. Finding her Sabbath candlesticks in a packing box prompts the widow into unpacking and making their new quarters into a welcoming home. The round, chunky illustrations and an unself-conscious text explain Jewish Sabbath rituals in an affecting way.

MUFARO'S BEAUTIFUL DAUGHTERS: AN AFRICAN TALE [464]

Written and illustrated by John Steptoe

Cloth: Lothrop, Lee & Shepard
Paper: Dragonfly
Published: 1987 **Prizes: Caldecott Honor**

This West African tale tells about Mufaro's two beautiful but totally different daughters—Manyara, who is ambitious and mean, and Nyasha, who is kind and helpful. Guess which one ends up marrying the king? The illustrations are sumptuous.

MY FIRST PICTURE DICTIONARY [465]

Written by Katherine Howard
Illustrated by Huck Scarry

Cloth: Random House
Published: 1978

A slim, simply arranged paperback that is both a useful dictionary—over two hundred words are illustrated in cheerful fashion—but also an introduction to the idea of dictionaries and reference books.

MY LITTLE ISLAND [466]

Written and illustrated by Frane Lessac

Cloth: HarperCollins
Paper: Harper Trophy
Published: 1985

The lucky narrator describes a wonderful holiday visit to an island in the Caribbean that he takes with his best friend, who was born there. Their holiday trip is captured in exuberant, brightly colored primitive-style paintings. Lucky boys.

MY NAME IS GEORGIA: A PORTRAIT [467]

Written and illustrated by Jeanette Winter

Cloth: Harcourt Brace
Published: 1998

This "portrait" of Georgia O'Keeffe is told in short first-person narrative sentences and illustrated with paintings, many of which are homages to images the great American artist painted in a long, productive lifetime. The same author has done storybook biographies of Johann Sebastian Bach, Diego Rivera, and other artists.

[469]

THE MYSTERIES OF
HARRIS BURDICK [468]

Written and illustrated by Chris Van Allsburg

Cloth: Houghton Mifflin
Paper: Houghton Mifflin
Published: 1984   **Prizes: New York Times Best Illustrated Book**

Strange, even weird, fragments of text, illustrated in totally unexpected ways by a master draftsman. This is a contemporary picture book that speaks to teenagers and adults as strongly as to older children. A book for discussion and to use in making up games and plays.

NANA UPSTAIRS & NANA
DOWNSTAIRS [469]

Written and illustrated by Tomie dePaola

Cloth: Putnam
Paper: Puffin
Published: 1973

As a grown-up, Tommy remembers the rituals of his visits to the house his active grandmother (Nana Downstairs) shared with his bedridden, ninety-four-year-old great-grandmother (Nana Upstairs), both of whom he loved dearly. Death is a fact, presented and accepted. Even now Tommy sees the Nanas' spirits in shooting stars. A very fine book that remains fresh.

NED AND THE JOYBALOO [470]

Written by Hiawyn Oram
Illustrated by Satoshi Kitamura

Cloth: Farrar, Straus & Giroux
Paper: Sunburst
Published: 1989

Ned's Joybaloo is "big and beautiful, with a funny leathery nose and a breath full of paper roses." The fantasy creature is his companion in escape from the ordinary, and what blissful escape it is. But when the time comes for Ned to go on alone, the Joybaloo helps him with the separation. The artist and writer collaborated on *Angry Arthur,* which is similarly satisfying. The accomplished

watercolor drawings are best when freest—as when Ned and the Joybaloo go sailing through the deep blue sky.

A NEW COAT FOR ANNA   [471]

Written by Harriet Ziefert
Illustrated by Anita Lobel

Cloth: Knopf
Paper: Knopf
Published: 1986

Someplace in Europe after World War II, Anna's mother bargains and barters with a sheep farmer, a spinner, a weaver, and a tailor so that Anna will have a new coat the following winter. This story, accompanied by appealing illustrations, is of greatest interest to early-grade children, especially girls, but holds the attention of younger listeners.

THE NIGHT IGUANA LEFT HOME   [472]

Written by Megan McDonald
Illustrated by Ponder Goembel

Cloth: DK Ink
Published: 1999

It's very cold in the winter in Schenectady, New York, where Iguana lives with Alison, so the lizard heads for the Florida Keys. All right, it's ridiculous, but Iguana's adventures in the Keys are very funny, and after doing a stint licking stamps at the Post Office, the lizard figures out how to get back to Alison for summer vacations. A regional favorite for obvious reasons.

NIM AND THE WAR EFFORT   [473]

Written by Milly Lee
Illustrated by Yangsook Choi

Cloth: Farrar, Straus & Giroux
Published: 1997

The setting is San Francisco during World War II and Nim is caught up in the paper drive, part of the home-front war effort. Her deter-

[474]

mination to win the drive takes her out of Chinatown, and means missing Chinese lessons. The illustrations capture the city and the young heroine's serious purpose.

NOAH'S ARK   [474]

Written and illustrated by Peter Spier

Cloth: Doubleday
Paper: Yearling
Published: 1977

Prizes: Caldecott Medal
New York Times Best Illustrated Book

The only text in this prizewinning version of the story of Noah is a seventeenth-century Dutch poem describing the menagerie. The rest of this account is narrative illustration. There are double-page spreads showing minute details of the construction of the ark and habits of the animals, contrasted with double-page spreads of the tiny boat on wind-tossed, rainy seas. The crowding, chaos, and tension of the ark just before the end are palpable. This book holds the attention of a wide age range, from toddlers through middle graders. For what happened next, see *Aardvarks, Disembark*. There are many many other editions of the Noah story.

OFFICER BUCKLE AND GLORIA   [475]

Written and illustrated by Peggy Rathmann

Cloth: Putnam
Published: 1995

Prizes: Caldecott Medal

[475]

Officer Buckle, a veteran policeman, and his trusted dog, Gloria, do a kind of vaudeville act, teaching safety to schoolchildren. They become an entertainment sensation. Gloria is the funny one.

OL' PAUL: THE MIGHTY LOGGER [476]

Written and illustrated by Glen Rounds

Cloth: Holiday House
Paper: Holiday House
Published: 1936

Here's a dandy collection of stories about the giant logger's adventures and achievements. Rounds is the author-illustrator of another Bunyan tale, called *The Morning the Sun Refused to Rise,* which is also comic and far-fetched. There are other Paul Bunyan stories in print, including Stephen Kellogg's exuberant full-color picture-book version, and it's worth looking for the reissue of the distinguished, more sober volume, illustrated by Rockwell Kent, which is now out of print.

OLD HENRY [477]

Written by Joan Blos
Illustrated by Stephen Gammell

Cloth: Morrow Junior Books
Paper: Mulberry
Published: 1987

Old Henry just doesn't keep house the way his neighbors think he ought to, but when he up and leaves, they find they miss him. A small morality play about tolerance, illustrated with great wit in a style reminiscent of *The Relatives Came,* by Cynthia Rylant.

THE OLD SYNAGOGUE [478]

Written and illustrated by Richard Rosenblum

Cloth: Jewish Publication Society
Published: 1989

Some European Jews who came to the United States in the late nineteenth century founded a neighborhood synagogue in the city where they settled. The story of the synagogue, the neighborhood, and, implicitly, the unnamed city is told in detailed drawings and spare text. As time passed, things changed—the sidewalk hustle and bustle faded, people moved away, the synagogue fell into disuse, the neighborhood into decay. But this is a story of both religious and urban renewal, and a contemporary wave of migrants arrived, people who wanted both to live in the city and renew their faith. The slim book is rich in messages and morals.

[479]

OLIVE, THE OTHER REINDEER [479]

Written by Vivian Walsh and J. Otto Siebold
Illustrated by J. Otto Siebold

Cloth: Chronicle
Published: 1997

Olive, a spotted dog with style and dedication, misunderstands the holiday song about Rudolph and thinks "all of the other reindeer" refers to her. So she sets off to serve. It's a long way to the North Pole, but once there, she pitches in and succeeds in guiding a memorable ride.

ONE ROUND MOON AND A STAR FOR ME [480]

Written by Ingrid Mennen
Illustrated by Niki Daly

Cloth: Orchard Books
Published: 1994

The setting for this story about the birth of a new baby is among the Lesotho of South Africa, but it speaks to the universal concern when a new baby is coming. The engrossing illustrations are filled with symbolic images—of the moon itself; of the stars falling into Papa's brown blanket, one for the boy, one for the baby—and also with fine specific details such as young girls balancing buckets on their heads bringing water for the baby.

OOH-LA-LA (MAX IN LOVE)   [481]

Written and illustrated by Maira Kalman

Cloth: Viking Press
Published: 1991   **Prizes: New York Times Best Illustrated Book**

The most satisfying of the very hip books about Max Stravinsky, "the dog poet from New York" who also appears in *Swami on Rye* and *Max in Hollywood, Baby,* describes the canine romance with Paris and "the divine Dalmatian" Crepes Suzette.

OUTSIDE OVER THERE   [482]

Written and illustrated by Maurice Sendak

Cloth: HarperCollins
Paper: Harper Trophy   **Prizes: Caldecott Honor**
Published: 1981   **New York Times Best Illustrated Book**

Sendak's most visually lavish book has a spare text and addresses potent, emotional issues—siblings and abandonment. Ida is left in charge of her baby sister, who is kidnapped. Ida determines to rescue the baby and enters a baffling dream world from which they both emerge with new understanding. The painterly illustrations, full of elaborate symbolism and historical references, are worth studying closely. As with Sendak's other books, children tend to see them differently as they grow older rather than outgrow them.

[484]

[481]

OWL MOON [483]

Written by Jane Yolen
Illustrated by John Schoenherr

Cloth: Philomel
Published: 1987

Prizes: Caldecott Medal

This is the sort of book that makes city children ache to live in the country. The very idea of going out late on a moonlit winter's night with your father and calling for owls is quite magical, as is this story, with its snowy, night-lit illustrations.

OX-CART MAN [484]

Written by Donald Hall
Illustrated by Barbara Cooney

Cloth: Viking Press
Paper: Puffin
Published: 1979

Prizes: Caldecott Medal
New York Times Best Illustrated Book

Historical context can be conveyed in stories for young children, as this splendid book clearly shows. The text is by a distinguished writer and poet; the beautiful prizewinning illustrations are in the folk tradition. Their collaborative evocation of a year of domestic life in a nineteenth-century rural New England area is rich with detail and insight. It reads aloud very well.

PADDLE-TO-THE-SEA   [485]

Written and illustrated by Holling C. Holling

Cloth: Houghton Mifflin
Paper: Houghton Mifflin
Published: 1941

This book is both very old-fashioned to look at and thrillingly modern in its idea and organization. A boy living in the Great Lakes region sets a toy Indian lad into a canoe and sends them downstream. The story follows the waterways to the ocean. More than half a century has passed since it was written and a great deal has changed—technology the least of it—and yet the book is compelling and full of things to talk about.

[486]

PAMELA CAMEL   [486]

Written and illustrated by Bill Peet

Cloth: Houghton Mifflin
Paper: Houghton Mifflin
Published: 1984

Circus life makes Pamela Camel cross and irritable. She runs away along a railroad track, where she happens upon a broken tie, recognizes the danger it represents, and later is able to prevent a wreck by bravely stopping a train. A hero, she returns to the circus a star. There are several dozen books by Bill Peet, most of them still in print. They are lightly told, often rhymed fables, with illustrations that suggest his background as a Walt Disney studio artist. They are endearing, unpretentious, and satisfying. Look for *Zella, Zack, and Zodiac,* about a zebra and an ostrich chick; *Buford, the Little Bighorn,* or *The Caboose Who Got Loose.*

PAPA GATTO: AN ITALIAN FAIRY TALE   [487]

Written and illustrated by Ruth Sanderson

Cloth: Little, Brown
Paper: Little, Brown
Published: 1995

Pappa Gatto needs someone to care for his eight motherless kittens, for he must go and serve the prince. Lovely Sophia covets

Papa G's jewels; her sister, Beatrice, loves his kittens. Guess which one ends up marrying the prince? Lush, elaborate costume illustrations.

PAPER JOHN [488]

Written and illustrated by David Small

Cloth: Farrar, Straus & Giroux
Paper: Sunburst
Published: 1987

Paper John is a mysterious fellow who makes wonderful things, including his own house, out of folded paper. He does battle with a devil who has only one trick, but it is the potent one of controlling the winds and it threatens to destroy Paper John and the town as well. Handsomely illustrated.

PATRICK'S DINOSAURS [489]

Written by Carol Carrick
Illustrated by Donald Carrick

Cloth: Clarion
Paper: Houghton Mifflin
Published: 1983

Patrick listens carefully to his big brother Hank's description of dinosaurs and then scares himself with some fantasies about what it would be like if they were around today. In the even funnier *Return of Patrick's Dinosaurs,* he claims they are back, and the illustrations show clearly how the creatures enrich the ordinary things in life.

PAUL BUNYAN [490]

Written and illustrated by Steven Kellogg

Cloth: Morrow Junior Books
Paper: Mulberry
Published: 1984

A rambunctious version of the legend of the mighty logger and his blue ox, Babe. The illustrations are exuberant. The author-illustrator has also retold the story of Pecos Bill.

A PEACEABLE KINGDOM:
THE SHAKER ABECEDARIUS [491]

Written and illustrated by Alice Provensen

Cloth: Viking Press
Paper: Puffin
Published: 1978   **Prizes: New York Times Best Illustrated Book**

This splendid abecedarius (or alphabet book) shows a grand procession of real and imaginary animals parading in a setting that is also a vision of Shaker society. Parents who choose can go on to explain more about the American religious sect whose designs are so prized today.

THE PEOPLE COULD FLY:
AMERICAN BLACK FOLKTALES [492]

Written by Virginia Hamilton
Illustrated by Leo Dillon

Cloth: Knopf
Paper: Knopf
Published: 1985   **Prizes: New York Times Best Illustrated Book**

Twenty-four black American folktales are retold by a distinguished contemporary writer. There are animal stories, supernatural tales, and slave tales of freedom, all told in sharp, precise prose. The mystical illustrations are affecting. Wonderful to read aloud. (The tape is particularly good.)

[491]

192

PERFECT THE PIG [493]

Written and illustrated by Susan Jeschke

Cloth: Holt
Paper: Scholastic
Published: 1981

Sometimes getting what you wish for leads to serious complications. Perfect the Pig wishes for wings, but the results are not what he expected, even though he and his friend Olive end up just where they want to be in this charming and roundabout story.

[492]

PETER AND THE WOLF [494]

Written by Sergei Prokofiev
Illustrated by Jorg Miller

Cloth: Knopf
Paper: Mulberry
Published: 1986

This version of the story with music that is so often a child's real introduction to the orchestra is persuasively placed in a lush theatrical setting—a European opera house. The relationship of the musical instruments to the characters thus becomes clear, and even the role of the conductor makes sense. There are other good editions around, by such illustrators as Charles Mikolaycak, and even a pop-up version by Barbara Cooney.

THE PHILHARMONIC
GETS DRESSED [495]

Written by Karla Kuskin
Illustrated by Marc Simont

Cloth: HarperCollins
Paper: Harper Trophy
Published: 1982

As a winter day ends, 105 people bathe, get dressed, and go to work. They are members of an orchestra who live in and around a big city. The text and illustrations are both witty and economical and offer a great deal to talk about at bedtime (or any other time, for that matter). The equally delightful companion book is *The Dallas Titans Get Ready for Bed*.

PIGEONS [496]

Written by Miriam Schlein
Illustrated by Margaret Miller

Cloth: HarperCollins
Published: 1989

Country children, even suburban children, see nature and science everywhere; city children are often not so sure, or so some people think. There are many stylish black-and-white photographs of city pigeons here, including a windowsill perspective on the hatching and rearing of pigeon young and an album of metropolitan pigeon sightings. The photographs accompany a brightly written text, bringing science, nature, and photography together nicely.

PIGS FROM A TO Z [497]

Written and illustrated by Arthur Geisert

Cloth: Houghton Mifflin
Paper: Houghton Mifflin
Published: 1986   **Prizes: New York Times Best Illustrated Book**

A rich and imaginative book in which seven piglets build a tree house. The illustrations are in fact intricate etchings. This alphabet book seems especially appealing to boys. This is one of a number of Geisert's pig books, some of which, such as *Pa's Balloon* and *Other Pig Tales,* are out of print, but worth looking for.

THE PILGRIMS OF PLIMOTH [498]

Written and illustrated by Marcia Sewall

Cloth: Atheneum
Paper: Aladdin
Published: 1986

[499]

The narrator gives a detailed and appreciative account of daily life in the Plymouth colony as well as a brief history of its establishment, culminating, of course, with Thanksgiving. The oil-painting illustrations are unusually evocative, luminous canvases with precise details. The sequel, *People of the Breaking Day,* describes daily life in the same period from the Indian point of view. These scrupulously researched and thoughtful books approach illustrated history seriously and are appreciated by children in the lower and middle grades.

PINK AND SAY   [499]

Written and illustrated by Patricia Polacco

Cloth: Putnam
Published: 1994

The author's great-great-grandfather, Say, was a fifteen-year-old flag bearer in an Ohio regiment in the Civil War, left for dead in a Georgia pasture. He was rescued by Pinkus Aylee, a young bluecoat with skin "the color of polished mahogany," and nursed back to health by Pink's mother. Pink was later executed in the Andersonville Prison; Say survived. The moving story with its themes of slavery and freedom is a tribute to Pink.

PINKERTON, BEHAVE!   [500]

Written and illustrated by Steven Kellogg

Cloth: Dial
Paper: Pied Piper
Published: 1979

Even as a puppy, Pinkerton (who is really a Great Dane) is as big as a pony and as eager as a monkey, not to mention amiable, awkward, and full of mischief and goodwill. In *A Rose for Pinkerton,* the family gives him a kitten, who, it turns out, wants to be a great Dane, too. There are also *Tallyho, Pinkerton* and *Prehistoric Pinkerton,* all with illustrations in the author's recognizable wild, funny style.

THE POLAR EXPRESS   [501]

Written and illustrated by Chris Van Allsburg

Cloth: Houghton Mifflin   **Prizes: Caldecott Medal**
Published: 1985   **New York Times Best Illustrated Book**

An unseen adult narrator remembers a mysterious Christmas Eve when he rode the special train to the North Pole and was selected

by Santa Claus to receive the first Christmas gift. Haunting illustrations in rich, subtle colors make this a very magical book indeed.

A PRAIRIE BOY'S WINTER   [502]

Written and illustrated by William Kurelek

Cloth: Houghton Mifflin
Paper: Houghton Mifflin
Published: 1973   **Prizes: New York Times Best Illustrated Book**

A prairie farm in winter during the 1930s is vividly recalled in a book distinguished by the quality of both prose and full-page illustrations. The companion volume is *A Prairie Boy's Summer*.

PRINCESS FURBALL   [503]

Written by Charlotte Huck
Illustrated by Anita Lobel

Cloth: Greenwillow
Paper: Mulberry
Published: 1989

[505]

This variation on "Cinderella" tells how the beautiful and clever princess escapes marrying an ogre and captures the heart of the true prince. She tells her father she must have "three bridal gifts—one dress as golden as the sun, another as silvery as the moon, and a third as glittering as the stars. In addition . . . a coat made out of a thousand different kinds of fur," and then sets off on her own. The illustrations are all appealing; those set outdoors in the winter are haunting.

PRISCILLA TWICE   [504]

Written and illustrated by Judith Caseley

Cloth: Greenwillow
Paper: Mulberry
Published: 1996

Priscilla feels quite literally torn apart by her parents' divorce, so when asked to draw a picture of her family, she divides the page, puts her parents on either side, and gives each a tiny Priscilla. It's tough, direct, and affecting. There's no therapeutic solution either, but the affirming benefits of the passage of time, good humor, and unconditional love are clear.

[501]

THE PURPLE COAT   [505]

Written by Amy Hest
Illustrated by Amy Schwartz

Cloth: Four Winds
Paper: Aladdin
Published: 1986

Every year Gabrielle's grandfather makes her a new navy blue coat
in his tailor shop in the city. This year Gabrielle wants a purple coat,
and her mother says no. Grandfather finds a way. The quirky, cartoonish illustrations are precise and full of details to explore, especially those of the tailor shop. The affectionate sequel is *Gabby
Growing Up.*

PUSS IN BOOTS   [506]

Written by Charles Perrault
Illustrated by Fred Marcellino

Cloth: Farrar, Straus & Giroux
Paper: Sunburst
Published: 1990   **Prizes: Caldecott Honor**

The miller left his youngest son a cat, but oh, what a cat! This version of the well-loved French tale first told by Charles Perrault is
particularly sumptuous: the lush, period-perfect illustrations gleam
with silk and velvet. The cat who brings such good fortune is sly and

fine. Another, wordless version of the story, by John Goodall, is particularly pleasing to share with younger children.

[506]

RABBIT MAKES A MONKEY OUT OF LION: A SWAHILI TALE   [507]

Written by Verna Aardema
Illustrated by Jerry Pinkney

Cloth: Dial
Paper: Puffin
Published: 1989

Lion learns the hard way that "rabbits are just too hard to catch" in this laugh-out-loud East African trickster story. The watercolor illustrations have a velvety softness.

THE RAG COAT   [508]

Written and illustrated by Lauren Mills

Cloth: Little, Brown
Published: 1991

Minna is old enough and wants to go to school, but she is embarrassed that she has no coat. Mama's quilting group makes her a coat out of scraps, and when the children tease her, she shows them the patches that transform the "rag coat" into a coat of many stories—indeed, stories of their own lives. Delicate illustrations.

THE RAINBABIES   [509]

Written by Laura Krauss Melmed
Illustrated by Jim LaMarche

Cloth: Lothrop, Lee & Shepard
Paper: Mulberry
Published: 1992

A dozen "rainbabies" magically appear one day on the front lawn of a childless elderly couple. They care for the special babies, and endure special trials and temptations until one day they are given a real baby girl. The storytelling style is old-fashioned, even florid; the illustrations, luminous and fine, are quite beautiful.

THE RANDOM HOUSE BOOK OF MOTHER GOOSE [510]

Written and illustrated by Arnold Lobel

Cloth: Random House
Published: 1986

This generous edition of the canon, including 306 verses, shows a fine artist at the top of his roly-poly form. An ebullient collection, with selections appropriate for all ages.

[511]

RAPUNZEL [511]

Written and illustrated by Paul O. Zelinsky

Cloth: Dutton
Published: 1997

Prizes: Caldecott Medal

This version of the well-known and provocative fairy tale about the cloistered girl who lets down her hair is set sometime during the Italian Renaissance, not in the Germany of the Brothers Grimm. Lush painterly illustrations, filled with period detail, give young readers much to discuss in addition to the story. In a more traditional edition illustrated by Maja Dusikova, Rapunzel looks genuinely childlike.

RARE TREASURE: MARY ANNING AND HER REMARKABLE DISCOVERIES [512]

Illustrated by Don Brown

Cloth: Houghton Mifflin
Published: 1999

The bicentennial of the birth of Mary Anning, the British fossil hunter, prompted three story books about her work and life. While still a little girl, she uncovered the fossil of an ichthyosaur on the southern shore of England, and she spent her life carefully combing beaches and cliffs for more remains of prehistoric creatures. *Rare Treasure* is crisp and unsentimental, the illustrations delicate and inviting. *Mary Anning and the Sea Dragon* by Jeannine Atkins is more dramatic and *Stone Girl, Bone Girl* by Laurence Anholt speaks more directly to younger readers.

RED RANGER CAME CALLING: A GUARANTEED TRUE CHRISTMAS STORY [513]

Written and illustrated by Berkeley Breathed

Cloth: Little, Brown
Paper: Little, Brown
Published: 1994

It was 1939 and the cartoonist's father was a boy who lusted for a Buk Tween Two-Speed Crime-Stopper Star-Hopper bicycle. It's a slightly scary, surprising story with a startlingly unexpected ending. Good for reading aloud, but don't peek.

RIKKI-TIKKI-TAVI [514]

Written by Rudyard Kipling
Illustrated by Jerry Pinkney

Cloth: Morrow Junior Books
Published: 1997

The Kipling tale from the *Just-So Stories* of the brave little mongoose who battles and ultimately defeats the clever and dangerous cobras who threaten a British family in nineteenth-century India has been handsomely reillustrated in a large-format book, perfect for holding lap listeners' attention.

ROOTABAGA STORIES: PART ONE [515]

Written by Carl Sandburg
Illustrated by Michael Hague

Cloth: Harcourt Brace
Paper: Odyssey
Published: 1936; 1988

The American poet and biographer also wrote glorious nonsense and stories for his own daughters. "The Potato Face Blind Man" still beguiles, and so does "The Two Skyscrapers Who Decided to Have a Child." This new edition is in a large, pleasing format, with period-style illustrations. Easy to read, but better still to read aloud. The old edition, with illustrations by Maud and Miska Petersham, is still available in paperback. *More Rootabagas,* with illustrations by Paul O. Zelinsky, is out of print but worth finding as well. Individual stories are also available.

ROTTEN ISLAND   [516]

Written and illustrated by William Steig

Cloth: David Godine
Published: 1984

This is a revised edition of a splendid fantasy, first published in the 1960s, about a horrible, ghastly, ugly, vicious island populated with hideous monsters, disgusting creatures, thorny plants, and awful things. A flower appears one day and sets off an earth-shattering brawl. The wondrously imaginative illustrations are printed in fluorescent color. It is one of Steig's best books.

[513]

RUMPELSTILTSKIN [517]

Written and illustrated by Paul O. Zelinsky

Cloth: Dutton
Paper: Puffin
Published: 1986

Prizes: Caldecott Honor

A version of the familiar folktale placed in a medieval setting—turreted castles, peasants in the fields—executed in technically accomplished oil paintings. The straw and gold truly gleam. The text is from Grimm. The illustrator has done an equally lavish setting of *Hansel and Gretel* in the style of seventeenth-century Dutch landscape painting, not to mention *Rapunzel* (see separate entry). There are other Rumpelstiltskins, including an almost cartoonishly high-spirited one illustrated by Paul Galdone and a lush Russian-style one by Gennady Spirin that is out of print but worth finding.

RUSHMORE [518]

Written and illustrated by Lynn Curlee

Cloth: Scholastic
Published: 1999

The story of the monumental stone faces carved on Mount Rushmore between 1927 and 1941 is a tale of obsession, imagination, art, and engineering. The design and execution were the work of Gutzon Borglum, an autocratic and determined artist whose name is not carved on the mountain—the only thing modest about his achievement. Stunning, almost photorealistic paintings convey the engineering problems and the scale of the endeavor. The text, which deals with the history of the project as well as the technology and the danger, is engrossing.

SADAKO AND THE THOUSAND PAPER CRANES [519]

Written by Eleanor Coerr
Illustrated by Ronald Himler

Cloth: Putnam
Paper: Yearling
Published: 1979

Sadako was a toddler when the atomic bomb fell on Hiroshima. Years later, when she was hospitalized with the "atomic bomb sick-

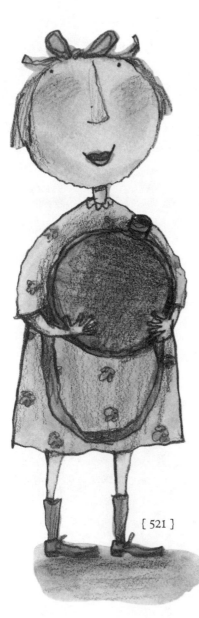

[521]

ness," a friend brought her some gold foil paper and reminded her of the saying that if you folded one thousand paper cranes, a sick person would be cured. Sadako died of leukemia at the age of twelve, but her story has been celebrated around the world.

ST. GEORGE AND THE DRAGON [520]

Written by Margaret Hodges
Illustrated by Trina Schart Hyman

Cloth: Little, Brown
Paper: Little, Brown
Published: 1984

**Prizes: Caldecott Medal
New York Times Best Illustrated Book**

Based on Spenser's *Faerie Queen*, this is a retelling of St. George's three-day battle with the dragon. The prizewinning illustrations are in the style of illuminated manuscripts; the text has been simplified but remains courtly. *The Kitchen Knight* is equally well told.

[522]

SAVING SWEETNESS [521]

Written by Diane Stanley
Illustrated by G. Brian Karas

Cloth: Putnam
Published: 1996

Sweetness, the smallest child in the wretched orphanage run by Mrs. Sump, runs away several times, and each time it is she who rescues the sheriff who is sent to rescue her. It's a Texas-style tall story, with sly illustrations and a delightful sequel, *Raising Sweetness*. In it the sheriff ends up with all the orphans and Sweetness decides he needs a wife.

SAYONARA, MRS. KACKLEMAN [522]

Written and illustrated by Maira Kalman

Cloth: Viking Press
Paper: Puffin
Published: 1989

Lulu takes her little brother, Alexander, on a totally madcap tour of Japan—the Tokyo subway, the noodle shops, a rock garden, and details of food, games, and films. Lulu is something of a know-it-all;

Alexander has great aplomb. The artist's style is a pastiche of wit imposed on chaos and too busy for many younger children but rewarding to pore over as sly jokes reveal themselves. In *Hey, Willy, See the Pyramids,* Lulu and Willy take another trip.

THE SCRAMBLED STATES OF AMERICA   [523]

Written and illustrated by Laurie Keller

Cloth: Henry Holt
Published: 1998

Suppose, just suppose the states are all hanging out and Kansas is bored and invites the others to a party, and at the party they all decide to change places. Mayhem ensues and then they all go home to their traditional spots. Anthropomorphic maps? Why not? Great fun, and great help as geography looms.

THE SELFISH GIANT   [524]

Written by Oscar Wilde
Illustrated by Lisbeth Zwerger

Cloth: Picture Book
Paper: Scholastic
Published: 1984

The Christian parable about children seeking access to a giant's garden is illustrated here by an unusually talented Viennese artist who takes an oblique view of the tale in her delicate watercolor paintings. She has also illustrated Wilde's *The Canterville Ghost.* The story reads aloud well and has a lasting appeal for adults as well as for children. There are many other editions.

THE SELKIE GIRL   [525]

Written by Susan Cooper
Illustrated by Warwick Hutton

Cloth: Margaret K. McElderry
Paper: Aladdin
Published: 1986

The haunting tale, from the Irish and Scots islands, of the young lad who loves and marries the maiden who is really a seal is beautifully told in this distinguished collaboration. The watercolor illustrations have a simplicity that is distinctive. The author and illustrator also worked together on the Welsh tale *The Silver Cow* and on *Tamlin*. Their books are increasingly difficult to find, but well worth the trouble.

SEVEN BLIND MICE   [526]

Written and illustrated by Ed Young

Cloth: Philomel
Paper: Puffin
Published: 1992

Prizes: Caldecott Honor

This reworking of the Indian folktale about the blind men and the elephant has seven little mice, who are the colors of the rainbow plus white, trying to figure out a thing that is really a pachyderm standing near a pond. The illustrations are collage, stark and stunning, and there are a number of concepts embedded in the amusing escapade: numbers, color, counting—both ordinal and cardinal. It's a rich entertainment as the mice think they encounter a pillar, a cliff, a fan, etc. Much to discuss.

SEVEN BRAVE WOMEN   [527]

Written by Betsy Hearne
Illustrated by Bethanne Andersen

Cloth: Greenwillow
Published: 1997

Each chapter is a short sketch of one of the author's female forebears who did great things in this country, but did not fight in wars. Simply told and wonderfully inspiring stories about women who lived difficult and complicated lives, raised and cared for families, each and all of which remind readers that "there are a million ways to be brave." In contrast to the crispness of the prose, the illustrations have a lush, romantic quality.

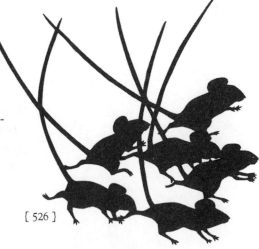

[526]

THE SEVEN CHINESE BROTHERS

[528]

Written by Margaret Mahy
Illustrated by Jean Tseng

Cloth: Scholastic
Paper: Scholastic
Published: 1990

Seven seemingly identical siblings are each endowed with some spectacular physical ability, which comes in handy here. They protect the slave laborers working on the Great Wall as the dread Chinese emperor Chin Shih Huang attempts to brutally consolidate his power. Basically, this is the same story as the long-ago favorite *The Five Chinese Brothers,* but without racial stereotyping, and with great dollops of wit in the text.

SHADOW [529]

Written by Blaise Cendrars
Illustrated by Marcia Brown

Cloth: Scribner
Paper: Aladdin
Published: 1982   **Prizes: Caldecott Medal**

The text, translated from the French, describes the mysterious eeriness of the shadow figure in African tribal life. The illustrations are dramatic collages.

THE SHADOW OF A FLYING BIRD: A LEGEND FROM THE KURDISTANI JEWS [530]

Written and illustrated by Mordicai Gerstein

Cloth: Hyperion
Published: 1994

This is a retelling of a midrash, a rabbinical commentary on the Scriptures—in this case a Kurdistani meditation on the inevitability of death. Moses, having been brought to the mountain from which he sees the land of milk and honey, learns that it is time for him to die. It is a difficult and beautiful story about grief and acceptance. The illustrations are cosmic and God appears consistently in negative space, defined by stars, clouds, mountains, and rivers.

SHAKA: KING OF THE ZULUS   [531]

Written and illustrated by Diane Stanley

Cloth: Morrow Junior Books
Paper: Mulberry
Published: 1988   **Prizes: Caldecott Honor**

In life, Shaka (1787–1828) was a brilliant military leader, heroic by any measure, and then, near the end of his twelve-year reign as king and mighty leader, quite horribly, cruelly insane. This stunning large-format story book biography decorated with Zulu artifacts and shields has a clear, dispassionate text that deals tactfully with the most terrifying parts of his life. The book is accessible as a read-aloud to young children but is most exciting to middle graders, for whom historical figures are becoming real.

[531]

SHE'S WEARING A DEAD BIRD ON HER HEAD!   [532]

Written by Kathryn Lasky
Illustrated by David Catrow

Cloth: Hyperion
Paper: Hyperion
Published: 1995   **Prizes: New York Times Best Illustrated Book**

The Massachusetts Audubon Society was started by Harriet Hemenway and her cousin Minna Hall, proper Bostonian ladies who were outraged by the turn-of-the-century fashion for women to wear feathers and even entire stuffed birds on the brims of their hats. What could be a dry account of the bird protection movement is enlivened by sprightly prose that captures the spirit of those Bostonians and colorfully detailed illustrations showing some of those hats.

SNOWFLAKE BENTLEY   [533]

Written by Jacqueline Briggs Martin
Illustrated by Mary Azarian

Cloth: Houghton Mifflin
Published: 1998   **Prizes: Caldecott Medal**

Wilson A. Bentley, native Vermonter and self-taught scientist, was obsessed with snowflakes, and in the late nineteenth century began photographing them. His 1931 text is still in use. This storybook biography, handsomely illustrated with distinctive woodcuts, conveys a sense of winter wonder as well as appreciation of Bentley's determination and achievements. Several of his photographs are included along with an excellent bibliography.

SONG OF THE SWALLOWS   [534]

Written and illustrated by Leo Politi

Cloth: Scribner's
Paper: Aladdin
Published: 1949   **Prizes: Caldecott Medal**

The story of the swallows who come each year to Capistrano is told here through young Juan and old Julian, who lived in the town a long time ago. Although the story remains fresh and interesting, to adult eyes the prizewinning art may seem cartoonish and dated.

SPINKY SULKS   [535]

Written and illustrated by William Steig

Cloth: Farrar, Straus & Giroux
Paper: Sunburst
Published: 1988   **Prizes: New York Times Best Illustrated Book**

For reasons too silly to bear much inspection, Spinky has gone into a world-class sulk, and nothing his parents or his reprehensible siblings or even his grandmother do is going to persuade him to come out of the yard. In this glorious, hilarious, painfully wonderful book, text and illustrations are seamlessly united to convey the palpable rage of a real tantrum and the delicacy needed to negotiate a way out.

[535]

STARRY MESSENGER: GALILEO GALILEI [536]

Written and illustrated by Peter Sis

Cloth: Farrar, Straus & Giroux
Published: 1996   **Prizes: Caldecott Honor**

A brilliantly illustrated account of the life of the astronomer at the Medici court whose heliocentric views threatened the Roman Catholic church. The text itself is spare; the margins are filled with data interesting to both children and adults. The illustrations—with symbolic motifs and exquisite details—reward close study. A storybook for middle grade children, full of potential for family discussion.

STEPHEN BIESTY'S INCREDIBLE CROSS SECTIONS [537]

Written by Richard Platt
Illustrated by Stephen Biesty

Cloth: Knopf
Published: 1992   **Prizes: New York Times Best Illustrated Book**

Incredible? Not easily imaginable would be more accurate. In any event, just what happens inside a castle, say, or an ocean liner or a submarine? This large-format book of exquisitely detailed drawings is something to pore over for the immediate pleasure and revelations it offers, and then return to when the subjects come up in other contexts or classroom projects.

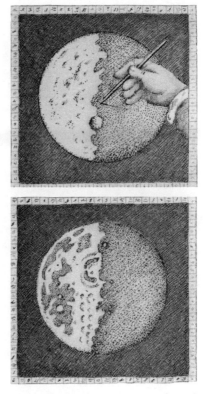

[536]

THE STINKY CHEESE MAN AND OTHER FAIRLY STUPID TALES [538]

Written by Jon Scieszka
Illustrated by Lane Smith

Cloth: Viking Press   **Prizes: Caldecott Honor**
Published: 1992   **New York Times Best Illustrated Book**

Smart-aleck central. In this raucous collection of retellings, the ugly ducking grows up to be an ugly duck, and the little red hen gets eaten by the giant from "Jack in the Beanstalk." There's a blithe, if mean-spirited, energy in both the text and the clever, angular, layered illustrations.

STONE SOUP: AN OLD TALE [539]

Written and illustrated by Marcia Brown

Cloth: Scribner
Paper: Aladdin
Published: 1947

This is a large-format, old-fashioned, and very charming version of the familiar story featuring distinctively French peasants and soldiers. No one in the village will offer hospitality to the three hungry soldiers; the stone soup they prepare teaches the virtue of cooperation. There are many other editions of the story, some with slightly different titles, such as *Bone Button Borscht* by Aubrey Davis.

[538]

STORIES TO SOLVE: FIFTEEN FOLKTALES FROM AROUND THE WORLD [540]

Written by George Shannon
Illustrated by Peter Sis

Cloth: Greenwillow
Paper: Beech Tree
Published: 1985

Oh, so clever, these fifteen very short folktales that pose problems, twisty problems. Two fathers and two sons went fishing . . . What did the bride say to persuade her mother-in-law that she hadn't

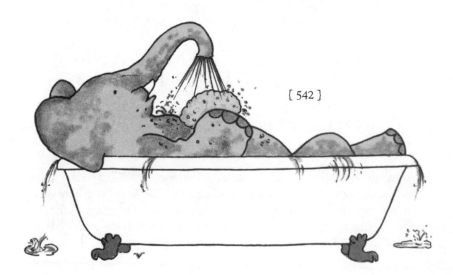

[542]

eaten all the chickpeas? Witty illustrations add to the fun. The temptation is to devour them like peanuts. Better still to read aloud one or two at a time and savor the wit. There is always *More Stories to Solve, Still More Stories to Solve,* or *True Lies: Eighteen Tales for You to Decide.*

THE STORY ABOUT PING [541]

Written by Marjorie Flack
Illustrated by Kurt Wiese

Cloth: Viking Press
Paper: Puffin
Published: 1933

Ping lives with his extended family on a boat on the great Yangtze River. One day, to avoid getting a spanking for being last back on board at the end of the day, Ping ventures off. Miraculously, he finds his way home. After more than half a century, this remains a compelling, even thrilling, story of nearly universal appeal to children just discovering the wide world beyond their own daily routines.

THE STORY OF BABAR [542]

Written and illustrated by Jean De Brunhoff

Cloth: Random House
Paper: Random House
Published: 1933   **Prizes: Carnegie Medal**

This is the classic French tale of a baby elephant, cruelly orphaned, who reaches the city, is civilized (even acquiring a handsome green suit), and eventually returns home to be king. The cast of characters includes his wife, Queen Celeste, their children, their relatives, and the splendid Old Lady. Some readers have seen the politics of colonialism in the stories, but that has not deterred generations of children in many countries from adoring them. The series includes *The Travels of Babar, Babar and His Children,* and *Babar the King.* The author's son Laurent has written and illustrated many additional titles, but most are now out of print.

[542]

211

THE STORY OF FERDINAND [543]

Written by Munro Leaf
Illustrated by Robert Lawson

Cloth: Viking Press
Paper: Puffin
Published: 1936

Ferdinand the bull does not want to go into the ring and fight; he really wants to sit under the cork tree and smell the flowers. A funny, wise story more than half a century old, and fresh as the daisy Ferdinand loves so well. (Some things change, but adults will be pleased to see that corks still grow on the cork trees here.)

THE STORY OF MRS. LOVEWRIGHT AND PURRLESS HER CAT [544]

Written by Lore Segal
Illustrated by Paul O. Zelinsky

Cloth: Knopf
Paper: Dragonfly
Published: 1985   **Prizes: New York Times Best Illustrated Book**

Mrs. Lovewright, who lives alone, inherits a kitten and plans on being cozy with it. But Purrless, who grows to giant size, has a different, sometimes bruising definition of cozy. Adults may detect a wry parable on marriage here, but children take the story more literally. The stylized illustrations are raucous.

STREGA NONA [545]

Written and illustrated by Tomie dePaola

Cloth: Prentice Hall
Paper: Aladdin
Published: 1975   **Prizes: Caldecott Honor**

The first of the inspired storybooks about the magic witch of Calabria in which we meet Strega Nona and her doltish helper Big Anthony and are introduced to Strega Nona's powers. Delightful to read aloud. Among the others in the series, *Merry Christmas, Strega Nona* is outstanding, and *Big Anthony: His Story* gives the lad's side of the legend.

[543]

STRINGBEAN'S TRIP TO
THE SHINING SEA [546]

Written by Vera B. Williams
Illustrated by Vera B. and Jennifer Williams

Cloth: Greenwillow
Paper: Scholastic
Published: 1988   **Prizes: New York Times Best Illustrated Book**

[545]

This sophisticated account of a trip the boy nicknamed Stringbean took with his uncle to the West Coast is told in witty postcards that come complete with cancellation stamps and photo or illustration credits. It is at once a very simple and very complicated book, appealing strongly to middle and upper grade schoolchildren, who are often good readers, enjoy working on elaborate projects, and know at least a little about geography and travel.

THE STUPIDS HAVE A BALL [547]

Written by Harry Allard
Illustrated by James Marshall

Cloth: Houghton Mifflin
Paper: Houghton Mifflin
Published: 1978

The Stupids manage to justify their name in the series of silly, clamorous books by the Allard/Marshall team that also produced the manic Miss Nelson tales. In this installment, they celebrate the fact that Buster and Petunia have failed every school subject—including recess. Don't miss *The Stupids Step Out, The Stupids Die,* and *The Stupids Take Off.*

SUNDAY POTATOES,
MONDAY POTATOES [548]

Written by Vicky Shiefman
Illustrated by Louise August

Cloth: Simon & Schuster
Published: 1994

Why potatoes? because in the European village charmingly illustrated in this tale, a poor family like to eat—and, let's face it, pota-

213

toes are better than nothing. They can be delicious, especially if you have potato pudding for supper on Saturday night. Recipe included.

SUSANNA OF THE ALAMO: A TRUE STORY [549]

Written by John Jakes
Illustrated by Paul Bacon

Cloth: Harcourt Brace
Paper: Voyager
Published: 1986

Susanna Dickinson played a crucial role in the early history of Texas because she and her baby survived the siege of the Alamo in 1836, and Susanna brought General Santa Anna's warning and challenge to Sam Houston. Her story was lost or overlooked for a long time, and this book helps straighten out the record.

SWAMP ANGEL [550]

Written by Anne Isaacs
Illustrated by Paul O. Zelinsky

Cloth: Dutton
Paper: Puffin
Published: 1994

Prizes: Caldecott Honor
New York Times Best Illustrated Book

Here's the tongue-in-cheek tall tale about Angelica Longrider, a Tennessee Paul Bunyanesque heroine whose escapades, including her struggle with a bear called Thundering Tarnation, are stylishly illustrated in witty paintings done on wood veneer. The denouement, which explains the creation of the Great Plains, is very amusing.

SWAN LAKE [551]

Written by Margot Fonteyn
Illustrated by Trina Schart Hyman

Cloth: Harcourt Brace
Published: 1989

You can virtually hear the music as you go through the great ballerina's telling of one of the best-known stories in the standard classical repertory. She makes it a very human story told from the perspective of a prince named Siegfried, who falls in love with a maiden imprisoned in a swan's body, and incorporates stage details echoed in the lush period illustrations. The gestures, poses, and costumes all suggest the ballet. There are a number of other editions of *Swan Lake,* none as true to the dance and music. Fonteyn has also told *Coppelia* with illustrations by Steve Johnson and Lou Fancher.

SYLVESTER AND THE MAGIC PEBBLE [552]

Written and illustrated by William Steig

Cloth: Farrar, Straus & Giroux
Paper: Sunburst
Published: 1970   **Prizes: Caldecott Medal**

Sylvester is a donkey who collects interesting things . . . like rocks and pebbles. He's contemplating a wish from a magic pebble when he's frightened by a lion and wishes he were a rock. But when he becomes one, he can't escape or make another wish. His parents, as you can imagine, are in despair. Ultimately, of course, he is restored to donkey state and all is well. Glorious language, droll illustrations.

THE TALE OF THE MANDARIN DUCKS [553]

Written by Katherine Paterson
Illustrated by Leo and Diane Dillon

Cloth: Lodestar
Paper: Puffin
Published: 1990   **Prizes: New York Times Best Illustrated Book**

Once in imperial Japan, a cruel lord took a fancy to a beautiful wild drake and had it captured and brought to his estate. The drake, pining for his mate, is helped to escape by the lord's chief steward, Shozo. The clever ducks find a way for Shozo and his love, the kitchen maid, to escape into the forest. The lush and beautiful illustrations, styled after Japanese ukyo-e paintings, are in the mottled colors of ducks' plumage.

[557]

TALES OF PAN [554]

Written and illustrated by Mordicai Gerstein

Cloth: HarperCollins
Published: 1986

A giddy, boisterous, infectious, and therefore utterly suitable collection of stories about the Greek god Pan and his mischievous ways. The colorful line-drawing illustrations are as light as confetti.

TAMBOURINE MOON [555]

Written by Joy Jones
Illustrated by Terry Widener

Cloth: Simon & Schuster
Published: 1999

Night in the big city is scary, so as they walk, Grandaddy tells Noni the story of the dark night in Alabama long ago, when by the light of the tambourine moon he first met Grandma Ismay. It's a soothing and very romantic story, and the tambourine moon, at least in these illustrations, has a comforting personality.

TAP-TAP [556]

Written by Karen Lynn Williams
Illustrated by Catherine Stock

Cloth: Clarion
Paper: Clarion
Published: 1994

In Haiti, a tap-tap is a brightly painted truck that picks up passengers in the countryside and stops when they tap on it to get the driver's attention. They can be very crowded with people, packages, and even livestock. Sasifi and Mama walk to market, but the little girl longs to ride home on the tap-tap. A modest adventure, but well told, with charming illustrations.

TAR BEACH [557]

Written and illustrated by Faith Ringgold

Cloth: Crown
Paper: Dragonfly
Published: 1991

**Prizes: Caldecott Honor
New York Times Best Illustrated Book**

Cassie Louise Lightfoot lives in Harlem in the 1930s, and while her daddy works on bridges and tunnels, he is kept out of the union. But on a summer night, on the rooftop tar beach, Cassie can dream of sailing across all the sky as though "I owned all I could see." The dazzling faux-primitive illustrations derive from quilts.

TASTY BABY BELLY BUTTONS [558]

Written by Judy Sierra
Illustrated by Meilo So

Cloth: Knopf
Published: 1999

Here's a skillful retelling of a traditional Japanese folktale about the melon princess, the little girl found inside a watermelon seed who rescues the town's babies from the oni, the terrible horned ogres who like to snack on belly buttons. The text, with Japanese phrases throughout ("boro boro" for babies crying, "tontoko, tontoko" for marching), is delightfully matched by bold watercolor illustrations.

TELL ME A MITZI [559]

Written by Lore Segal
Illustrated by Harriet Pincus

Cloth: Farrar, Straus & Giroux
Paper: Sunburst
Published: 1970

Three memorable stories about Mitzi and her little brother, Jacob: their secret attempt to visit Grandma, the whole family's cold, and an encounter with a presidential procession. The funny, awkward

illustrations combine fantasy and vivid detail in a way that complements the text perfectly. There is a related title, *Tell Me a Trudy,* illustrated by Rosemary Wells.

THE TENTH GOOD THING ABOUT BARNEY [560]

Written by Judith Viorst
Illustrated by Erik Blegvad

Cloth: Atheneum
Paper: Aladdin
Published: 1971

When Barney the cat dies, his young owner struggles to think of good things about his pet, and to understand both the finality of death and the unity of life. This is a splendid book, deservedly a classic, suitable for readers of all ages. In its simplicity and the genuine comfort it offers, it is one of the best books for children about death.

[558]

THREE DAYS ON A RIVER IN
A RED CANOE   [561]

Written and illustrated by Vera B. Williams

Cloth: Greenwillow
Paper: Mulberry
Published: 1981

Just what the title promises—an account of the trip a little girl, her cousin, and their mothers took, complete with instructions on how to set up a tent, make a fire, and cook. A charming travelogue.

THE THREE LITTLE WOLVES
AND THE BIG BAD PIG   [562]

Written by Eugene Trivizas
Illustrated by Helen Oxenbury

Cloth: Margaret K. McElderry
Paper: Aladdin
Published: 1993

This inside-out traditional story has the little wolves building a series of houses and ending up in a concrete bunker. The big bad pig who blows it up stays for a tea party with strawberries. The illustrations are so charming they deflect from the serious part of the story and make the surprisingly happy ending the more plausible.

THE THREE ROBBERS   [563]

Written and illustrated by Tomi Ungerer

Cloth: Atheneum
Paper: Roberts Rinehart
Published: 1962

This eternally modern, alarming, funny-scary story is in its original large format. The three fierce black robbers gallop across the pages unchecked until the girl named Tiffany changes their lives. The natural audience for the story is school-age children and adults.

THUMBELINA   [564]

Written by Hans Christian Andersen
Illustrated by Arelene Graston

Cloth: Delacorte Press
Published: 1997

The story of the tiny girl pursued by forest creatures who are determined to marry her is, in fact, quite alarming. The Danish text is clear and exciting; while the cover is benign, the illustrations convey the minute size of Thumbelina in comparison to the toad, fish, field mouse, and mole, and the bird who finally rescues her.

THUNDER CAKE   [565]

Written and illustrated by Patricia Polacco

Cloth: Philomel
Paper: Paper Star
Published: 1990

Grandmother's farm is in Michigan, but she came from the Ukraine, and her way of dealing with her granddaughter's fear of an approaching thunderstorm is . . . to bake a cake. The storm looms wonderfully in the watercolor illustrations as the little girl scurries about gathering the ingredients, a task that involves postponing and conquering her fears. The recipe for the cake, including the surprise ingredient, is at the end.

TOMIE DEPAOLA'S FAVORITE NURSERY TALES   [566]

Written and illustrated by Tomie dePaola

Cloth: Putnam
Published: 1986

A bright companion volume to dePaola's Mother Goose that includes more than twenty-five well-loved stories such as "Rumpelstiltskin," "The Frog Prince," and "The Emperor's New Clothes."

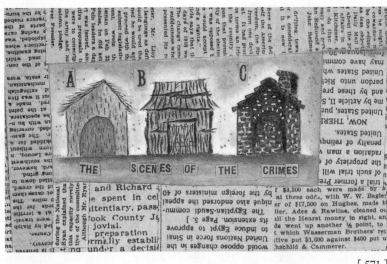

[571]

THE TOP OF THE WORLD: CLIMBING MOUNT EVEREST [567]

Written and illustrated by Steve Jenkins

Cloth: Houghton Mifflin
Published: 1999

Imaginative paper-collage illustrations increase the power of a simple but detailed text describing the mighty 29,028-foot Himalayan mountain and the "beauty, adventure, and danger" it poses to those who attempt to challenge it. Another stunning book by the same author-illustrator, *Hottest, Coldest, Highest, Deepest,* uses similar techniques to probe extremes.

TOTALLY UNCOOL [568]

Written by Janice Levy
Illustrated by Chris Monroe

Cloth: Carolrhoda
Published: 1999

Appearances can be deceiving. The narrator is complaining about her father's uncool new girlfriend, Sweet Potato, who plays the tuba, sings opera to her goldfish, and reads poems that don't rhyme. But it turns out she has possibilities after all; she pays attention and doesn't stay mad.

TRAPPED BY THE ICE!: SHACKLETON'S AMAZING ANTARCTIC ADVENTURE [569]

Written and illustrated by Michael McCurdy

Cloth: Walker and Co.
Published: 1997

The British explorer Sir Ernest Henry Shackelton set out in 1914 to be the first to cross the south polar ice cap, but his ship, the *Endurance,* was frozen into the ice. He and his men endured seemingly endless trials on the ice and at sea before reaching a whaling station. The text is plain and engrossing, the illustrations the pale colors of the ice and thin light. *Black Whiteness: Admiral Byrd Alone in the Antarctic* is a kind of companion volume, albeit dark. Drawing on his diaries, it tells the story of the American explorer who set out to spend the winter of 1934 alone on the ice. A fascinating pair of books about real adventurers.

THE TREK [570]

Written and illustrated by Ann Jonas

Cloth: Greenwillow
Paper: Mulberry
Published: 1985

Walking to school isn't what grown-ups think. Why, there are wild creatures hidden almost everywhere, and in these clever illustrations you can see them. Don't be afraid, though. You will get there safely.

[571]

THE TRUE STORY OF THE 3 LITTLE PIGS [571]

Written by Jon Scieszka
Illustrated by Lane Smith

Cloth: Viking Press
Paper: Puffin
Published: 1989

A chap calling himself Alexander T. Wolf ("You can call me Al") wants to straighten out the record about what happened with those pigs. Mr. Wolf claims he's been victimized by the press. His version—how he had a cold (the huffing and puffing) and went to the neigh-

bors to borrow some sugar and sneezed—is funny enough. What makes this account dazzling as well as hilarious are the excited, jazzy illustrations. If you have mastered the traditional story, and there are wonderful versions available, this is great fun. It is also good to read with middle grade children learning about "point of view."

THE TUB PEOPLE   [572]

Written by Pam Conrad
Illustrated by Richard Egielski

Cloth: HarperCollins
Paper: Harper Trophy
Published: 1989

The tub people are little dolls who look startlingly like Fisher-Price toys, live on the bathtub ledge, and play in the water. One day the little tub boy is sucked down the drain. Never fear, he is rescued. The illustrations are large, round, stolid, and although charming, seem static to an adult eye at first or even thirtieth reading. But the very young hear the emotions described in the text, concentrate, and believe in those pictures—believe in them intensely. The stories continue in *The Tub Grandfather* and *The Tub People's Christmas*.

TWELVE TALES: HANS CHRISTIAN ANDERSEN   [573]

Written by Hans Christian Andersen
Illustrated by Erik Blegvad

Cloth: Margaret K. McElderry
Paper: Aladdin
Published: 1994

Here's a beautifully made book, a collection of stories not as familiar as they once were, yet as haunting and engrossing and sometimes

hilarious as ever. The fluent translations are easy to read aloud; the illustrations are thoughtful and apt.

A VISIT TO WILLIAM BLAKE'S INN: POEMS FOR INNOCENT AND EXPERIENCED TRAVELERS [574]

Written by Nancy Willard
Illustrated by Alice and Martin Provensen

Cloth: Harcourt Brace
Paper: Voyager
Published: 1981

Prizes: National Book Award
Newbery Medal
Caldecott Honor

A collection of intriguing poems inspired by William Blake's *Songs of Innocence* and *Songs of Experience*, with stylized, witty illustrations capturing a mysterious sense of nineteenth-century London. While this is a book meant for older children and adults, younger children who are used to listening to poetry may well be interested.

[575]

[575]

WHEN WE WERE VERY YOUNG   [575]

Written by A. A. Milne
Illustrated by Ernest H. Shepard

Cloth: Dutton
Paper: Puffin
Published: 1924

A collection of verse for young children that has been considered classic for generations, full of fantasy and vignettes to remember for a lifetime. Household pets, kings and queens, games, illness, pirates, and prayers—and lilting, sometimes silly rhymes. The line drawings are models of illustration balancing the sometimes fey poems. *Now We Are Six* is the companion volume.

WHISKERS & RHYMES   [576]

Written and illustrated by Arnold Lobel

Cloth: Greenwillow
Paper: Mulberry
Published: 1985

In this collection of delightful nonsense verses, the conceit is that they are all illustrated by cats—dandified cats in old-fashioned costumes, perhaps visiting from the eighteenth century.

WHITE DYNAMITE AND CURLY KIDD   [577]

Written by Bill Martin, Jr., and John Archambault
Illustrated by Ted Rand

Cloth: Henry Holt
Paper: Henry Holt
Published: 1986

A grand account of White Dynamite, a mean old bull, and Curly Kidd, the toughest rodeo rider around. Designed for reading aloud.

[577]

WHY MOSQUITOES BUZZ IN PEOPLE'S EARS: A WEST AFRICAN TALE   [578]

Written by Verna Aardema
Illustrated by Leo and Diane Dillon

Cloth: Dial
Paper: Puffin
Published: 1975   **Prizes: Caldecott Medal**

This is an eccentric and wonderful story based on an odd chain of events. Mosquito tells a lie that ultimately results in the sun's not rising. When the animals, led by lion, figure out just what happened, Mosquito is punished. A fine read-aloud text is supported by stylized illustrations.

WHY THE SUN & MOON LIVE IN THE SKY   [579]

Written and illustrated by Niki Daly

Cloth: Lothrop, Lee & Shepard
Paper: Mulberry
Published: 1995   **Prizes: New York Times Best Illustrated Book**

This adaptation of a Nigerian creation myth remembers that Sun (a young man) and Moon (a young woman) once lived together in a grand house. The extroverted Sun loved to travel, while Moon stayed home. Infatuated by Sea, Sun invited her home and she and her children inundated the house. Elegant watercolor illustrations give rich character to the deceptively simple story.

WORSE THAN WILLY! [580]

Written and illustrated by James Stevenson

Cloth: Greenwillow
Published: 1984

This is one of the many raucous, improbable, and soothing stories Grandpa tells Louie and Mary Ann about the childhood he shared with Uncle Wainwright. The layout is half story book, half cartoon. Some other titles in the series include *Could Be Worse* and *What's Under My Bed?* In addition, Stevenson has written a splendid series of autobiographical stories including *When I Was Nine, Higher on the Wall,* and *Don't You Know There's a War On?* that are out of print but well worth finding.

THE YEAR OF THE PERFECT CHRISTMAS TREE: AN APPALACHIAN STORY [581]

Written by Gloria Houston
Illustrated by Barbara Cooney

Cloth: Dial
Paper: Puffin
Published: 1988

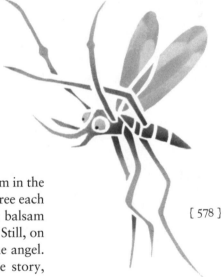

[578]

It's 1918 in the mountains of North Carolina, and the custom in the village is for one family to select and donate the Christmas tree each year. In the spring, Ruthie and her father choose a perfect balsam high on a rocky crag. Then Father goes off to World War I. Still, on Christmas Eve the tree is in the church and Ruthie plays the angel. The winning illustrations perfectly match the tone of the story, which comes from the author's family.

YERTLE THE TURTLE AND OTHER STORIES [582]

Written and illustrated by Dr. Seuss

Cloth: Random House
Published: 1958

Dr. Seuss from his classic period: three modern fables with improbable characters, illustrations, and story lines all in verse—but with very real morals.

[579]

YOU BE GOOD AND I'LL BE NIGHT: JUMP-ON-THE-BED POEMS   [583]

Written by Eve Merriam
Illustrated by Karen Lee Schmidt

Cloth: Morrow Junior Books
Paper: Mulberry
Published: 1989

The title of these playful bedtime verses captures the affectionate spirit that gives the collection such appealing charm. Lots of gentle jokes for small lap listeners, and beguiling illustrations as well.

ZIN! ZIN! ZIN! A VIOLIN   [584]

Written by Lloyd Moss
Illustrated by Marjorie Priceman

Cloth: Simon & Schuster
Paper: Aladdin
Published: 1995   **Prizes: New York Times Best Illustrated Book**

A lighthearted verse introduction to the instruments of the orchestra with exuberant illustrations that are fanciful and colorful at the same time. The cellist is dressed like Pierrot, the flutist like a harlequin; there are cats, dogs, a whole menagerie swirling around as the instruments assemble and reassemble in combinations from duets to nonets. After the concert, on the last page, a stagehand sweeps up and the animals go to sleep.

Early Reading Books

These well-illustrated books are designed for children who are learning to read and making the transition into "chapter books." Some of them are a particular pleasure to read aloud to attentive younger children.

26 FAIRMOUNT AVENUE [585]

Written and illustrated by Tomie dePaola

Cloth: Putnam
Published: 1999　　　　　**Prizes: Newbery Honor**

In easy-to-read chapters, the well-known author and illustrator tells about his Irish and Italian family and their move to a new home when he was a little boy in the 1930s.

A, MY NAME IS ALICE [586]

Written by Jane E. Bayer
Illustrated by Steven Kellogg

Cloth: Dial
Paper: Dutton
Published: 1984

An assortment of animals jump rope and bounce balls to those familiar rhymes that pass from generation to generation, with only minor and gradual changes.

THE ADVENTURES OF PINOCCHIO

[587]

Written by Carlo Collodi
Illustrated by Attilio Mussino

Cloth: Macmillan
Published: 1925

The most enchanting edition of the classic story of the little wooden puppet who wants to become a real boy appeared in Italy in 1911, in the United States in 1925, and was reissued in the late 1980s. It's now out of print again, but worth searching for in a library. The large, open format that sets off both the stylish illustrations and the gracefully displayed text make it easy to read aloud. The original story was written for newspaper serialization in 1882, so the narrative is somewhat jerky at times. Of course, if you are reading it aloud at bedtime, you may not notice. There are many abridged and coyly illustrated editions around, but nothing approaches the bookmaking excellence of this one, though an interesting and handsome adaptation by Ed Young appeared in 1996. Incidentally, children weaned on the Disney version, which is quite wonderful in its own right, should be warned that the book is much harsher and more sinister.

[588]

AMANDA PIG AND HER BIG BROTHER OLIVER [588]

Written by Jean Van Leeuwen
Illustrated by Ann Schweninger

Cloth: Dial (Easy to Read)
Paper: Puffin
Published: 1982

One of the finest early-reader series is also particularly astute about sibling rivalry and sibling strength and affection. It features a family of plausible pigs and their endearing children in a range of domestic adventures that will resonate with the lives of most young readers. These books are a pleasure to read to children until they can read them to each other. Titles include *Amanda Pig on Her Own; Oliver, Amanda, and Grandmother Pig; Tales of Oliver Pig; More Tales of Oliver Pig;* and *More Tales of Amanda Pig.*

AMELIA BEDELIA [589]

Written by Peggy Parish
Illustrated by Fritz Seibel

Cloth: HarperCollins
Paper: Harper Trophy
Published: 1963

The Amelia Bedelia books have been published in two series by Harper and Greenwillow with no diminution in their wacky charm and appeal. (The publishers are now united, the newest books written by Parish's heirs.) The literal-minded housekeeper was first hired by Mr. and Mrs. Rogers nearly forty years ago, when social class in this country was less of an issue, but she remains beloved by beginning readers. She goes on "dressing" chickens, "separating" the eggs, and earnestly misunderstanding. Happily, she always puts "a little of this" and "a little of that" together and bakes her way into job security. Other titles include *Come Back, Amelia Bedelia; Good Work, Amelia Bedelia; Amelia Bedelia and the Baby; Amelia Bedelia Goes Camping; Merry Christmas, Amelia Bedelia,* and *Amelia Bedelia and the Baby.*

[589]

AND THEN WHAT HAPPENED, PAUL REVERE? [590]

Written by Jean Fritz
Illustrated by Margot Tomes

Cloth: Coward
Paper: Paper Star
Published: 1973

[589]

A biography of Paul Revere for young readers that is good-natured and accessible as well as being accurate and good history. The prizewinning author has written a veritable history course of light-hearted but provocative biographies for children. Other fine titles include *Can't You Make Them Behave, King George?*; *Why Don't You Get a Horse, Sam Adams?*; and *What's the Big Idea, Ben Franklin?*

ARE YOU MY MOTHER? [591]

Written and illustrated by P. D. Eastman

Cloth: Random House (Beginner Books)
Published: 1960

In this classic beginning reader, a baby bird falls from the nest and tries to find his mother. The simple text is augmented by bright pictures. Watch out for abridgements and odd formats; this is a fine book as it is and deserves to be read in its original form.

ARTHUR'S HONEY BEAR [592]

Written and illustrated by Lillian Hoban

Cloth: HarperCollins
Paper: Harper Trophy
Published: 1974

Arthur the chimpanzee and his little sister, Violet, are two favorite siblings in the world of early-reader books. Their relationship and adventures are plausible and entertaining. The other titles include *Arthur's Prize Reader, Arthur's Pen Pal* (which has a good antisexist surprise in the plot), *Arthur's Christmas Cookies,* and *Arthur's Funny Money.*

"B" IS FOR BETSY [593]

Written and illustrated by Carolyn Haywood

Cloth: Harcourt Brace
Paper: Odyssey
Published: 1939

This is the first of a series of easy-to-read and perennially popular chapter books that follow Betsy from first to fourth grade in an idyllic town. Other titles include *Back to School with Betsy, Betsy and the Boys,* and *Betsy and Billy.*

A BEAR CALLED PADDINGTON [594]

Written by Michael Bond
Illustrated by Peggy Fortnum

Cloth: Houghton Mifflin
Paper: Dell Yearling
Published: 1960

The lovable bear from darkest Peru found by Mr. and Mrs. Brown in London's Paddington Station makes his debut here. There are ten books in the original series and nearly half a dozen others, plus all sorts of franchise paraphernalia and merchandise to be found everywhere. The original stories are still delightfully funny and hard, but challenging as early readers. The same author created Olga De Polga, a very imaginative guinea pig, who appears in three books.

[595]

THE BEAUTY OF THE BEAST: POEMS FROM THE ANIMAL KINGDOM [595]

Written by Jack Prelutsky
Illustrated by Meilo So

Cloth: Knopf
Published: 1997

A delightful anthology of poems about animals, and not just farm or jungle animals, but city creatures as well. The organization is by species—reptiles, birds, mammals—and the illustrations are enchantingly deft wet-in-wet watercolors that suit the subjects perfectly.

BEST ENEMIES [596]

Written by Kathleen Leverich
Illustrated by Susan Condie Lamb

Cloth: Greenwillow
Paper: Bullseye
Published: 1989

Felicity Doll was probably born a menace. Certainly by the time she enters the second grade and does her best to make Priscilla Robin's life a nightmare, she is. Felicity is like a snake in lavender ruffles, and these four short, funny stories capture her at her memorable worst—snitching, bullying, teasing, shaking her curls, and fussing. And Priscilla? She stands up for herself very nicely, thank you. Their adventures continue in *Best Enemies Again* and *Best Enemies Forever*.

BETSY-TACY [597]

Written by Maud Hart Lovelace
Illustrated by Lois Lenski

Cloth: HarperCollins
Paper: Harper Trophy
Published: 1940

The Betsy-Tacy series, set in Deep Valley, Minnesota, around the turn of the century, follows three girls, Betsy (WASP), Tacy (Irish), and Tib (German), from the time they are five on through high school, college, and marriage. It is a model of an enduring and appealing kind of series fiction in which the text increases in complexity with each book and the characters are fully developed as they grow up. The girls' concerns and adventures are more than plausible—they ring true even now. The first six titles are the childhood sequence and are available in a boxed paperback edition. They include *Betsy-Tacy and Tib, Betsy and Tacy Go Over the Big Hill, Betsy and Tacy Go Downtown, Heavens to Betsy,* and *Betsy in Spite of Herself.* The illustrations in the first books are by Lois Lenski; in the later books, by Vera Neville. Both are appropriate choices.

[594]

A BOOK OF AMERICANS [598]

Written by Rosemary and Stephen Vincent Benét
Illustrated by Charles Child

Cloth: Henry Holt
Paper: Henry Holt
Published: 1933; reissued 1986

A collection of fifty-six poems about historic Americans, both lesser and well known, written with style and wit more than half a century ago and reissued for new generations to enjoy. There are presidents and plain folk inventoried, and even a few villains here. Perfect for reading aloud. The woodcut illustrations are dramatic.

BUFFALO WOMAN [599]

Written and illustrated by Paul Goble

Cloth: Bradbury
Paper: Aladdin
Published: 1984

The young hunter's bride, scorned by his people, returns to her own—the Buffalo Nation. He follows and proves his love for her and their son with the son's help. The hunter is then transformed into a buffalo, too, and honor is given to all. Dramatic, eloquent, and beautifully illustrated in highly stylized full-color illustrations, this is a profound love story. Children in the early grades find it particularly thrilling.

BUNNICULA [600]

Written by Deborah and James Howe
Illustrated by Alan Daniel

[601]

Cloth: Atheneum
Paper: Aladdin
Published: 1979

Is Bunnicula really a vegetarian vampire bunny? Harold, the Monroe family's dog and the narrator of this comic novel, thinks so. This is the first of a funny series featuring Harold, Chester the dog, and Howie the dachshund puppy. Middle grade readers find them very entertaining. *The Celery Stalks at Midnight* is followed by *Nightly Nightmare, Howliday Inn* and finally, of course, *Bunnicula Strikes Again.*

THE CAT IN THE HAT   [601]

Written and illustrated by Dr. Seuss

Cloth: Random House (Beginner Books)
Published: 1956

The one—not the only, but certainly the original—contemporary beginning reader. (It makes no difference that it is nearly fifty years old.) One rainy afternoon, when Mother is out and there is nothing to do, the Cat in the Hat comes to visit, and mayhem ensues. It continues in *The Cat in the Hat Comes Back*.

CAT'S CRADLE, OWL'S EYES:
A BOOK OF STRING GAMES   [602]

Written by Camilla Gryski
Illustrated by Tom Sankey

Cloth: Mulberry
Published: 1984

A collection of forty string games, with clear instructions and fine photographs, beginning, of course, with cat's cradle. If you think about it, string games are more than fun, they are an introduction to math as well. If you get hooked on string, there is a sequel, *Many Stars,* and *More String Games*.

[599]

A CHILD'S CALENDAR   [603]

Written by John Updike
Illustrated by Trina Schart Hyman

Cloth: Holiday House
Published: 1999   **Prizes: Caldecott Honor**

A dozen verses tied to the months, describing a New England year, first published in 1969, were reillustrated to suggest the family life of a particularly appealing pair of brothers in a mixed-race family who lead a bucolic existence in a pretty rural place.

THE COBBLE STREET COUSINS   [604]

Written by Cynthia Rylant
Illustrated by Wendy Anderson Halperin

Cloth: Simon & Schuster
Published: 1999

Josie and Lily are sisters, and their cousin Tess lives with them in a pretty house on Cobble Street. Their adventures are modest—making a dollhouse that looks like Aunt Lucy's flower shop, for example—but vivid. The pencil and watercolor illustrations are as sweet as the stories. The first titles include *Some Good News* and *In Aunt Lucy's Kitchen.*

DANNY AND THE DINOSAUR   [605]

Written and illustrated by Syd Hoff

Cloth: HarperCollins
Paper: Harper Trophy
Published: 1958

A museum dinosaur spends a perfectly wonderful day wandering around the city with Danny. There is a Spanish-language edition of this perennial favorite in print as well. The author also created *Sammy the Seal* and *Chester the Horse* in the early-reader series.

DID YOU CARRY THE FLAG TODAY, CHARLEY? [606]

Written by Rebecca Caudill
Illustrated by Nancy Grossman

Cloth: Henry Holt
Paper: Yearling
Published: 1966

At Charley's school in Appalachia, you don't get to carry the flag unless you learn to behave. Mischievous Charley wins the honor in the end. An old-time story with great charm.

DIGGING UP DINOSAURS [607]

Written and illustrated by Aliki

Cloth: HarperCollins
Paper: Harper Trophy
Published: 1981

All right, dinosaur fans, just how did those bones get from the ground into the museums? This book provides serious answers in a lighthearted and informative way sure to please young scientists. The differences among the giant creatures is explained in simple text and clear illustrations in the author's *Dinosaurs Are Different*—for example, how to tell the meat eaters from the vegetarians. Essential for the fanatics, interesting to the merely curious.

THE DISAPPEARING ALPHABET [608]

Written by Richard Wilbur
Illustrated by David Diaz

Cloth: Harcourt Brace
Published: 1998

What would happen to our language if individual letters of the alphabet began to disappear? A Pulitzer Prize–winning poet gave an amusing and provocative answer in verse: "Since it is by words that we construe/The world, the world would start to vanish, too!" His imaginative examples go right through the alphabet. The illustrations are both clever and helpful. This is an alphabet book best

[612]

suited to children who can read and are writing and beginning to think about the subtleties of language. The poem was actually written for adults, so it's okay to be so entertained yourself.

THE ENORMOUS CROCODILE   [609]

Written by Roald Dahl
Illustrated by Quentin Blake

Cloth: Knopf
Paper: Puffin
Published: 1978

A droll story about an enormous crocodile who dares to leave the river and go to the town to find little children to eat. He poses as a coconut tree, a merry-go-round, and a picnic bench and is foiled each time by other animals. Witty illustrations.

FISH FACE   [610]

Written by Patricia Reilly Giff
Illustrated by Blanche Sims

Cloth: Delacorte
Paper: Dell Yearling
Published: 1984

This is one of the titles in "The Kids in the Polk Street School" series, which follows the adventures of the children in Ms. Rooney's room, especially Emily Arrow and Richard "Beast" Best, throughout the year. Here, Emily Arrow discovers that the girl who sits next to her, Dawn Tiffanie Bosco, is a thief. The illustrations are cheerful. The series is very popular with beginning readers. Some of the

[612]

other titles are *The Beast in Ms. Rooney's Room, The Valentine Star, Snaggle Doodles,* and *Say Cheese.*

FOX AND HIS FRIENDS [611]

Written by Edward Marshall
Illustrated by James Marshall

Cloth: Dial (Easy to Read)
Paper: Puffin
Published: 1982

Fox, an eager fellow, and his assorted friends appear in a funny series about life, school, and play, whose other titles include *Fox at School, Fox in Love, Fox on Wheels, Fox all Week,* and, of course, *Fox Out Foxed.*

FROG AND TOAD TOGETHER [612]

Written and illustrated by Arnold Lobel

Cloth: HarperCollins
Paper: Harper Trophy
Published: 1972   **Prizes: Newbery Honor**

There are four books about those amiable friends Frog and Toad and their modest but utterly engrossing adventures and activities—everything from planting a garden and dreaming of grandeur to getting the house clean or flying a kite. The language is pleasing, the illustrations amusing. *Days with Frog and Toad, Frog and Toad Are Friends,* and *Frog and Toad All Year* are the other titles. Younger children love hearing them, beginning readers pore over them, and adults remember them with abiding affection.

THE GREAT BRAIN [613]

Written by John Fitzgerald
Illustrated by Mercer Mayer

Cloth: Dial
Paper: Dell Yearling
Published: 1967

The first of a series of good-natured books based on the author's memories of growing up in Utah at the beginning of this century, in awe of his older brother, who was called the Great Brain. Other titles include *The Great Brain at the Academy, The Great Brain Does It Again, The Great Brain Reforms,* and *The Return of the Great Brain.* They are especially appealing to boys.

GREEN EGGS AND HAM [614]

Written and illustrated by Dr. Seuss

Cloth: Random House (Beginner Books)
Published: 1960

One of the fine Seuss early readers, with a limited vocabulary and a narrator who keeps insisting, "I do not like them, Sam I am," until he tastes those eggs. Just try not to laugh!

[615]

HALF MAGIC   [615]

Written by Edward Eager
Illustrated by N. M. Bodecker

Cloth: Harcourt Brace
Paper: Odyssey
Published: 1954

Four children wish on an ancient coin and—presto!—their dull summer turns into a series of splendid, exciting adventures, once they figure out that they'll get only half of what they bargain for. Other titles by Edward Eager include *Magic or Not?* and *Magic by the Lake.* For younger Harry Potter fans, the ones who listened, but couldn't quite read them alone, these are delightfully accessible. Good for reading aloud, too.

HAPPILY EVER AFTER   [616]

Written by Anna Quindlen
Illustrated by James Stevenson

Cloth: Viking Press
Published: 1998

The star shortstop of the Walker's Delicatessen Little League team, eight-year-old Kate, falls asleep reading a story about a princess, and finds herself in a stone tower in a pink dress. Next thing you know she's saving princes who want to marry her and rescuing herself, even if, as she sensibly points out, she's only in the fourth grade. *Rumplestiltskin's Daughter* is another funny feminist turn on traditional fairy tales.

[617]

THE HUNDRED DRESSES   [617]

Written by Elenor Estes
Illustrated by Louis Slobodkin

Cloth: Harcourt Brace
Paper: Voyager
Published: 1944

Prizes: Newbery Honor

The story of Wanda Petronski, the little Polish girl whose classmates did not believe she had a hundred dresses, has been a classic for several generations, teaching quiet, painful lessons of tolerance and dignity. The pale, delicate illustrations are memorable, too. The writing is simple enough for younger readers to manage independently and powerful enough so they never forget it.

IN A DARK, DARK ROOM: AND OTHER SCARY STORIES [618]

Written by Alvin Schwartz
Illustrated by Dirk Zimmer

Cloth: HarperCollins
Paper: Harper Trophy
Published: 1984

A nicely nasty collection of mysterious stories, based on traditional folktales but written for the beginning reader. If you like them, look for *Ghosts! Ghostly Tales from Folklore* or *No More Monsters for Me.*

JANE MARTIN, DOG DETECTIVE

[619]

Written by Eve Bunting
Illustrated by Amy Schwartz

Cloth: Harcourt Brace
Paper: Voyager
Published: 1984

For a fee of just twenty-five cents a day, Jane Martin finds missing dogs. Three short, easy-to-read detective stories with whimsical illustrations.

[621]

THE LAND I LOST: ADVENTURES OF A BOY IN VIETNAM [620]

Written by Quang Nhuong Nhuong
Illustrated by Vo-Dinh Mai

Cloth: HarperCollins
Paper: Harper Trophy
Published: 1982

This is the true story of the author's childhood in a Vietnamese hamlet, told with affectionate details about social customs and nature. This is one of the best of the easily obtainable books for children about Vietnam or Vietnamese culture.

LITTLE BEAR [621]

Written by Else Holmelund Minarik
Illustrated by Maurice Sendak

Cloth: HarperCollins
Paper: Harper Trophy
Published: 1957

One of the first and very finest series of early-reader books features Little Bear and his considerate friends, including Hen, Duck, Cat, his doting parents in their Victorian dress, and eventually his friend Emily and her doll Lucy. The use of a controlled vocabulary does not inhibit the stories, which appeal to toddlers and preschoolers almost as much as to the beginning readers. The other titles are *Little Bear's Friend, Father Bear Comes Home, Little Bear's Visit,* and *A Kiss For Little Bear,* in which the various animals deliver the kiss Grandma sends Little Bear in return for a picture.

LITTLE BROTHER OF THE WILDERNESS: THE STORY OF JOHNNY APPLESEED [622]

Written by Meridel Le Sueur
Illustrated by Suzy Sansom

Cloth: Holy Cow! Press
Paper: Holy Cow! Press
Published: 1947

John Chapman, who really did walk from Massachusetts to Indiana in the early nineteenth century planting apple seeds, is a heroic figure of the frontier. For contemporary children, who seem to consume gallons of apple juice daily, his achievement is both wonderful and genuinely relevant to their lives. This story of Johnny Appleseed is beautifully written and very easy to read—indeed, although tentative readers can manage it alone, it asks to be read aloud. Among the other accounts of his life and deeds available, Steven Kellogg's has a typically energetic quality, and Kathy Jakobsen did primitive-style illustrations incorporating quilt motifs to accompany a verse version by Reeve Lindbergh. Le Sueur's prose, however, is matchless.

[621]

[623]

LITTLE HOUSE IN
THE BIG WOODS   [623]

Written by Laura Ingalls Wilder
Illustrated by Garth Williams

Cloth: HarperCollins
Paper: Harper Trophy
Published: 1932

The Little House books follow the Ingalls family as they move west from Wisconsin into Indian lands and finally settle in the Dakota territory. The stories begin in the 1870s, when Laura, the central character, is not quite five, and continue through her girlhood and adolescence to her marriage to Almanzo Wilder, a young settler. His boyhood in New York State is described in

Farmer Boy. The prose becomes more sophisticated as Laura grows up. The details of pioneer life are vivid and exact, and the books are thrilling in their artless didacticism and portrayal of close and rewarding family life. There is an endlessly replaying television series very loosely based on the books, but with none of their charm. And alas, there are endless chopped-up and merchandised bits and chapters posing as books as well as brand-new books about other family members. Avoid the travesties—read the real books. The other titles include *Little House on the Prairie, On the Banks of Plum Creek, By the Shores of Silver Lake, The Long Winter, Little Town on the Prairie,* and *Those Happy Golden Years*. There is a boxed paperback edition of nine titles. *The Little House Cookbook: Frontier Foods from Laura Ingalls Wilder's Classic Stories* is out of print, but it is a genuinely good cookbook for children, drawing on the recipes that occur so naturally in the stories. Skip the junk version.

THE LITTLE PRINCE   [624]

Written and illustrated by Antoine de Saint-Exupéry

Cloth: Harcourt Brace
Paper: Harvest
Published: 1943

The mystical fairy tale storybook about a little prince who comes from another planet has been an adult cult title since it was first published and is most often read in French classes or by adults. A new edition translated by Richard Howard appeared this year.

LITTLE WITCH'S BIG NIGHT   [625]

Written by Deborah Hautzig
Illustrated by Marc Brown

Paper: Random House (Step into Reading)
Published: 1985

Little Witch has been so good she is punished and has to stay at home on Halloween. She takes three friends—a pirate, an astronaut, and a devil—riding on her broomstick. In *Happy Birthday Little Witch,* her friends manage to come to her birthday party. There's also *Little Witch Goes to School.*

[623]

LULU GOES TO WITCH SCHOOL   [626]

Written by Jane O'Connor
Illustrated by Emily Arnold McCully

Cloth: HarperCollins
Paper: Harper Trophy
Published: 1987

This Lulu, who starred in *Lulu and the Witch Baby,* has moved on to witch school, and she just loves it. She loves Miss Slime, her teacher, her cubby with the bat picture, the lizard tarts at snack time, and flying lessons. Eventually, she even makes friends with Sandy Witch. Lighthearted fun.

MORE STORIES HUEY TELLS   [627]

Written by Ann Cameron
Illustrated by Lis Toft

Cloth: Farrar, Straus & Giroux
Paper: Farrar, Straus & Giroux
Published: 1997

Huey is the spunky younger brother of that boy named Julian (*Stories Julian Tells*), and happily, he has a series of books of his own. Most of the series is out of print. Look for it anyway, because, for example, in this one, touchingly, Huey tries to save his dying sunflower forest.

THE MOUSE AND THE MOTORCYCLE   [628]

Written by Beverly Cleary
Illustrated by Louis Darling

Cloth: Morrow Junior Books
Paper: Avon
Published: 1965

The first of three engaging books about Ralph, a mouse, who is given a toy motorcycle and finds it is the vehicle of his dreams. In *Runaway Ralph,* the generation gap intrudes, and in *Ralph S. Mouse* (illustrated by Paul O. Zelinsky), the hero goes to school.

[624]

MOUSE TALES   [629]

Written and illustrated by Arnold Lobel

Cloth: HarperCollins
Paper: Harper Trophy
Published: 1972

Papa Mouse promises his boys one story each before bedtime. There are seven—all short, some funny, some wise, and all wonderful. Elements include a talking wishing well, a tall and a short mouse, a flood, and more. Engrossing for a beginning reader. *Mouse Soup* is a sequel of sorts.

MR. POPPER'S PENGUINS   [630]

Written by Richard and Florence Atwater
Illustrated by Robert Lawson

Cloth: Little, Brown
Paper: Dell Yearling
Published: 1938   **Prizes: Newbery Honor**

After more than sixty years, readers and listeners are still enchanted by the classic tale of Mr. Popper, a kindly housepainter in a town called Stillwater, who loved penguins. It's about how his family coped with the gift of one, Captain Cook, who was joined by another, Greta, and begat a small flock of penguins. The illustrations capture the humor of both penguins and the story. The essential curiosity of the penguins and Mr. Popper's goodwill are something children remember.

MR. PUTTER AND TABBY ROW THE BOAT [631]

Written by Cynthia Rylant
Illustrated by Arthur Howard

Cloth: Harcourt Brace
Published: 1997

Mr. Putter is a kindly elderly gent and Tabby is his cat. Their modest adventures—here on a hot summer afternoon they cool off at a pond with an assortment of friends and neighbors—are satisfying early readers. Other titles in the series include *Mr. Putter and Tabby Paint the Porch, Mr. Putter and Tabby Fly the Plane, Mr. Putter and Tabby Walk the Dog,* and *Mr. Putter and Tabby Pour the Tea.*

MY FATHER'S DRAGON [632]

Written by Ruth Stiles Gannett
Illustrated by Ruth Chrisman Gannett

Cloth: Random House
Paper: Knopf
Published: 1948   **Prizes: Newbery Honor**

The narrator's father, Elmer Elevator, sets out to rescue a baby dragon from the Wild Island. He uses his wits and imagination and only a few props. The illustrations, especially the endpaper maps, are enchanting. Good early chapter book for reading aloud or reading alone. There is a boxed paperback set that includes two other dragon titles, *Elmer and the Dragon* and *The Dragons of Blueland.*

[632]

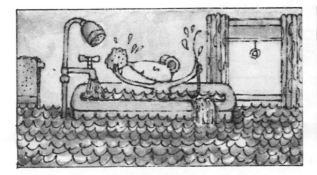 

[629]

NATE THE GREAT [633]

Written by Marjorie Weinman Sharmat
Illustrated by Marc Simont

Cloth: Coward
Paper: Dell Young Yearling
Published: 1972

Nate the Great is the neighborhood detective, a serious sleuth only three feet high. The hat's a little big, the sentences are short, the detecting pretty easy. Lots and lots of fun for beginning readers. Other titles include *Nate the Great and the Fishy Prize, Nate the Great and the Snowy Trail,* and *Nate the Great and the Missing Key.*

NO MORE MONSTERS FOR ME [634]

Written by Peggy Parrish
Illustrated by Marc Simont

Cloth: HarperCollins
Paper: Harper Trophy
Published: 1981

Minneapolis Simpkin is quite desperate to have a pet, and her mother didn't say she couldn't have a monster. So she brings home a baby one and then tries to keep it hidden. A fine, farcical early reader. The single-child/single-parent household is a given.

OLD MOTHER WEST WIND   [635]

Written by Thornton W. Burgess
Illustrated by Harrison Cady

Cloth: Little, Brown
Paper: Little, Brown
Published: 1910

This delightful collection of short, easy-to-read stories about Reddy Fox, Peter Rabbit, Danny Meadow Mouse, and the other creatures of the meadow and woods has been a favorite for generations and with good reason. The type is large and clear; the illustrations are old-fashioned and simple. Good for reading aloud to younger children, too. If you love it, then find *Old Mother West Wind's Children*.

OWL AT HOME   [636]

Written and illustrated by Arnold Lobel

Cloth: HarperCollins
Paper: Harper Trophy
Published: 1975

A touching set of stories about Owl, a rather stay-at-home fellow, who lets winter come in to visit with chilling results, makes tearwater tea, and finds a friend in the moon. Though a splendid early reader, it is also good for reading aloud to lap listeners.

PIPPI LONGSTOCKING   [637]

Written by Astrid Lindgren
Illustrated by Louis S. Glanzman

Cloth: Viking Press
Paper: Puffin
Published: 1950

[635]

Pippi is a scamp, a mischief maker, and a very nice little girl all in one. She lives all alone in a little house at the edge of the village. Her manners, housekeeping methods, and everything else about her are unconventional. The translation from the Swedish is slightly awkward and clumsy to read aloud, but listeners invariably want another chapter, please, or reread the books for themselves. Other Pippi books include *Pippi Goes on Board, Pippi on the Run,* and *Pippi in the South Seas.*

SAM THE MINUTEMAN   [638]

Written by Nathaniel Benchley
Illustrated by Arnold Lobel

Cloth: HarperCollins
Paper: Harper Trophy
Published: 1969

Here is one little boy's version of the beginnings of the American Revolution. The remarkably well-written story is both accurate and clear and makes a number of sophisticated points about the causes of the revolution in ways young children can absorb. The companion volume is *George the Drummer Boy*, about a British drummer boy.

SCARY STORIES TO TELL IN THE DARK: COLLECTED FROM AMERICAN FOLKLORE   [639]

Written by Alvin Schwartz
Illustrated by Stephen Gammell

Cloth: HarperCollins
Paper: HarperCollins
Published: 1981

Gather round and sit close by. Here's a dandy collection, including ghosts, folktales, and some modern scary stories. Ideal for campfires and reading aloud. The second volume is *More Scary Stories to Tell in the Dark*.

[631]

SCOOTER   [640]

Written and illustrated by Vera B. Williams

Cloth: Greenwillow
Published: 1993

In this richly illustrated and appealing novel, there is a sense of the hurly-burly of urban life in a crowded New York City neighborhood a few generations ago, as well as Scooter's unmistakable voice. Good for early independent readers, but also a fine book for reading aloud.

THE SHRINKING OF TREEHORN

[641]

Written by Florence Parry Heide
Illustrated by Edward Gorey

Cloth: Holiday House
Paper: Holiday House
Published: 1971   **Prizes: New York Times Best Illustrated Book**

This is the first of three wistfully comic tales about Treehorn, the sort of boy who is ignored by others, even his parents and teachers. He is actually fading away and they don't notice. The morbid and hilarious illustrations are by a master. There's also *Treehorn's Treasure* and *Treehorn's Wish*.

SMALL POEMS   [642]

Written by Valerie Worth
Illustrated by Natalie Babbitt

Cloth: Farrar, Straus & Giroux
Published: 1972

Here is a delightful series of small books of small poems, with small illustrations but great quantities of wit and style. The other titles, naturally, include *More Small Poems, Still More Small Poems,* and *Small Poems Again.* In paperback, there is a complete collection of *All the Small Poems and Fourteen More.*

[644]

THE STORIES JULIAN TELLS [643]

Written by Ann Cameron
Illustrated by Ann Strugnell

Cloth: Knopf
Paper: Random House
Published: 1981

In this chapter book for beginning readers—six stories about Julian and his modest, cheerful middle-class black family, including his engaging little brother, Huey—there is an appealing everydayness: losing a tooth, ordering a cat from a catalog. The sequel is *More Stories Julian Tells.*

TODAY WAS A TERRIBLE DAY [644]

Written by Patricia Reilly Giff
Illustrated by Susanna Natti

Cloth: Viking Press
Paper: Puffin
Published: 1984

Ronald Morgan is a hapless hero who suffers from acute bumbling and the problems of the second grade. His struggles continue in *Watch Out, Ronald Morgan!* and *Ronald Morgan Goes to Bat,* which are almost as funny as *The Almost Awful Play,* in which Ronald is the star, sort of, of the class play. He is Winky the Cat.

[637]

THE VELVETEEN RABBIT [645]

Written by Margery Williams
Illustrated by William Nicholson

Cloth: Doubleday
Paper: Camelot
Published: 1926

This slightly syrupy tale of the toy that so loved its boy that it did, ultimately, become real was a modest standard title until a surge of popularity with college students and younger adults gave it visibility in the late 1970s and early 1980s. Through carelessness, the copyright was allowed to expire, and presto, a half-dozen other editions appeared, including those illustrated by Michael Hague, David Jorgensen, and Tien Ho. This is the original and most affecting edition and comes plain or in a fancy slipcase.

[647]

WHITE BIRD   [646]

Written by Clyde Robert Bulla
Illustrated by Donald Cook

Cloth: Random House (Stepping Stone)
Published: 1966/1990

A long time ago, at the beginning of the nineteenth century, in a valley in Tennessee, a lonely and suspicious hermit, Luke, raised a foundling he called John Thomas. The boy trained a white bird, his only friend. When the bird was stolen from him, John Thomas disobeyed Luke and went to town. Although the story is short and easy to read, its poignance resonates and is affecting to much older children, too.

AMBER BROWN IS NOT A CRAYON

[647]

Written by Paula Danziger
Illustrated by Tony Ross

Cloth: Putnam
Paper: Scholastic
Published: 1994

The very personal account of the life of a very messy but quite delightful third grader whose parents have recently divorced and who breaks up with Justin Daniels, her best friend since preschool, perhaps because he's going to move from New Jersey to Alabama. In *You Can't Eat Your Chicken Pox, Amber Brown,* she's on her way to London and Paris. The series continues with *Amber Brown Goes Fourth,* and *Amber Brown is Feeling Blue.*

YOU READ TO ME, I'LL READ TO YOU   [648]

Written by John Ciardi
Illustrated by Edward Gorey

Cloth: HarperCollins
Paper: Harper Trophy
Published: 1962

A collection of thirty-five poems, mostly lighthearted, organized for a child and an adult to read out loud alternately and together. The illustrations are appropriately amusing, too.

[647]

Middle Reading Books

The books in this section are part of the rich treasure chest of childhood—adventures, fairy stories, chapter books, series—books to listen to, read, reread, and then reread again for the pleasure of knowing what is going to happen next. The appropriate age range for listening to these stories is very wide. Preschoolers can follow some of them; many teenagers comfortably read others. A number of titles were once considered appropriate for adolescent readers only. For good or ill, our children grow up too soon these days, and in a world made small by television, the electronic media, and the Internet, a parent should use judgment about what individual children know and understand. The annotations make such distinctions clear.

A GIRL NAMED DISASTER   [649]

Written by Nancy Farmer

Cloth: Orchard Books
Published: 1996   **Prizes: Newbery Honor**

It's her only chance to escape an arranged marriage to a cruel older man who already has three wives, so Nhamo, who isn't quite twelve years old, sets out alone in a canoe. She must follow the Musengezi River from Mozambique to Zimbabwe. Emotional support as she navigates through one adventure after another comes from persuasively communing with the spirits of her mother and Shona ancestors. Exciting and provocative.

A HISTORY OF US   [650]

Written by Joy Hakim

Cloth: Oxford University Press
Paper: Oxford University Press
Published: 1994

This ten-volume series, based on up-to-date academic research about American history is both inviting and accessible. It progresses chronologically, using examples of incidents, stories of real people and period illustrations, but the volumes are independent.

A LONG WAY FROM CHICAGO   [651]

Written by Richard Peck

Cloth: Dial
Published: 1998   **Prizes: Newbery Honor**

In seven humorous, chronological chapters, the narrator reminisces about the summer vacations Joey and his sister Mary Alice spent during the Depression in a small town in Illinois where the strangest things kept happening. It's a tall tale told straight.

ABEL'S ISLAND [652]

Written and illustrated by William Steig

Cloth: Farrar, Straus & Giroux
Paper: Sunburst
Published: 1976 **Prizes: Newbery Honor**

Abelard Hassam di Chirico Flint, an artist and a mouse, is swept away in a rainstorm and is stranded for a year on an island in the middle of a river. Splendid Steig for independent readers or reading aloud.

THE ABRACADABRA KID: A WRITER'S LIFE [653]

Written by Sid Fleischman

Cloth: Greenwillow
Paper: Mulberry
Published: 1996

It turns out that a childhood passion for magic can, one way or another, passing through adventures in World War II and later in Hollywood, lead a fellow to writing very good books for children. It's an engaging memoir of a favorite author.

THE ADVENTURES OF DOCTOR DOLITTLE [654]

Written by Hugh Lofting
Illustrated by Michael Hague

Cloth: Delacorte
Paper: Yearling
Published: 1920; reissued 1988 **Prizes: Newbery Medal**

The adventures of the good doctor from Puddleby-on-the-Marsh who understood the languages of animals have come back into print. The socially objectionable phrases have been removed, with the help of Lofting's son, without really diminishing the charm of the stories in the least. Young Tommy Stubbins, Polynesia the Parrot, Dab-Dab the Duck, and the Pushmipulu are as charming as you remember them. Half a dozen individual titles are available.

AFTERNOON OF THE ELVES [655]

Written by Janet Taylor Lisle

Cloth: Orchard Books
Paper: Scholastic
Published: 1989   **Prizes: Newbery Honor**

Sara-Kate, an odd child no one likes, is befriended by Hilary, the
very conventional fourth grader who lives next door. Soon it is
Hilary who is drawn into Sara-Kate's magical world—the miniature
village behind her house that the girl claims was built by elves. The
novel addresses many of the questions of loyalty, friendship, and
privacy that concern middle grade children.

ALAN AND NAOMI [656]

Written by Myron Levoy

Cloth: HarperCollins
Paper: Harper Trophy
Published: 1977

Naomi is a refugee child from Paris who moves into Alan Silver-
man's New York City apartment building during World War II. She
seems very peculiar, so he avoids her at first, but a genuine friendship ensues in the honestly told story.

ALL-OF-A-KIND FAMILY [657]

Written by Sidney Taylor
Illustrated by Helen John

Cloth: HarperCollins
Paper: Yearling
Published: 1951

There are five books in the well-loved series about a close-knit Jewish family living on New York City's Lower East Side in the early
part of this century. The five daughters are high-spirited and make
their own good times. And their little brother turns out to be a
charmer. Who can forget the library lady? The other titles include
All-Of-A-Kind Family Downtown, *All-Of-A-Kind Family Uptown*,
then *Ella of All-Of-A-Kind Family*, and *More of All-Of-A-Kind
Family*.

AN EXTRAORDINARY LIFE: THE STORY OF A MONARCH BUTTERFLY [658]

Written by Laurence Pringle
Illustrated by Bob Marstall

Cloth: Orchard Books
Published: 1997

The life cycle of that distinguished international traveler the monarch butterfly, which crosses borders and defies all manner of obstacles including dietary ones, is described with certain, appropriate awe. Handsomely organized and illustrated.

ANASTASIA KRUPNIK [659]

Written by Lois Lowry
Illustrated by Diane de Groat

Cloth: Houghton Mifflin
Paper: Yearling
Published: 1979

The heroine's name marks the beginning of an affectionate, comic series about the Krupnik family and Anastasia in particular. She is growing up bright and articulate in a contemporary Boston suburb. The other members of the family, especially her little brother, Sam, are vividly portrayed, too. The series begins in the fourth grade, and by the fifth book, Anastasia is a junior in high school. Other titles include *Anastasia at Your Service; Anastasia, Ask Your Analyst; Anastasia on Her Own;* and *Anastasia and Her Chosen Career.* Sam books include *All About Sam, Atta Boy Sam! See You Around Sam, Zooman Sam.*

...AND NOW MIGUEL [660]

Written by Joseph Krumgold
Illustrated by Jean Charlot

Cloth: HarperCollins
Paper: Harper Trophy
Published: 1953

Prizes: Newbery Medal

Miguel Chaven, a twelve-year-old boy, lives with his family of sheepherders in the Sangre de Cristo Mountains in New Mexico. He tells how he wishes to accompany the men and the sheep to their summer pasture, a journey that is both a rite of passage and a symbol of belonging to the community. This book has passed the test of time and remains engrossing.

AND THEN THERE WAS ONE: THE MYSTERIES OF EXTINCTION [661]

Written by Margery Facklam
Illustrated by Pamela Johnson

Cloth: Sierra Club
Published: 1990

Dinosaurs are among the examples of extinct species examined here along with giant tortoises, passenger pigeons, and the dodo. Good discussion of environmental risk.

ANNE FRANK: THE DIARY OF A YOUNG GIRL HIDING FROM THE NAZIS [662]

Written by Anne Frank

Cloth: Doubleday
Paper: Bantam
Published: 1947

The diary of the thirteen-year-old Jewish girl, hidden in an attic during the Nazi occupation of Holland, remains a powerful and poignant book. The universally appealing aspects—the singular problems of adolescence and Anne's family relationships as well as her optimism—are in shocking contrast to the terror of her situation. And, of course, there was no happy ending. Children often read this to themselves, but it needs to be discussed, often at length and sometimes in the middle of the night. The introduction to the hardcover edition is by Eleanor Roosevelt, who may also require some introduction for contemporary readers.

[659]

ANNE OF GREEN GABLES [663]

Written by L. M. Montgomery
Illustrated by Jody Lee

Cloth: Grosset & Dunlap
Paper: Dell
Published: 1908

Anne Shirley, the red-haired heroine of the perennially popular girls' series, moves to Canada's Prince Edward Island at the turn of the century. As the story begins, she is eleven and full of talk and troubles. She sorts out her relationship with her initially uneasy foster parents, Matthew and Merilla Cuthbert. In later installments she goes to college, returns to the island to teach, and eventually marries. The other titles include *Anne of Avonlea, Anne of the Island, Anne of Windy Poplars, Anne's House of Dreams,* and *Anne of Ingleside.*

ARE YOU THERE, GOD? IT'S ME, MARGARET [664]

Written by Judy Blume

Cloth: Bradbury
Paper: Laurel Leaf
Published: 1970

Almost twelve, both longing for and fearing adolescence, Margaret, who chats with God on a regular basis about her worries, is a heroine most children identify with, at least for a minute, as they move along the path toward growing up. Controversial when they were first published, the Blume books are part of the rites of passage for many, if not most, American children. Some of the other most popular titles are *Then Again, Maybe I Won't; Otherwise Known as Sheila the Great;* and *Tiger Eyes. Are You There, God?* is also available in Spanish.

AROUND THE WORLD IN EIGHTY DAYS [665]

Written by Jules Verne
Illustrated by Barry Moser

Cloth: Morrow Junior Books
Paper: Scholastic
Published: 1873; 1989

The story of how Phileas Fogg accepted a daring wager—to circumnavigate the globe in a ludicrously short period of time—was first published in 1873. In this elegant, well-translated new edition, he and his faithful manservant, Passepartout, race on boldly, pursued by Detective Fix. There are sixteen illustrations.

ARTHUR, FOR THE VERY FIRST TIME [666]

Written by Patricia MacLachlan
Illustrated by Lloyd Bloom

Cloth: HarperCollins
Paper: Harper Trophy
Published: 1980

It is a transitional summer for Arthur, a fussy ten-year-old who is spending time at his eccentric aunt and uncle's farm while his mother awaits a new baby at home. A charmingly illustrated and well-written story of self-discovery and assertion.

BABE THE GALLANT PIG [667]

Written by Dick King-Smith
Illustrated by Mary Raynor

Cloth: Crown
Paper: Random House
Published: 1993

Farmer Hogget rescues Babe, the piglet runt, never expecting that he would turn into a truly great herder. It's a wonderful tale of accomplishment and agriculture, and the movies aren't bad, either. The author is prolific and among his many other accessible and amusing tales are *Ace: The Very Important Pig* and *Harry's Mad*.

BALLET SHOES [668]

Written by Noel Streatfeild

Cloth: Random House
Paper: Dell Yearling
Published: 1937

This is the first in an internationally popular series of books for girls. It tells the story of the three Fossil girls, adopted by an ever-traveling professor, who has sent them to be raised in London and trained for the stage. They are plucky and determined and beguilingly British. Similarly appealing other families and their adventures are told in *Movie Shoes, Dancing Shoes, Skating Shoes, Theatre Shoes,* and other titles. There's a pretty 1990's edition with illustrations by Diane Goode.

BASEBALL IN APRIL: AND OTHER STORIES [669]

Written by Gary Soto

Cloth: Harcourt Brace
Paper: Odyssey
Published: 1990

These short stories set in Mexican-American neighborhoods in California are about youngsters caught in the dilemma of transformation. They are becoming American by popular culture and adult experiences, and yet their community is still Mexican. A bittersweet air of resignation pervades.

BE EVER HOPEFUL, HANNALEE [670]

Written by Patricia Beatty

Cloth: Morrow Junior Books
Paper: Troll
Published: 1989

Hannalee Reed is the heroine of an earlier historical novel, *Turn Homeward, Hannalee,* which follows the girl through much of the Civil War. This book, which can be read as a sequel or independently, begins as the family returns to the devastated city of Atlanta in the summer of 1865. Unusually ambitious and well researched.

THE BEARS' HOUSE   [671]

Written by Marilyn Sachs

Cloth: Dutton
Paper: Puffin
Published: 1971

Fran Ellen is a nine-year-old who has a great many real problems with her family and in school. Her greatest pleasure is in visiting the classroom dollhouse, the Bears' House, which she loves. This is a beautifully written short novel about struggle and maturation and a steady favorite among middle grade readers. The out-of-print sequel is *Fran Ellen's House*.

BEAUTY: A RETELLING OF THE STORY OF BEAUTY AND THE BEAST   [672]

Written by Robin McKinley

Cloth: HarperCollins
Paper: Harper Trophy
Published: 1978

Here is a first-person fantasy novel that retells the fairy tale with great style in conventional northern European form and setting and is particularly appealing to upper grade readers. Twenty years later, the author returned to the story and told it as a lush fairy- and flower-filled fantasy, *Rose Daughter*.

BEHIND THE ATTIC WALL   [673]

Written by Sylvia Cassedy

Cloth: Avon/Camelot
Paper: Camelot
Published: 1983

This satisfying novel is in a classic tradition. As it begins, twelve-year-old Maggie, who has been shunted from school to school, pale, unhappy, and unwanted, is sent off to Uncle Morris and the two great-aunts. They don't seem like prizes, and the house, Adelphi Hills Academy, really is creepy, with strange sounds. Ghosts. Stylishly told.

BEHIND THE MASK: THE LIFE OF QUEEN ELIZABETH I [674]

Written by Jane Resh Thomas

Cloth: Clarion
Published: 1998

Far and away the best biography for young readers of the great queen who gave her name to an age. Addressing and disputing popular myths about Gloriana, Good Queen Bess, and the Virgin Queen, the author sets the complicated facts of Elizabeth's tempestuous life in social and political context. The carefully chosen illustrations include full-color reproductions of many of the best-known portraits of the monarchs. There is ample help for readers who have only moviegoing experience of English history, including a cast of characters, a chronology, and a fine bibliography.

BEN AND ME [675]

Written and illustrated by Robert Lawson

Cloth: Little, Brown
Paper: Little, Brown
Published: 1939

This is one of a series of confidential biographies of historical figures as narrated by a pet or animal with inside information and a lighthearted view of history, in this case Benjamin Franklin as seen by a mouse. Other titles include *Mr. Revere and I* and *Captain Kidd's Cat*. Generations of middle grade schoolchildren have adored these.

THE BEST CHRISTMAS PAGEANT EVER [676]

Written by Barbara Robinson
Illustrated by Judith Gwyn Brown

Cloth: HarperCollins
Paper: Harper Trophy
Published: 1972

What is the true meaning of Christmas? When the ramshackle, chaotic, impossible Herdman children are cast in the annual Christmas pageant, some important lessons are learned all around the community. This could have been treacle, but it's told so deftly it

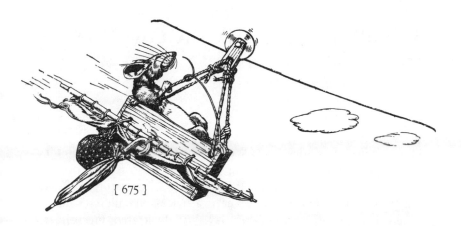

[675]

has become a classic. Good to read aloud. *The Best School Year Ever* is a pale sequel.

THE BFG   [677]

Written by Roald Dahl
Illustrated by Quentin Blake

Cloth: Farrar, Straus & Giroux
Paper: Puffin
Published: 1982

Here is the story of the Big Friendly Giant who kidnapped Sophie, an eight-year-old orphan, and took her to Giantland. It was the author's favorite and for many adults is the most appealing of his books. The wordplay of the gentle giant as he bottles dreams and protects Sophie from the nine giants who eat children is dazzling. The absurdly funny plot turns and turns again, and eventually, with the help of the queen of England herself, is resolved. As in all Dahl books, there is a proper ending. Splendid.

BIG RED   [678]

Written by Jim Kjelgaard
Illustrated by Bob Kuhn

Cloth: Holiday House
Paper: Bantam Skylark
Published: 1945

[675]

An enduring and appealing dog-and-boy story, in this case a champion Irish setter and a trapper's son. The sequels are *Irish Red* and *Outlaw Red*.

BILL PEET: AN AUTOBIOGRAPHY

[679]

Written and illustrated by Bill Peet

Cloth: Houghton Mifflin
Paper: Houghton Mifflin
Published: 1989

Prizes: Caldecott Honor

Bill Peet's first memories are of World War I. He came of age in the Midwest in the 1920s and during the Great Depression drove to California, where he became a top writer and illustrator for Walt Disney, all before he began a career as a successful children's book writer. His plainly written but lavishly illustrated memoir is enthralling. He is unsparing of himself and the difficulties he faced, and generous to others, including Disney. The drawings, which fill half or more of most pages, seem to race along.

BLACK BEAUTY [680]

Written by Anna Sewell
Illustrated by Fritz Eichenberg

Cloth: Grosset & Dunlap
Paper: Grosset & Dunlap
Published: 1877; reissued 1945

There are many abridged editions of the best-known horse story of all. This is the full text of the story of the beautiful black animal who is traded into many adventures and ultimately rescued. The

[677]

[677]

1986 edition illustrations are by Susan Jeffers. An award-winning contemporary novelist, Robin McKinley, adapted the ultimate horse story in somewhat simplified language. The lush illustrations fairly gallop across the page. This version works well for younger readers.

THE BLACK CAULDRON [681]

Written by Lloyd Alexander

Cloth: Henry Holt
Paper: Dell Yearling
Published: 1965　　　　　　　　**Prizes: Newbery Honor**

This is the best-known volume of a favorite fantasy quintet about the imaginary land of Prydain, which has some basis in Welsh legend and traditional mythology. In this volume, a council of warriors face villainy. The first book is *The Book of Three*, and others are *The Castle of Llyr, Taran Wanderer*, and *The High King*.

THE BLACK PEARL [682]

Written by Scott O'Dell

Cloth: Houghton Mifflin
Paper: Dell Yearling
Published: 1967　　　　　　　　**Prizes: Newbery Honor**

A thrilling adventure story set off the Baja California coast tells about a village of pearl divers, rivalry, and a giant manta ray guarding a huge black pearl.

THE BLACK STALLION   [683]

Written by Walter Farley

Cloth: Random House
Paper: Random House
Published: 1941

One of the all-time favorite animal series—there are nineteen tales about that mighty champion the black stallion and his various relations. Titles include *The Black Stallion and Flame, The Black Stallion Challenged!,* and *The Black Stallion's Sulky Colt.*

THE BORROWERS   [684]

Written by Mary Norton
Illustrated by Beth and Joe Krush

Cloth: Harcourt Brace
Paper: Odyssey
Published: 1953

Prizes: Carnegie Medal

The first volume of a series of grand novels about Pod, Homily, and Arrietty, a family of little people who lived under the kitchen floor in a quiet house some time not that long ago, perhaps around the end of the nineteenth century. The idea of these little people often appeals to children who otherwise have no taste for whimsy. The fine line illustrations certainly add to their charm. Other titles include *The Borrowers Afield, The Borrowers Afloat, The Borrowers Aloft,* and *The Borrowers Avenged.* A boxed paperback edition is available.

[684]

BOY: TALES OF CHILDHOOD   [685]

Written by Roald Dahl

Cloth: Farrar, Straus & Giroux
Paper: Puffin
Published: 1984

The story of the author's childhood in Norway and (mostly) in England is filled with incidents as peculiar, sharp, funny, and sometimes awful as those in his stories. The memoir is illustrated with excerpts from schoolboy letters and photographs. The second volume, *Going Solo,* is for older readers and describes Dahl's experience in Africa and as a pilot during World War I.

BRIDGE TO TERABITHIA [686]

Written by Katherine Paterson
Illustrated by Donna Diamond

Cloth: HarperCollins
Paper: Harper Trophy
Published: 1977   **Prizes: Newbery Medal**

This is an astonishingly powerful novel about an improbable friendship between Jess, a poor local boy, and Leslie, the willful, brilliantly imaginative girl who moves into a house nearby. They
establish a secret hiding place they call Terabithia and develop a rich
friendship that is severed when Leslie is accidentally killed. There
are only a few novels for children about death and they are generally unsatisfactory. This one succeeds brilliantly and speaks to the
resolution of grief among the living. But because the writing is so
fine and persuasive, the impact on readers of all ages is deep. This
is a six-Kleenex late-night-talk-time story, and worth the effort.

BROTHERS OF THE HEART [687]

Written by Joan Blos

Cloth: Scribner
Paper: Aladdin
Published: 1985

A historical novel set in the far north in the mid-nineteenth century,
during a bitter-cold winter. Shem, a boy from an Ohio family who
moved to Michigan and later on was hired as clerk to a fur-trading
expedition, is found in an isolated cabin by an elderly Ottowan
Indian woman. Their relationship becomes the core of the story.

BUD, NOT BUDDY [688]

Written by Christopher Paul Curtis

Cloth: Delacorte
Published: 1999   **Prizes: Newbery Medal**

The telling is good-natured, often funny, but it is a poignant story
ten-year-old Bud Caldwell tells about leaving his third foster home
in Flint, Michigan, in 1936, four years after his mother died. Bud is
determined to find Herman E. Calloway, a bass fiddle player in
Grand Rapids who just might be his father. Calloway and Lefty

Lewis, a pitcher in the Negro baseball leagues, are characters based on the author's grandfathers, and fine men they both are.

CADDIE WOODLAWN   [689]

Written by Carol Ryrie Brink
Illustrated by Trina Schart Hyman

Cloth: Macmillan
Paper: Aladdin
Published: 1935   **Prizes: Newbery Medal**

This popular novel about pioneer life in Wisconsin in the late 1860s, reillustrated in 1973, is still convincing and compelling reading.

CALL IT COURAGE   [690]

Written and illustrated by Armstrong Sperry

Cloth: Macmillan
Paper: Aladdin
Published: 1939   **Prizes: Newbery Medal**

Set in the South Pacific, this is a timelessly interesting adventure story about Mafatu, the son of the Great Chief of Hikueru, who conquers his fear of the sea.

CANYON WINTER   [691]

Written by Walt Morey

Cloth: Dutton
Paper: Puffin
Published: 1972

Pete, a fifteen-year-old boy, is stranded in a canyon after a plane crash. He finds his way to the cabin of Omar, a solitary old man, and spends the whole winter with him. There is an underlying theme of conservation and a concern for ecology and nature. Among Morey's other boys-and-nature books are *The Lemon Meringue Dog, Sandy and the Rock Star,* and *The Year of the Black Pony.*

THE CAT ATE MY GYMSUIT [692]

Written by Paula Danziger

Cloth: Delacorte
Paper: Dell Yearling
Published: 1974

Marcy's view is that life is rotten: her social life, her weight, her parents—the usual. Then she encounters a remarkable teacher and things begin to change fast. Inside the humor is a lesson about social protest. The sequel is *There's a Bat in Bunk Five.*

THE CAT WHO WENT TO HEAVEN

[693]

Written by Elizabeth Coatsworth

Cloth: Macmillan
Paper: Aladdin
Published: 1930   **Prizes: Newbery Medal**

This short novel tells of a starving young artist in long-ago Japan, his faithful servant, a white cat, and a rare commission. And there is a Buddhist miracle. Religious values are subtly conveyed within the story.

CATHEDRAL: THE STORY OF ITS CONSTRUCTION [694]

Written and illustrated by David Macaulay

Cloth: Houghton Mifflin
Paper: Houghton Mifflin   **Prizes: Caldecott Honor**
Published: 1977   **New York Times Best Illustrated Book**

A remarkable re-creation of the building of a French Gothic cathedral. The illustrations are pen and ink; the text is utterly clear. If you are mesmerized by this explanation, then look for *Castle* and *Pyramid* or the brilliant fantasy *Unbuilding.* There is another twenty-fifth anniversary edition retitled *Building the Book Cathedral,* explaining how it was written. It corrects and readjusts the original and is as clear about bookmaking as it is about constructing a cathedral.

CATHERINE, CALLED BIRDY   [695]

Written by Karen Cushman

Cloth: Clarion
Paper: Harper Trophy
Published: 1994   **Prizes: Newbery Honor**

It's the end of the thirteenth century in England, 1290 to be precise, and in that medieval environment girls are married off early. Catherine, who is fourteen, is keeping a diary of the way she avoids the various suitors her father chooses. The humor is broad and the attitude modern, which makes it very entertaining, but it needs to be read with context about women's and girls' lives in the Middle Ages. A richer, more detailed novel, *The Ramsay Scallop,* is set at the same time and is about a pilgrimage Eleanor Ramsay and her husband-to-be, Thomas, make to the shrine of Santiago de Compostela.

CHARLIE AND THE CHOCOLATE FACTORY   [696]

Written by Roald Dahl
Illustrated by Joseph Schindelman

Cloth: Knopf
Paper: Puffin
Published: 1963

The story of how poor but honest Charlie Bucket came to visit Willie Wonka's fantastic and marvelous chocolate factory in the company of a memorable band of truly obnoxious children (all of whom get their just desserts, ha, ha) is one of the deserved, and certainly the most delicious, modern classics. There is an adaptation in play form available in paperback from Puffin, and a sequel, *Charlie and the Great Glass Elevator.*

[697]

CHARLOTTE'S WEB [697]

Written by E. B. White
Illustrated by Garth Williams

Cloth: HarperCollins
Paper: Harper Trophy
Published: 1952   **Prizes: Newbery Honor**

Wilbur, an innocent and amiable pig, is saved from slaughter by a true friend and a fine writer, Charlotte, the gray spider in the barnyard door. The language, the subplots, the details (especially the science and nature observations), and the moral seem more insightful and rewarding with each reading. The feature-length cartoon is not a travesty and does not usually dissuade children from listening to, or reading, the book. As Charlotte herself wrote, "Terrific."

A CHILD'S CHRISTMAS IN WALES [698]

Written by Dylan Thomas
Illustrated by Trina Schart Hyman

Cloth: Holiday House
Paper: New Directions
Published: 1985

The Welsh poet's evocative memoir of Christmas early in the century is full of snow, cats, aunties, and boyish adventure. This is a fine edition with affectionate watercolor illustrations (the cats in the snow are especially appealing), nicely sized to hold in small hands. There is another beautifully drawn version, illustrated by the British artist Edward Ardizzone.

THE CHILDREN OF GREEN KNOWE [699]

Written by Lucy Boston
Illustrated by Peter Boston

Cloth: Harcourt Brace
Paper: Odyssey
Published: 1954

A lonely boy called Tolly is sent to stay with his ancient great-grandmother, who lives in an eccentric house in England called

Green Knowe. It has belonged to the family for hundreds of years. Tolly finds the toys and possessions of other children who lived and played there, and gradually he finds that the seventeenth-century siblings, Toby, Linnet, and Alexander, still do. Totally mysterious and magical, the writing in these elegant novels is superb. The series includes *Treasure of Green Knowe, The River at Green Knowe,* and *A Stranger at Green Knowe,* which won the Carnegie Medal. The best way to begin is to read aloud in dark December so you reach the memorable Christmas scenes at the appropriate time.

THE CHILDREN'S HOMER: THE ADVENTURES OF ODYSSEUS AND THE TALE OF TROY [700]

Written by Padraic Colum
Illustrated by Willy Pogany

Paper: Aladdin
Published: 1918

This is a splendid use of paperback publishing—making available to new readers the beautifully illustrated 1918 edition of Homer told by the distinguished Irish poet. The prose is brilliant, and the fine line drawings are fairly breathtaking. The companion volume, *The Golden Fleece: And the Heroes Who Lived Before Achilles,* which tells many Greek myths within the framework of the story of Jason and the Argonauts, is also again in print. Barry Moser has illustrated a hardcover edition of the same text called *The Trojan War and the Adventures of Odysseus.*

CHOCOLATE FEVER [701]

Written by Robert Kimmel Smith
Illustrated by Gioia Fiammenghi

Paper: Dell Yearling
Published: 1978

Henry Green ate so much of the yummy stuff he caught chocolate fever. How was he cured? Read and find out. Funny enough to read aloud with middle grade listeners.

THE CHOCOLATE TOUCH   [702]

Written by Patrick Skene Catling
Illustrated by Margot Apple

Cloth: Morrow Junior Books
Paper: Dell
Published: 1979

Chocoholics, beware! Imagine the Midas story, only the object of lust has turned from gold to rich, dark, chocolatey brown. Here it is, and now imagine what happens to John when everything he touches turns to . . . chocolate. Funny, and sweetly moral.

A CHRISTMAS CAROL   [703]

Written by Charles Dickens
Illustrated by Trina Schart Hyman

Cloth: Holiday House
Paper: Holiday House
Published: 1983

Bless us every one. Here's a setting of the familiar text set off with decorated initials and six color plates by a well-known contemporary artist. There are many other good, legible (important if you are reading out loud) editions available, including those illustrated by Michael Foreman, Roberto Innocenti, and Lisbeth Zwerger.

CHRISTMAS IN THE BIG HOUSE, CHRISTMAS IN THE QUARTERS

[704]

Written by Patricia C. and Fredrick McKissack
Illustrated by John Thompson

Cloth: Scholastic
Paper: Scholastic
Published: 1994

Using a wide range of historical documents, the authors have imagined the holiday season of 1859 on a fictional Tidewater Virginia plantation, complete with songs, recipes, and political topics of conversation appropriate to the Big House and the Quarters.

THE CHRONICLES OF NARNIA [705]

Written by C. S. Lewis
Illustrated by Pauline Baynes

Cloth: Macmillan
Paper: HarperCollins
Published: 1950

This seven-volume allegorical Christian fantasy has steadily gained worldwide popularity since it was first published in the 1950s. In the beginning, Aslan, the white lion, freed Narnia from the spell of the White Witch, but that was just the beginning. These tales are very good for reading aloud. The titles are *The Lion, the Witch, and the Wardrobe; Prince Caspian; The Voyage of the "Dawn Treader"; The Silver Chair; The Horse and His Boy; The Magician's Nephew;* and *The Last Battle.*

CITY: A STORY OF ROMAN PLAN-NING AND CONSTRUCTION [706]

Written and illustrated by David Macaulay

Cloth: Houghton Mifflin
Paper: Houghton Mifflin
Published: 1974

The planning and construction of an imaginary Roman city is set forth in clear pen-and-ink illustrations and a lucid text. The idea of rational city planning is explicit.

THE CLAY MARBLE [707]

Written by Minfong Ho

Cloth: Farrar, Straus & Giroux
Paper: Sunburst
Published: 1991

Most of the story of twelve-year-old Dara, her family and her new friend, Jantu, is set in a Cambodian refugee camp located inside the Thai borders in the early 1980s. The author sees the Cambodians as "not the victims of war but its victors . . . who had, against all odds, survived."

COLOUR FAIRY BOOKS [708]

Written by Andrew Lang

Paper: Dover
Published: 1889; reissued 1978

These are facsimiles of the famed colour fairy books—blue, green, pink, red, and yellow—in their original, 1889/90/92 editions. They are a trove of lore and provide nearly endless hours of delight for older readers who like fairy tales.

COMMODORE PERRY IN THE LAND OF THE SHOGUN [709]

Written by Rhoda Blumberg

Cloth: Lothrop, Lee & Shepard
Published: 1985   **Prizes: Newbery Honor**

The story of the American expedition to Japan led by Commodore Matthew Perry in 1853. Not only is the text well written, but the large-format book is unusually well designed, with reproductions of Japanese illustrations of the period.

COUSINS [710]

Written by Virginia Hamilton

Cloth: Philomel
Paper: Scholastic
Published: 1990

Cammy didn't get along with her practically perfect cousin Patty Ann, but she holds herself responsible for the freak accident that takes place in this short, accessible novel. Cammy and her gram— who may be old and frail, but is sharp and wise—are vivid characters. *Second Cousins* takes place a year later and is about Cammy and her cousin Elodie.

THE CRICKET IN TIMES SQUARE

[711]

Written by George Selden
Illustrated by Garth Williams

Cloth: Farrar, Straus & Giroux
Paper: Dell Yearling
Published: 1960

The first of a fine series of heartwarming adventures involving Harry the cat, Tucker the mouse, Chester the musical cricket, and their friends in the Times Square newsstand. Other titles include *Tucker's Countryside, Chester Cricket's New Home, Harry Cat's Pet Puppy,* and the prequel *Harry Kitten and Tucker Mouse.*

THE CUCKOO'S CHILD   [712]

Written by Suzanne Freeman

Cloth: Greenwillow
Paper: Disney Press
Published: 1996

Mia wishes she could be a normal American, but she and her sisters are living in Beirut, Lebanon. Then after their parents' accidental deaths they are sent to live with an aunt in Tennessee and are forced to confront complex issues. There's dark humor mixed into the serious story.

DADDY-LONG-LEGS   [713]

Written by Jean Webster

Paper: Puffin
Published: 1912

Today's young readers may be infinitely more sophisticated, but this remains a timeless, romantic favorite. Miraculously, a mysterious benefactor sends seventeen-year-old Jerusha, an orphan, to college. Her only obligation is to write him progress reports.

DANNY THE CHAMPION OF THE WORLD   [714]

Written by Roald Dahl
Illustrated by Jill Bennett

Cloth: Knopf
Paper: Puffin
Published: 1975

In the Dahl canon, the story of Danny and his dad, living happily in a gypsy caravan parked behind a filling station in rural England and masterfully poaching pheasants, is possibly the sunniest and most purely humorous. Dad's technique for trapping pheasants is wonderfully ingenious and must be encountered, not described. Great fun to read out loud.

THE DARK IS RISING   [715]

Written by Susan Cooper
Illustrated by Alan Cober

Cloth: Margaret K. McElderry
Paper: Aladdin
Published: 1973   **Prizes: Newbery Honor**

The second of five in a thrilling cycle of fantasy novels—including *Over Sea, Under Stone; Greenwitch; The Grey King;* and *Silver on the Tree*—that deal with Will Stanton, his siblings, the ancient sleepers, a crystal sword, and good and, of course, evil.

THE DARK-THIRTY: SOUTHERN TALES OF THE SUPERNATURAL   [716]

Written by Patricia C. McKissack
Illustrated by Brian Pinkney

Cloth: Knopf
Paper: Knopf
Published: 1992   **Prizes: Newbery Honor**

The title refers to that mysterious last half hour after the sun has set but before it is dark, when children must wind up their play and get

safely home—or else. These original, short, and ghostly stories, which come with brief historical introductions placing them in the American South, are grand for reading aloud.

DEAR MR. HENSHAW   [717]

Written by Beverly Cleary
Illustrated by Paul O. Zelinsky

Cloth: Morrow Junior Books
Paper: Avon
Published: 1983   **Prizes: Newbery Medal**

A fine novel about that painful issue—divorce. Leigh Botts, who is not only the new kid in school but also adjusting to his parents' divorce, follows a class assignment and writes confidingly to his favorite author.

THE DEVIL IN VIENNA   [718]

Written by Doris Orgel

Cloth: Dial
Paper: Puffin
Published: 1978

An affecting autobiographical novel told in diary form of a Jewish girl in Vienna and her friend, the daughter of a Nazi, during the Anschluss.

A DOG ON BARKHAM STREET   [719]

Written by Mary Stolz
Illustrated by Leonard Shortall

Cloth: HarperCollins
Paper: Harper Trophy
Published: 1960

Edward wants a dog and he wants to be free of Martin Hastings, the bully who lives next door. *The Bully of Barkham Street* reveals Martin's problems clearly. There is also *The Explorer of Barkham Street*. These are good books about preadolescent boys and favorite first books for independent reading.

THE DOG WHO WOULDN'T BE   [720]

Written by Farley Mowat
Illustrated by Paul Galdone

Cloth: Little, Brown
Paper: Bantam
Published: 1957

The much-loved autobiographical account of growing up on the
Canadian Plains with Mutt, a perfect, if unpedigreed, dog.

THE DOLL'S HOUSE   [721]

Written by Rumer Godden

Paper: Puffin
Published: 1948

The story of Charlotte and Emily's great-grandmother's dollhouse,
restored after World War II for the dolls who think of themselves as
the Plantagenet family, is skillfully written. The story is about Tot-
tie, the brave farthing doll, and the villainess is a kidskin doll,
Marchpane, too beautiful to be played with, only to be admired. A
grand girls' book.

DOMINIC   [722]

Written and illustrated by William Steig

Cloth: Farrar, Straus & Giroux
Paper: Sunburst
Published: 1972

Dominic is a hero and a multitalented gent, as well as being a dog. He sets out to see the world and tests his many talents to wide acclaim.

DRAGONWINGS   [723]

Written by Laurence Yep

Cloth: HarperCollins
Paper: Harper Trophy
Published: 1975   **Prizes: Newbery Honor**

The setting is San Francisco in the first years of the century. A Chinese immigrant father and son build a flying machine shortly after the Wright brothers build theirs. The immigrant perspective on the turbulent period and place is particularly interesting. The author's other novels on similar themes include *Dragon's Gate, The Lost Garden,* and *Dragon of the Lost Sea.*

THE EAR, THE EYE, AND THE ARM   [724]

Written by Nancy Farmer

Cloth: Orchard Books
Paper: Puffin
Published: 1994   **Prizes: Newbery Honor**

A futuristic adventure story set in Zimbabwe in 2194 begins in the technologically advanced and isolated home of the military dictator. The thirteen-year-old hero and his younger siblings escape and find themselves in traditional villages. Engrossing.

THE EGYPT GAME [725]

Written by Zilpha Keatley Snyder
Illustrated by Alton Raible

Cloth: Macmillan
Paper: Dell Yearling
Published: 1967   **Prizes: Newbery Honor**

April and Melanie are eleven years old and best friends in a small town in California. They are deeply interested in ancient Egypt, and the game they invent leads them into real-life criminal investigation. Inventive plotting. Great fun for middle grade readers.

ELEANOR ROOSEVELT: A LIFE OF DISCOVERY [726]

Written by Russell Freedman

Cloth: Clarion
Paper: Clarion
Published: 1993

This account of the life of the activist wife of Franklin Delano Roosevelt, who entered public life reluctantly after her husband had polio, was controversial for her political involvements throughout his three and a half terms in office, and continued her crusading work as a widow, has been carefully told here. There is no speculation about her private life, but the difficulties she encountered in being taken seriously by the public are explained clearly. Barbara Cooney's *Eleanor* is a storybook account of her difficult early years.

ELLA ENCHANTED [727]

Written by Gail Carson Levine

Cloth: HarperCollins
Paper: Harper Trophy
Published: 1997   **Prizes: Newbery Honor**

Ella's fairy godmother gave her the gift of obedience, making her powerless against a direct command. The setting is a modestly magical long-ago kingdom, where Ella, a spunky heroine, is determined to break the spell and thus free herself from the possibility of doing something really stupid just because she has been told to. A high-spirited, comic first novel. *The Princess Tales* honors the spirit, if not the full development, of *Ella*.

ENCYCLOPEDIA BROWN [728]

Written by Donald J. Sobol
Illustrated by Leonard Shortall

Cloth: Morrow Junior Books
Paper: Bantam
Published: 1963

Idaville's chief of police, Mr. Brown, nicknamed his son Leroy "Encyclopedia" because of all the facts he knows and his methodical way of observing and using his mind. Thus was a hero born. There are several dozen books available from several publishers in hardcover and paperback. Most of the books consist of ten cases the boy detective solves. Some of the titles are *Encyclopedia Brown: Boy Detective, Encyclopedia Brown and the Case of the Midnight Visitor,* and *Encyclopedia Brown Finds the Clues.*

EVERY LIVING THING [729]

Written by Cynthia Rylant
Illustrated by S. D. Schindler

Cloth: Bradbury
Paper: Aladdin
Published: 1985

The well-written short stories in this collection are about people whose lives are affected by animals ranging from a stray puppy and other household pets to a nesting robin.

THE EXAMINATION [730]

Written by Malcolm Bosse

Cloth: Farrar, Straus & Giroux
Paper: Sunburst
Published: 1994

The setting is sixteenth-century China, during the Ming Dynasty, where the examination system offered the only possible avenue of social mobility for a poor but clever boy. Chen is a gifted Confucian scholar, but naive in the ways of the world. His brother Hong is clever in a different way and hot-tempered. Beginning with a cricket fight in the countryside, the novel follows the brothers' engrossing adventures.

THE FAMILY TREASURY OF
JEWISH HOLIDAYS [731]

Written by Malka Drucker
Illustrated by Nancy Patz

Cloth: Little, Brown
Published: 1994

An inviting compendium of information about the Jewish holidays
and how they are celebrated, along with poems, songs, and recipes.
There are traditional stories and some modern ones as well. Very
helpful for secular or non-Jewish families seeking basic information.

FIRST CHILDREN: GROWING UP
IN THE WHITE HOUSE [732]

Written by Katherine Leiner
Illustrated by Katie Keller

Cloth: Tambourine
Published: 1996

Here are seventeen profiles of lives of children whose fathers happened to be presidents of the United States—Roosevelt, Lincoln,
Nixon, Carter, Clinton, and others. There are photographs and
period engravings to supplement the text and formal scratchboard
portraits that begin each chapter.

FIVE CHILDREN AND IT [733]

Written by E. Nesbit

Cloth: Morrow Junior Books
Paper: Puffin
Published: 1902/1999

Long ago, in the mid-nineteenth century, five English children on a
summer holiday were just digging for fun in the sand of a gravel pit
when they encountered it, a mysterious creature with the power to
grant wishes. The two other books about Cyril, Anthea, Robert,
Jane, and the baby are *The Phoenix and the Carpet* and *The Story
of the Amulet*. It is often hard to persuade children to begin reading "classic" titles, like this older fantasy and adventure novel. But
if you begin them as bedtime read-aloud books, they often prove
irresistible. The 1999 edition illustrated by Paul O. Zelinsky is
charming.

THE FLEDGLING   [734]

Written by Jane Langton

Cloth: HarperCollins
Paper: Harper Trophy
Published: 1980   **Prizes: Newbery Honor**

A fine fantasy, set at Walden Pond, about a girl named Georgie who longs to fly. She meets a mysterious Canada goose, and her dream comes true. Her cousins, Eleanor and Eddie, are prominent in the fantasies *The Astonishing Stereoscope* and *The Diamond in the Window.*

THE FLUNKING OF JOSHUA T. BATES   [735]

Written by Susan Richards Shreve
Illustrated by Diane de Groat

Cloth: Knopf
Paper: Scholastic
Published: 1984

Life in the middle grades can be really hard, and sometimes children, especially boys, are held back in school even if they are smart. To his dismay, Joshua T. Bates was supposed to repeat the entire third grade, but he was lucky enough to have a very sympathetic teacher. In *Joshua T. Bates in Trouble Again,* he rejoins his class in the middle of fourth grade and it's not smooth sailing, while *Joshua T. Bates Takes Charge* deals with some challenges in fifth grade.

THE FOLK KEEPER   [736]

Written by Fanny Billingsley

Cloth: Atheneum
Published: 1999

Corinna disguises herself as a Folk Keeper, someone who acts as a buffer between the human world above ground and the supernatural creatures below, as a way of escaping from abusive caretakers. She does not know that she herself is a Selkie (a seal maiden), or of the complex adventures that lie ahead of her.

FRANKLIN DELANO ROOSEVELT

[737]

Written by Russell Freedman

Cloth: Clarion
Paper: Clarion
Published: 1990

The thirty-second president of the United States, the first president fully recorded on film and sound, was probably the most complex and interesting American political leader of the twentieth century. He is a historical figure to today's young readers, who may hear only grandparents or great-grandparents speak of him. This handsomely illustrated biography has a soundly researched, gracefully written introduction.

FREAKY FRIDAY   [738]

Written by Mary Rogers

Cloth: HarperCollins
Paper: HarperCollins
Published: 1972

Imagine that you are Annabel Andrews, a thirteen-year-old girl, and you wake up one Friday—in your mother's body. It's a funny premise, told with great style and conviction. In *A Billion for Boris,* the upstairs neighbor has a get-rich-quick scheme for exploiting his television set, which shows everything one day in advance. In *Summer Switch,* Annabel's twelve-year-old brother, Ben, trades bodies with his father. These books remain fresh, appealing, and popular.

FREDDY THE DETECTIVE   [739]

Written by Walter R. Brooks
Illustrated by Kurt Wiese

Cloth: Overlook
Paper: Overlook
Published: 1942/1999

The delightful porcine detective Freddy, who first charmed readers more than half a century ago, is back in facsimile editions, including

Freddy Goes Camping and *Freddy Goes to Florida*. On the Beans' farm, where many animals speak English, the political maxims are cooperate and organize. There's Felix the cat and Mrs. Wiggins the cow as well. Some adults remember with joy the interpretation of R.S.V.P.—Refreshments Served Very Promptly. Although these are long chapter books and look old-fashioned, once started they are popular with younger independent readers. They are very funny and read aloud very well.

FROM THE MIXED-UP FILES OF MRS. BASIL E. FRANKWEILER [740]

Written and illustrated by E. L. Konigsburg

Cloth: Atheneum
Paper: Yearling
Published: 1967   **Prizes: Newbery Medal**

Living inside the Metropolitan Museum of Art in New York City turns out to have some unexpected problems for Claudia and Jamie, who try it. It's part of Claudia's scheme to escape from the suburbs. The children are smart, but Mrs. Frankweiler, the rich old lady whose files reveal all, is the really clever one. The museum interiors have changed quite a lot since the book was published, but the story remains unalterably fresh and entertaining.

A GATHERING OF DAYS: A NEW ENGLAND GIRL'S JOURNAL, 1830–32 [741]

Written by Joan Blos

Cloth: Atheneum
Paper: Aladdin
Published: 1979   **Prizes: Newbery Medal**

A haunting work of historical fiction, this novel takes the form of a New Hampshire farm girl's diary written in the 1830s, full of the stuff of everyday life. It is both evocative and poignant.

THE GATHERING ROOM   [742]

Written by Colby Rodowsky

Cloth: Farrar, Straus & Giroux
Paper: Sunburst
Published: 1981

This remarkable novel is set in a graveyard. Mudge's parents cannot cope with the world and become caretakers there, and Mudge has grown up happily in this unusual environment. An aunt wants to bring the family back into the more conventional world.

THE GENIE OF SUTTON PLACE   [743]

Written by George Selden

Cloth: Farrar, Straus & Giroux
Paper: Sunburst
Published: 1973

In his father's archaeological notebooks, Tim finds an ancient spell for calling up a genie, which he thinks he needs because his aunt is insisting that he give up his dog, Sam. The genie turns out to be trapped in a museum nearby. Delightful fantasy for those who would like a little more magic in their lives.

GENTLE BEN   [744]

Written by Walt Morey
Illustrated by John Schoenherr

Cloth: Dutton
Paper: Puffin
Published: 1965

A boy and a bear in Alaska long ago—that is, before statehood: friendship and adventure popular for decades, especially with middle grade boy readers.

THE GETTYSBURG ADDRESS [745]

Written by Abraham Lincoln
Illustrated by Michael McCurdy

Cloth: Houghton Mifflin
Published: 1995

Lincoln's battlefield speech is obviously not a children's text, but this stark and stunning edition, illustrated with black-and-white woodcuts of battlefield and wartime scenes, is a fine book to read aloud, study, and include in any family discussions of American history or the Civil War. *Lincoln: In His Own Words* is a larger collection of documents and speechs, handsomely illustrated.

A GIRL CALLED AL [746]

Written by Constance C. Greene
Illustrated by Byron Barton

Cloth: Viking Press
Paper: Puffin
Published: 1969

The first of a series of books about Al(exandra)—bright, fat, nonconformist, and vulnerable. The other titles include *I Know You, Al; Your Old Pal, Al; Al(exandra) the Great;* and *Just Plain Al.* Good fiction about real-life growing up.

THE GIVER [747]

Written by Lois Lowry

Cloth: Houghton Mifflin
Paper: Houghton Mifflin
Published: 1993   **Prizes: Newbery Medal**

For his life's work assignment, Jonas is chosen at the age of twelve to become the conscience of the cult community in which he has been raised. Controversy, pain, and choice have been eliminated, but he doesn't know that. The implications of conscience and the realization of the dimensions of the cult and the consequences of taking action are set out like a silken thread, drawing the reader into the complexity of the story with great skill. A provocative novel, one that parents should read along with their children.

THE GIVING TREE [748]

Written and illustrated by Shel Silverstein

Cloth: HarperCollins
Published: 1964

A much-loved story about a boy and a tree, one growing, the other giving generously. It is perhaps corny but not mawkish, and generations of faithful fans quote lines back and forth to each other.

GO HANG A SALAMI! I'M A LASAGNA HOG!: AND OTHER PALINDROMES [749]

Written and illustrated by Jon Agee

Cloth: Farrar, Straus & Giroux
Published: 1992

If the original price of the book ($12.21) strikes you as funny, the visible entries—"tahiti hat," "Pooh's hoop," an orchestral clarinetist saying "Not a banana baton!" to the conductor—will strike you as hilarious. And it only gets better (or worse, depending on your vision) in the two companion volumes, *Sit on a Potato Pan, Otis!* and *"So Many Dynamos."*

THE GOATS [750]

Written by Brock Cole

Cloth: Farrar, Straus & Giroux
Paper: Sunburst
Published: 1988

Two preadolescent misfits at summer camp are stripped of their clothes and left for the night on an island in the middle of a lake. Instead of going to pieces from fear and cold, they manage to escape and spend a few days exploring their newfound strength and courage. The novel is wonderfully controlled and convincing and has quickly become a popular favorite but it is not just for vacation reading.

THE GOLD CADILLAC [751]

Written by Mildred Taylor
Illustrated by Michael Hays

Cloth: Dial
Paper: Puffin
Published: 1987

A short, easy-to-read, but very powerful story about a black family living in Ohio in 1950. 'lois's daddy buys a gold Cadillac and tries to take the family home to Mississippi. The proud, loving family and the shock of their harsh encounter with institutionalized racism are skillfully described in a book that stands as fiction and history and is suitable for early grade children.

THE GOLDEN COMPASS: HIS DARK MATERIALS, BOOK ONE [752]

Written by Philip Pullman

Cloth: Knopf
Paper: Del Rey
Published: 1996

The most ambitious high-fantasy series in recent years, this first volume of a trilogy begins as Lyra climbs on a great bear's back and sets off into the Arctic to save the world. In that world humans are paired with loving animal "daemons," and they cannot separate without fading and dying. Children's daemons are shape shifters. The second volume, *The Subtle Knife,* and the third, *The Amber Spyglass,* can be read satisfactorily separately.

THE GOLDEN KEY [753]

Written by George MacDonald
Illustrated by Maurice Sendak

Cloth: Farrar, Straus & Giroux
Paper: Sunburst
Published: 1967

This is a fine illustrated edition of one of the classic Victorian fairy tales, here a boy and girl who must find the keyhole that fits the rainbow's key. Sendak also illustrated MacDonald's *The Light Princess.* These are titles contemporary children don't pick up, but often listen to with interest and then might read for themselves.

THE GOLEM [754]

Written by Barbara Rogasky
Illustrated by Trina Schart Hyman

Cloth: Holiday House
Published: 1996

One of the best-known tales of Jewish mysticism, a staple of folk-lore, and a predecessor of Frankenstein's monster is the golem. A creature made of clay, he was brought to life by Rabbi Judah Loew in sixteenth-century Prague to protect the Jews from their enemies. This is an episodic account of the story, richly written. David Wisniewski's dramatic cut-paper storybook version, *Golem,* won the Caldecott Medal.

GONNA SING MY HEAD OFF! AMERICAN FOLK SONGS FOR CHILDREN [755]

Written by Kathleen Krull
Illustrated by Allen Garns

Cloth: Knopf
Paper: Knopf
Published: 1992

Here are sixty-eight songs that older parents and grandparents surely remember, even if they can't quite get the words straight. Most of these aren't exactly folk tunes, they were written by individuals, but they are so much a part of American melodic memory they might as well be—Woody Guthrie tunes, "City of New Orleans," "Take Me Out to the Ball Game," "Joe Hill," and more. Accompanied by simple keyboard arrangements.

THE GREAT FIRE [756]

Written by Jim Murphy

Cloth: Scholastic
Published: 1995   **Prizes: Newbery Honor**

The Chicago fire of 1871 was one of the turning points of American urban history, and this account, filled with eyewitness reports, historic photos, newspaper clippings, and memoirs, is engrossing.

THE GREAT GILLY HOPKINS [757]

Written by Katherine Paterson

Cloth: HarperCollins
Paper: Harper Trophy
Published: 1978

**Prizes: Newbery Honor
National Book Award**

Gilly Hopkins is a tough, angry girl who has been shunted from foster home to foster home and is determined not to fit in at this new house of misfits and eccentrics: fat Trotter, little William Ernest, and old Mr. Randolph, who is blind. But she does. It's a fine novel that deals sensitively with issues of racism and class as well as the more obvious problems the plot presents, but it is likely to draw young readers because of the story itself and Gilly's strong, absolutely believable voice—especially her "creative cursing."

GROWING UP AMISH [758]

Written by Richard Ammon

Cloth: Atheneum
Paper: University Editions
Published: 1989

This account of the daily life of a girl named Anna and her Amish family on a farm in Pennsylvania addresses both the myths and the realities of the Anabaptist sect, most popularly known for their traditional dress and conscientious objection to military service. The text is unusually thoughtful, and the photographs are well chosen.

HARRIET THE SPY [759]

Written and illustrated by Louise Fitzhugh

Cloth: HarperCollins
Paper: Harper Trophy
Published: 1964

This justly acclaimed modern classic is about Harriet, a clever little girl who wants to be a writer, so she watches and takes notes about everything she sees and hears. Which is fine until her notebooks fall into the wrong hands.

HARRY POTTER AND
THE SORCERER'S STONE   [760]

Written by J. K. Rowling
Illustrated by Mary Grandpré

Cloth: Scholastic
Published: 1998

They're funny, they're smart, they're scary, there's no telling what will happen next term. The boarding-school adventures of the young orphan wizard with the lightning scar on his forehead were the most popular novels for children and adults at the end of the twentieth century. Wildly successful all around the world. The next titles in the planned series of seven are *Harry Potter and the Chamber of Secrets, Harry Potter and the Prisoner of Azkaban,* and *Harry Potter and the Goblet of Fire.* Read 'em all. In order.

HARRY'S MAD   [761]

Written by Dick King-Smith
Illustrated by Jill Bennett

Cloth: Crown
Paper: Knopf
Published: 1987

[760]

An American relative he never knew has left young Harry his African gray parrot named Madison, or Mad. The bird proves a tremendous asset to the British family and speaks both British and American, indeed, full sentences of both. Very funny.

HATCHET   [762]

Written by Gary Paulsen

Cloth: Bradbury Press
Paper: Aladdin
Published: 1987   **Prizes: Newbery Honor**

Tersely written, filled with precise detail of activity and anxiety, the story of what happens when the light plane taking thirteen-year-old Brian to visit his father in Canada crashes into a lake in the wilderness, stranding the boy for fifty-four days, is a classic adventure. There are three other short novels following Brian after he returns

to civilization and adolescence and he's never the same: *The River, Brian's Winter,* and *Brian's Return.* The other books are interesting. *Hatchet* is thrilling.

HENRY HUGGINS   [763]

Written by Beverly Cleary
Illustrated by Louis Darling

Cloth: Morrow Junior Books
Paper: Camelot
Published: 1950

Because Henry Huggins lives on Klickitat Street, he is sometimes lost in the shadow of his neighbors the Quimbys—Beezus and Ramona. But Henry is a champion himself, the kind of boy you would like to have for a neighbor. On his own he first appears in third grade, adopting, or being adopted by, his splendid mutt, Ribsy. Their adventures continue in *Henry and Ribsy* and *Henry and the Clubhouse.*

HERSTORIES: AFRICAN AMERICAN FOLKTALES, FAIRY TALES, AND TRUE TALES   [764]

Written by Virginia Hamilton
Illustrated by Leo and Diane Dillon

Cloth: Scholastic
Published: 1995

A powerful, carefully annotated collection of traditional tales about strong black women, some of them based in fact and real lives, some in the supernatural, some involving animals. The individual stories are meant to be read aloud, but there is helpful background information for the curious.

THE HERO AND THE CROWN [765]

Written by Robin McKinley

Cloth: Greenwillow
Paper: Ace
Published: 1984   **Prizes: Newbery Medal**

The prizewinning sequel to *The Blue Sword,* a high fantasy involving the adventures of the Damarian king's daughter, Aerin. A favorite with fantasy fans.

HITTY: HER FIRST HUNDRED YEARS [766]

Written by Rachel Field
Illustrated by Dorothy P. Lathrop

Cloth: Macmillan
Paper: Yearling
Published: 1929   **Prizes: Newbery Honor**

Hitty is a doll who was carved out of a piece of white ash one winter in Maine nearly two hundred years ago. She belonged to Phoebe Prible, who took her everywhere till she tumbled away into her own adventures. It's an old-fashioned historical novel with charm. A large-format 1999 edition has been re-edited by Rosemary Wells and lavishly illustrated by Susan Jeffers. It tidies up the story and gives it more politically correct incidents.

HOB AND THE GOBLINS [767]

Written by William Mayne
Illustrated by Norman Messenger

Cloth: Dorling Kindersley
Published: 1994

He's not a ghost or a goblin. Rather Hob is a protective household spirit who takes care of the family dwelling, keeping it free of small worries. He's become attached to a nice family, and in this novel he must take on a serious task, goblins being larger and stronger than his usual opponents, because the family have occupied the most dangerous cottage in England. Everything is on a small, not very scary scale, and the language is graceful and invites reading aloud. *The Book of Hob Stories* contains the whole series. Worth looking for.

THE HOBBIT [768]

Written by J. R. R. Tolkien
Illustrated by Michael Hague

Cloth: Houghton Mifflin
Paper: Ballantine
Published: 1937

The background volume to the *Lord of the Rings* trilogy tells the story of Bilbo Baggins and the Hobbits. It can be read to or by younger children, who may not be ready to absorb the other novels, which are richer and more complex.

HOMESICK: MY OWN STORY [769]

Written by Jean Fritz
Illustrated by Margot Tomes

Cloth: Putnam
Paper: Dell Yearling
Published: 1982

**Prizes: Newbery Honor
American Book Award**

A historian who writes for children, Jean Fritz was born and raised in China. Here she remembers that world and what it was like in the mid-1920s to be "homesick" for the United States, giving a vivid picture of life where she actually was. Her return to China, after the book was published in 1982, is described in *China Homecoming*.

HOOPS [770]

Written by Robert Burleigh
Illustrated by Stephen T. Johnson

Cloth: Harcourt Brace
Published: 1997

Poems and illustrations that together offer a lush, stop-action view of the fast and fabulous game.

THE HOUSE OF DIES DREAR   [771]

Written by Virginia Hamilton

Cloth: Macmillan
Paper: Aladdin
Published: 1968

This lushly written novel tells about a contemporary black family who buy the house in Ohio in which, a century earlier, Dies Drear and two slaves he had been hiding were murdered. (The house was a stop on the Underground Railroad.) At its simplest level, this is an entertaining mystery, yet it can be read as a parable. In the sequel, *The Mystery of Drear House,* the Small family deals with hidden treasure.

THE HOUSE WITH A CLOCK IN ITS WALLS   [772]

Written by John Bellairs
Illustrated by Edward Gorey

Cloth: Dial
Paper: Puffin
Published: 1973

The first of a dozen mysteries about a boy and his uncle, who is a kind of wizard, illustrated by an artist whose style is in itself mysterious. One of the most popular mystery series for children, it's clanic in form, reasonably well written, and reasonably scary. The other titles include *The Figure in the Shadows* and *The Letter, the Witch, and the Ring.*

HOW TO EAT FRIED WORMS   [773]

Written by Thomas Rockwell
Illustrated by Emily McCully

Cloth: Franklin Watts
Paper: Bantam
Published: 1973

Billy accepted the bet, and now he has to eat fifteen worms in fifteen days. The story moves along pell-mell, in short, boisterous chapters, as Billy comes up with some pretty inventive ways to get the wigglers down. Will he succeed? This is a book that holds the attention of even the most restless listeners and readers.

I, JUAN DE PAREJA [774]

Written by Elizabeth Borton De Trevino

Cloth: Farrar, Straus & Giroux
Paper: Sunburst
Published: 1965   **Prizes: Newbery Medal**

This compelling historical novel takes the form of the autobiography of Juan de Pareja, the son of a black African woman and a white Spaniard, who was willed to the Spanish artist Velázquez. Their lifelong relationship evolved toward equality and friendship. Challenging but worth it.

ICE STORY: SHACKLETON'S LOST EXPEDITION [775]

Written by Elizabeth Cody Kimmel

Cloth: Clarion
Published: 1999

A fine account of Sir Ernest Shackleton's 1914 expedition to cross the polar ice cap and the fate of his ship, the *Endurance*, illustrated handsomely with some of the historic photographs. Michael McCurdy's *Trapped by the Ice!* tells the same terrifying survival story.

IN THE BEGINNING: CREATION STORIES FROM AROUND THE WORLD [776]

Written by Virginia Hamilton
Illustrated by Barry Moser

Cloth: Harcourt Brace
Paper: Harcourt Brace
Published: 1988

Here are twenty-five creation myths from nearly every continent, richly told in singing language. A lot of cultural conventions adults know are turned upside down—for example, in a Melanesian story, "In the beginning, there was light. It never dimmed, this light over darkness." People are never too young or too old to listen to myths—to hear how other people explain what we think we know. The mysterious illustrations enhance the charms of this collection. Read aloud.

IN THE YEAR OF THE BOAR AND JACKIE ROBINSON [777]

Written by Bette Bao Lord
Illustrated by Marc Simont

Cloth: HarperCollins
Paper: Harper Trophy
Published: 1984

Shirley Temple Wong arrives in Brooklyn able to speak only two words of English. She works her way into the American dream via the classic route, baseball—turning into a fan and a player the same season Jackie Robinson joins the Dodgers. It is an old-fashioned middle grade story, told humorously and well. The illustrations are both stylish and witty.

INCIDENT AT HAWK'S HILL [778]

Written by Allan W. Eckert
Illustrated by John Schoenherr

Cloth: Little, Brown
Paper: Little, Brown
Published: 1971   **Prizes: Newbery Honor**

On a mild June day in 1870, on the broad Canadian prairie, a shy six-year-old boy, Ben McDonald, slipped away into the tall grasses and was lost for nearly six months. His adventures, including a

[777]

[777]

remarkable relationship with a female badger, are at the core of the much-loved story. A sequel, *Return to Hawk's Hill* involving the evil trapper, George Burton, was published more than twenty-five years later.

THE INCREDIBLE JOURNEY [779]

Written by Sheila Burnford
Illustrated by Carl Burger

Paper: Yearling
Published: 1961

This immensely popular story tells about three loyal house pets, Tao, a Siamese cat, Bodger, a bull terrier, and Luash, a Labrador retriever, who follow "their" family, a kind man, through many an adventure across 250 miles of Canada to their new home.

INDIAN CHIEFS [780]

Written by Russell Freedman

Cloth: Holiday House
Published: 1987

Here is a good introduction to six of the great American Indian chiefs who led their people against the encroaching pioneers—Red Cloud, Santana, Quanah Parker, Washakie, Joseph, and Sitting Bull—illustrated with memorable historic photographs.

THE INDIAN IN THE CUPBOARD

[781]

Written by Lynne Reid Banks
Illustrated by Brock Cole

Cloth: Doubleday
Paper: Camelot
Published: 1981

Omri, a boy living near London, is given an old bathroom cupboard as an odd sort of birthday present. The key his mother digs up to unlock it has magical powers, so that when Omri puts one of his toys, a miniature plastic Indian, in the cupboard and locks the door, the figure is brought to life. Little Bear, a warrior from another civilization, with his bow and arrow, and others who travel through the cupboard into the modern world teach Omri and his friend Patrick a great deal. The adventure story is exciting, sometimes thrilling. Young readers, like Omri himself, brood about taking responsibility for and interfering in other people's lives. The sequel, *The Return of the Indian,* in which Omri's friends are caught up in war, is equally rewarding; the third book, *The Secret of the Indian,* is less so. Terrific for reading aloud with middle grade children, especially boys.

INSIDE THE WHALE: AND OTHER ANIMALS [782]

Written by Steve Parker
Illustrated by Ted Dewan

Cloth: Doubleday
Published: 1992

The next best thing to a biology class and a lot less messy, this menagerie of twenty-one animals and insects including the blue whale, dromedary camel, brown bat, giant tortoise, blue-ringed octopus, common chicken, honeybee, and mosquito, is shown in remarkable detail and clarity. For parents as well as children.

THE IRON GIANT [783]

Written by Ted Hughes
Illustrated by Andrew Davidson

Cloth: Knopf
Published: 1968

The rich fantasy written by the British poet laureate as the Vietnam War raged remains potent although power in the world has shifted so dramatically that the allegorical message may be lost. From the memorable opening scene as the Iron Giant rebuilds itself on a rocky beach to the end, an ingenious battle between the giant and the space-bat-angel and the melodic conclusion, it's gripping.

ISLAND OF THE BLUE DOLPHINS

[784]

Written by Scott O'Dell
Illustrated by Milton Johnson

Cloth: Houghton Mifflin
Paper: Dell Yearling
Published: 1960 **Prizes: Newbery Medal**

A memorable adventure and coming-of-age novel about Karana, an Indian girl who spends eighteen years alone on a rocky island off the coast of California in the early nineteenth century. It is based on the true experiences of "The Lost Woman of San Nicolas." *Zia* is the sequel. A popular title with older grade schoolchildren of both sexes. A commemorative hardcover edition, also published by Houghton Mifflin, came out in 1990, with new illustrations.

IT'S LIKE THIS, CAT [785]

Written by Emily Cheney Neville

Cloth: HarperCollins
Paper: HarperCollins
Published: 1963 **Prizes: Newbery Medal**

This dandy coming-of-age novel tells about Dave, who is fourteen and lives near Gramercy Park in New York City. He has family troubles, acquires a cat, and is launched into adventures in the neighborhood. The absence of drugs as a fact of life gives the story an old-fashioned quality, but Dave's relationship with his parents rings true.

IT'S PERFECTLY NORMAL: A BOOK ABOUT CHANGING BODIES, GROWING UP, SEX, AND SEXUAL HEALTH [786]

Written by Robie H. Harris
Illustrated by Michael Emberley

Cloth: Candlewick Press
Published: 1995 **Prizes: Caldecott Honor**

The inspired cartoon illustrations in this genuinely instructive book about sex and reproduction allow the author and illustrator to be honest without losing their sense of humor or patronizing any potential readers. This is a book to leave out for the whole family to read or look at, although probably not everyone together. Younger independent readers can find information and some important definitions, preadolescents will want to check on what they think they know but is explicitly clear in the illustrations, and adolescents may absorb some sound advice about sexual survival. Also look at the splendid companion volume for younger children *It's So Amazing*.

JAMES AND THE GIANT PEACH [787]

Written by Roald Dahl
Illustrated by Lane Smith

Cloth: Knopf
Paper: Puffin
Published: 1961/1996

A Dahl fantasy about how James escapes from dreary life with his two aunts by crawling inside a giant peach. This is one of those scary, wonderful books, best read aloud the first time. Quite, er, delicious. The 1996 edition illustrated by Lane Smith is eccentric and edgy but true to the book as well.

A JAR OF DREAMS [788]

Written by Yoshiko Uchida

Cloth: Margaret K. McElderry
Paper: Aladdin
Published: 1981

This is the first of three novels about Rinko, a Japanese-American girl growing up in Berkeley, California, in the 1930s. The extended family, the conflicting cultural influences, and the warmth of the characters are appealing. The other titles are *The Best Bad Things* and *The Happiest Ending*.

JELLY BELLY [789]

Written by Robert Kimmel Smith
Illustrated by Bob Jones

Cloth: Delacorte
Paper: Dell Yearling
Published: 1981

The kids tease Ned because he's so fat, calling him Jelly Belly, so his family sends him off to diet camp. His bunk mate turns out to be a cheater, but Ned learns a lot over that summer about life as well as diet. This is good fiction for upper grade readers, not just bibliotherapy.

JIP: HIS STORY [790]

Written by Katherine Paterson

Cloth: Lodestar
Published: 1996

The setting is a "poor farm" in Vermont in 1855. The hero—and he does become a hero—is an orphan called Jip ("on account of I fell off the back of a wagon and some says it was a gypsy wagon"). He's an appealing and brave boy, and some of the issues that appear naturally, without feeling forced or inappropriate, in the narrative include welfare, treatment of insanity, slavery, and literacy. The title character from the author's other Vermont historical novel *Lyddie* makes a crucial appearance as well.

JOHNNY TREMAIN [791]

Written by Esther Forbes

Cloth: Houghton Mifflin
Paper: Laurel Leaf
Published: 1943

Prizes: Newbery Medal

It's 1775 in Boston, and after a tragic accident in the silversmith's shop, the young apprentice becomes involved in political activity leading to the American Revolution. A popular favorite for generations, in book and film form.

JOURNEY TO AMERICA [792]

Written by Sonia Levitin
Illustrated by Charles Robinson

Cloth: Atheneum
Paper: Aladdin
Published: 1970

This is the compelling fictionalized story of how one Jewish family, the Platts, fled from Hitler's Germany and managed to get to Switzerland and eventually to the United States. *Silver Days* is the sequel, describing their new life in Los Angeles, and *Annie's Promise* picks up the story of the youngest daughter in 1945, at the end of World War II.

JULIE OF THE WOLVES [793]

Written by Jean Craighead George
Illustrated by John Schoenherr

Cloth: HarperCollins
Paper: Harper Trophy
Published: 1972   **Prizes: Newbery Medal**

The memorable story of Julie, a thirteen-year-old Eskimo girl. She gets lost on the tundra and is protected by a wolf pack. The story continues in *Julie,* a weaker volume more about her relationship to her father and his new wife, and concludes with *Julie's Wolf Pack.* The last is perhaps the most exciting and provocative tale, told from the perspective of the wolves and containing some thrilling descriptive writing as well as a cleverly plotted ecological warning. *Water Sky* also deals with the Eskimos.

[794]

THE JUNIPER TREE: AND OTHER TALES FROM GRIMM [794]

Written by Jacob and Wilhelm Grimm
Illustrated by Maurice Sendak

Cloth: Farrar, Straus & Giroux
Paper: Noonday Press
Published: 1973   **Prizes: New York Times Best Illustrated Book**

This two-volume set of twenty-seven stories by the brothers Grimm was translated with scrupulous care and tact by Lore Segal and

Randall Jarrell and illustrated with equal grace by Maurice Sendak. It's a labor of love that shows no age. The stories are by turn heart-breaking and terrifying, gentle and sharp, poignant and funny. If you want one edition of Grimm, to read or to read aloud, this is the most satisfying one available.

JUST SO STORIES   [795]

Written by Rudyard Kipling
Illustrated by Michael Foreman

Cloth: Viking Press
Paper: Puffin
Published: 1902/1987

Listen, O Best Beloved, to the wondrous tales of animals—the little elephant child, the whale, the leopard, the cat, and others. Listen carefully, for these stories should be heard first and read independently later. They are among the greatest short fictions for children in the language and fairly roll off the reader's tongue. There are many picture-book editions of individual stories; some packaged with audio- or videotapes as well. This 1987 edition, illustrated by a distinguished British artist, is appealing and comprehensive.

KENNEDY ASSASSINATED! THE WORLD MOURNS: A REPORTER'S STORY   [796]

Written by Wilborn Hampton

Cloth: Candlewick Press
Published: 1997

The author of this account was a very young reporter in the Dallas office of United Press International on November 22, 1973. His account alternates between what he actually saw and the events taking place beyond his view. The handsomely designed book uses photographs and documents of the time on almost every page, and the result is a fine example of modern documentary history. Parents and grandparents may find it equally compelling.

THE KID FROM TOMKINSVILLE [797]

Written by John R. Tunis

Cloth: Harcourt Brace
Paper: Odyssey
Published: 1940

Several generations of sports fans have grown up with the series of splendid baseball novels known collectively as Baseball Diamonds. The others include *World Series, Keystone Kids,* and *Rookie of the Year.* The writing is always deft, and the action on the field is sensational and easy to follow even for non-fans.

KIDS ON STRIKE! [798]

Written by Susan Campbell Bartoletti

Cloth: Houghton Mifflin
Published: 1999

Here are concise chapters on eight episodes of American labor history involving children and issues about child labor beginning in Lowell, Massachusetts, in 1836. The text moves around the country and includes newspaperboys, the coal mines, garment workers, and finally back to the Lawrence mills in 1912. The sourcing is excellent, the writing is vivid, and the fine photographs include many famous images. A properly provocative book.

KING OF SHADOWS [799]

Written by Susan Cooper
Cloth: Margaret K. McElderry
Published: 1999

A remarkably deft time-tripping novel takes Nat Field, an American boy actor belonging to a troupe scheduled to perform at the new Globe Theater in London, back to 1599 and the Globe Theater when Will Shakespeare was in residence. A good deal of information about acting, performance technique, and Elizabethan customs is woven through the story.

KNEEKNOCK RISE [800]

Written and illustrated by Natalie Babbitt

Cloth: Farrar, Straus & Giroux
Paper: Sunburst
Published: 1970   **Prizes: Newbery Honor**

Villagers in Instep think that Kneeknock Rise (which is really little more than a hill) has mysterious properties. They think a fearsome creature they call a Megrimum lives at the top of the rise and is the source of strange sounds on stormy nights. Fine and persuasive, a little bit funny and a great deal wise.

THE LANDRY NEWS [801]

Written by Andrew Clements

Cloth: Simon & Schuster
Published: 1999

Mr. Larson's fifth grade classroom is like a "giant educational glacier," where nothing happens. Mr. Larson has effectively stopped teaching, leaving his students to fend for themselves. Then Cara Landry, who loves to read newspapers, starts her own, *The Landry News,* with a scathing editorial about her teacher. It becomes a class project and a political issue. While the story gallops along and celebrates journalism, honoring the motto "Truth and Mercy," the good humor makes the message palatable. *Grindle* and *The Janitor's Boy* are also set in middle school.

THE LEMMING CONDITION [802]

Written by Alan Arkin
Illustrated by Joan Sandin

Cloth: HarperCollins
Paper: Harper San Francisco
Published: 1976

An allegory about Bubber, an un-lemminglike lemming who persists in asking questions and considering the consequences. A good choice for philosophical young readers.

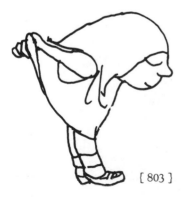

[803]

A LIGHT IN THE ATTIC [803]

Written and illustrated by Shel Silverstein

Cloth: HarperCollins
Published: 1981

By turns happy, sad, funny, and affecting, this is an immensely popular collection of poetry, verse, and illustration. It is idiosyncratic but maintains a firm moral stance and appeals to all ages.

LILY'S CROSSING [804]

Written by Patricia Reilly Giff

Cloth: Delacorte
Published: 1997   **Prizes: Newbery Honor**

It's the summer of 1944, the time of the Allied invasion of Europe, and on the home front, specifically the Rockaway beachfront of New York City, ten-year-old Lily Mollahan is spending the summer with her grandmother. Despite her bravado, Lily is lonely and anxious and not particularly nice, which makes her an interesting main character. Vivid period details.

LINCOLN: A PHOTOBIOGRAPHY

[805]

Written by Russell Freedman

Cloth: Clarion
Published: 1987   **Prizes: Newbery Medal**

This sympathetic and well-balanced biography of Abraham Lincoln, accessible for middle grade readers, sets out his life and career without minimizing the complexity of many of the issues he addressed, including slavery. The subtitle, *A Photobiography,* underscores the fact that Lincoln was the first president whose life was recorded by the camera; however, the illustrations include documents and artifacts as well as photographs.

[803]

A LITTLE PRINCESS   [806]

Written by Frances Hodgson Burnett
Illustrated by Tasha Tudor

Cloth: HarperCollins
Paper: Harper Trophy
Published: 1963

Sweet-natured Sara Crewe, left by her father in a British boarding school, falls onto hard times and is badly treated after her father's death overseas. She is, of course, virtuous and is rescued and brought back to high estate by a rich gentleman who was her father's friend. It is old-fashioned soap opera, charming on its antiquated terms, and told confidently. For many years, this was the only edition available in the United States. But, as with all the other Burnett novels, the copyright has expired and numerous editions in hard- and softcover have appeared. Avoid clumsy and unnecessary abridgments. A great favorite for reading aloud.

LITTLE WOMEN   [807]

Written by Louisa May Alcott
Illustrated by Jessie Wilcox Smith

Cloth: Little, Brown
Paper: Penguin; Bantam; Signet
Published: 1868

The March girls—Meg, Jo, Beth, and Amy—and how they grew up in Massachusetts during the Civil War. Well over a century later, this is still one of the most affecting and powerful novels written for girls, although contemporary parents may wish to give some running commentary about the narrow definition of female roles. The sequels include *Jo's Boys* and, of course, *Little Men* and *Rose in Bloom*. Because the titles are in the public domain, there are many editions: avoid abridgments, and browse before you buy. Several of the paperback editions have interesting introductions by contemporary writers.

LIVES OF THE MUSICIANS: GOOD TIMES, BAD TIMES (AND WHAT THE NEIGHBORS THOUGHT) [808]

Written by Kathleen Krull
Illustrated by Kathryn Hewitt

Cloth: Harcourt Brace
Paper: Harcourt Brace
Published: 1993

The first in a successful series of collections of witty biographical sketches in this case of musicians. An amusing and insightful full-color, caricature-style illustration accompanies each profile. There are other *Lives* as well: *Lives of the Writers: Comedies, Tragedies (And What the Neighbors Thought), Lives of the Presidents: Fame, Shame (And What the Neighbors Thought)*, also artists and athletes.

THE LOST FLOWER CHILDREN [809]

Written by Janet Taylor Lisle

Cloth: Philomel
Published: 1999

The orphaned Olivia and her little sister, Nellie, have been put in the care of Great-Aunt Minty. Nellie, almost paralyzed by grief for her mother, lives by an elaborate, inhibiting set of rules. Then, in Aunt Minty's wild, overgrown garden, the children find a tiny china cup. The old lady says it belonged to a party of children who were turned into flowers long ago by a band of fairies. A wonderful adventure ensues, with healing results.

[803]

LUCIE BABBIDGE'S HOUSE [810]

Written by Sylvia Cassedy

Cloth: HarperCollins
Paper: Camelot
Published: 1989

At the same time that Lucie Babbidge is Goosey-Loosey, the unkempt, unpopular girl at Norwood Hall School, she is loved and admired at home, even if the family is a little eccentric. Keep reading through the rich prose, because all is not as it seems; it's much

more complicated, particularly the "family." Know that Lucie will survive and triumph, bringing her fantasies to her own aid. A memorable novel.

LYDDIE   [811]

Written by Katherine Paterson

Cloth: Lodestar
Published: 1991

In this novel of the Industrial Revolution in New England, Lyddie's family loses their farm in rural Vermont and breaks up; the thirteen-year-old girl is first hired out to the tavern. Eventually she finds her way to Lowell and work in the mill. Lyddie is plucky and brave, but the conditions in the mills, the boardinghouses, and the town are forbidding and fraught with trials. Still, a heroine finds her way.

M. C. HIGGINS, THE GREAT   [812]

Written by Virginia Hamilton

Cloth: Macmillan
Paper: Aladdin
Published: 1974   **Prizes: Newbery Medal**

In this remarkable novel about thirteen-year-old M. C. Higgins, the black boy helps care for the younger children and dreams of escape for himself and his family from poverty and the slow-moving slag heap left from the strip mine. He fantasizes unrealistic possibilities and then realizes some real opportunities. The author's language is rich and subtle, demanding and worthwhile.

MAGIC ELIZABETH   [813]

Written by Norma Kassirer
Illustrated by Joe Krush

Cloth: Knopf/Bullseye
Paper: HarperCollins
Published: 1966

Sally is sent to spend the end of the summer with gloomy old Aunt Sarah, in her gloomy old house. In the child's room is a painting from long ago of another girl named Sally and her doll, Elizabeth. Magically, modern-day Sally visits them, and Elizabeth ends up in the present.

THE MAN IN THE CEILING [814]

Written and illustrated by Jules Feiffer

Cloth: HarperCollins
Paper: HarperCollins
Published: 1993

Jimmy draws comics—he's good at it, and it's a way of rearranging the experiences and conditions in the real world to make things better. He portrays his overworked father as a hero, celebrates his own smallness by creating Mini-Man, a micro hero. This is an affecting, sophisticated novel that looks, because of the wonderful drawings, more lighthearted than it is.

MAN O'WAR [815]

Written by Walter Farley

Paper: Random House
Published: 1962

Here is a novel based on the life of the great racehorse, full of information about the racing world and the excitement of thoroughbreds.

MANIAC MAGEE [816]

Written by Jerry Spinelli

Cloth: Little, Brown
Paper: Little, Brown
Published: 1990   **Prizes: Newbery Medal**

This is told as a kind of Paul Bunyan story, a larger-than-life folktale about Magee, the boy who bolted from the school auditorium at the age of eleven and ran away to lead a daredevil life in and near his hometown in western Pennsylvania. In fact, he's looking for a home, a real home. The story fairly gallops along and deals deftly with poverty, intolerance, and racism along the way.

MARTHA GRAHAM: A DANCER'S LIFE [817]

Written by Russell Freedman

Cloth: Clarion
Published: 1998

An unusually sophisticated and candid biography of the legendary American dancer and choreographer. Stunning black-and-white photographs might well intrigue young readers who have never heard of Graham before.

MARTIN THE WARRIOR [818]

Written by Brian Jacques
Illustrated by Gary Chalk

Cloth: Philomel
Paper: Putnam
Published: 1993

Although published out of sequence, this installment takes readers to the beginning of the Redwall books, telling about that brave mouse, Arthur, who founded the Redwall Abby deep in the Moss-flower Woods and whose spirit inspires the series. The form is classic: a complete, complicated, detailed world in which the good guys, both male and female, are very good; the villains, also both male and female, are deliciously wicked. The line drawings are distinctive and helpful to reluctant readers who are enthralled by the stories.

[821]

MARY POPPINS: REVISED EDITION

[819]

Written by P. L. Travers
Illustrated by Mary Shepard

Cloth: Harcourt Brace
Paper: Odyssey
Published: 1934/1962

This is the first in the perennially popular series of books about the British nanny with magical abilities who arrives at the Banks family home on Cherry Tree Lane with the east wind. Other titles in the series include *Mary Poppins Comes Back, Mary Poppins in the Park,* and *Mary Poppins Opens the Door.* "Revised Edition" refers to the elimination of the unfortunately explicit racism of the original edition. The movie version is not true to the stories, which have elements of mysticism and make subtle references to classical texts.

[819]

THE MASTER PUPPETEER [820]

Written by Katherine Paterson
Illustrated by Haru Wells

Cloth: HarperCollins
Paper: Harper Trophy
Published: 1976   **Prizes: National Book Award**

It is eighteenth-century Japan in this historical novel. Most of the story is set inside the Hanaza puppet theater in Osaka during a period of famine. Jiro, the son of a starving puppet maker, runs away from home and apprentices in the theater. It is an extraordinarily well-written and compelling novel, filled with detail. Brace yourself for the chilling ending. The author has written two other novels set in Japan's historical periods—*Of Nightingales That Weep* and *The Sign of the Chrysanthemum*—as well as many fine books set in the United States.

MATILDA [821]

Written by Roald Dahl
Illustrated by Quentin Blake

Cloth: Viking Press
Paper: Puffin
Published: 1988

Matilda is a frighteningly precocious child burdened by wretched, selfish, silly parents and a fiendish headmistress, Miss Trunchbull. Happily, Matilda has a gift for creative naughtiness, a good friend in Lavender, a wonderful teacher in the enchanting Miss Honey, and best of all, an inspired creator in Roald Dahl, who somehow makes it all believable.

MEAN MARGARET   [822]

Written by Tor Seidler
Illustrated by Jon Agee

Cloth: HarperCollins
Published: 1997

They were a very nice woodchuck couple, leading a very orderly nice life, when that tyrannical toddler Margaret entered their lives, and suddenly there was chaos. A very funny story, with very funny illustrations, about behavior and its consequences.

THE MENNYMS   [823]

Written by Sylvia Waugh

Cloth: Greenwillow
Paper: Camelot
Published: 1994

The family of the title in an appealing series of British novels are life-size rag dolls who were made by an eccentric old lady, a seamstress, who lived at 5 Brocklehurst Grove. They—Vinetta and Joshua, the parents, Appleby, the fifteen-year-old, Sir Magnus and blue Soobie—came to life shortly after their maker's death. In this and subsequent novels, *The Mennyms in the Wilderness* and *Mennyms Under Siege* they deal with the modern world and human beings. In the great tradition of *The Borrowers*.

[822]

MISSING MAY [824]

Written by Cynthia Rylant

Cloth: Orchard Books
Paper: Yearling
Published: 1992   **Prizes: Newbery Medal**

It's been six months since Aunt May died, and twelve-year-old Summer, the narrator, and her uncle Ob are not reconciled to her absence. After her mother's death, when she was a baby, Summer had been passed around by relatives until settling in with Uncle Ob and Aunt May. They had made themselves a family of three, and now they are trying to come to terms with their loss. They set off to visit Reverend Miriam B. Conklin, "Small Medium at Large," in hopes of contacting May.

MISTY OF CHINCOTEAGUE [825]

Written by Marguerite Henry
Illustrated by Wesley Dennis

Cloth: Macmillan
Paper: Aladdin
Published: 1947

Is there a more romantic vision than wild ponies galloping on the beach of Chincoteague Island? Generations of readers have doubted it, and the ever-popular series includes *Stormy: Misty's Foal* and *Sea Star: Orphan of Chincoteague*.

[822]

THE MOORCHILD [826]

Written by Eloise McGraw

Cloth: Margaret K. McElderry
Paper: Aladdin
Published: 1996   **Prizes: Newbery Honor**

Her father is human, her mother comes from the Moorfolk, and the child born Moql was first raised by the fairies, then exchanged with a human child in a rural village. She is now a girl called Saaski and her strangeness is hated and feared by the local folk. Folkloric themes.

MORNING GIRL [827]

Written by Michael Dorris

Cloth: Hyperion
Paper: Hyperion
Published: 1992

Morning Girl and her brother Star Boy live on a beautiful, if not precisely idyllic island in this gentle, kindly novel of family life that, the reader knows from the beginning, is actually set in 1492. Christopher Columbus comes over the horizon at the very end. The issue is cultural perspective, the lesson is gracefully taught.

MRS. FRISBY AND THE RATS OF NIMH [828]

Written by Robert C. O'Brien
Illustrated by Zena Bernstein

Cloth: Atheneum
Paper: Aladdin
Published: 1971   **Prizes: Newbery Medal**

A prizewinning novel about Mrs. Frisby, a widowed mouse, and the rats of NIMH (National Institute of Mental Health), a well-educated group who are about to set up their own culture. The sequel is *Rasco and the Rats of NIMH*, completed by the author's daughter, Jane Conly.

MRS. PIGGLE-WIGGLE [829]

Written by Betty MacDonald
Illustrated by Hilary Knight

Cloth: HarperCollins
Paper: Harper Trophy
Published: 1957

These well-loved and easy-to-read books make up a kind of catalog of childhood misbehavior and pranks, all cured by the delightful old lady who never scolds but has some very clever ideas about how to handle children who aren't really naughty but are, for example, Never-Want-to-Go-to-Bedders or Tattle-Tales or Fraidy-Cats. The series includes *Hello, Mrs. Piggle-Wiggle; Mrs. Piggle-Wiggle's Farm;* and *Mrs. Piggle-Wiggle's Magic.* There are some individual chapters told as picture books—stick to the real thing.

MY BROTHER SAM IS DEAD [830]

Written by James Lincoln Collier and Christopher Collier

Cloth: Four Winds
Paper: Scholastic
Published: 1974

The Revolutionary War has come to the Tory town of Redding, Connecticut, and this remarkably rich novel details how it affects the Meekers, a nonpartisan family. One of the most sophisticated and powerful historical novels for young readers.

MY SIDE OF THE MOUNTAIN [831]

Written and illustrated by Jean Craighead George

Cloth: Dutton
Paper: Puffin
Published: 1959   **Prizes: Newbery Medal**

The author, a distinguished nature writer, skillfully blends themes of nature, courage, curiosity, and independence in this novel about Sam Gribley, who built himself a tree house in the Catskill Mountains north of New York City, lives off the land, and raises a peregrine falcon. The details and technical illustrations have charmed and thrilled generations. *On the Far Side of the Mountain,* published thirty years later, is essentially about Sam's sister's adventure. *Frightful's Mountain,* published forty years later and told from the perspective of adult falcons, is very exciting and beautifully written.

NICK OF TIME [832]

Written by Anne Lindbergh

Cloth: Little, Brown
Published: 1994

The Mending Wall School is an eccentric place, but still, this new boy Nick does seem to be going through walls into the future. A hilarious time-tripping novel.

THE NIGHT JOURNEY [833]

Written by Kathryn Lasky
Illustrated by Trina Schart Hyman

Cloth: Viking Press
Paper: Puffin
Published: 1981

Nana Sashie enjoys her afternoon visits with thirteen-year-old Rachel and eventually confides in her to tell the story of her Jewish family's escape from czarist Russia. Moving and well written. Good to read aloud.

NO PRETTY PICTURES: A CHILD OF WAR [834]

Written by Anita Lobel

Cloth: Greenwillow
Published: 1998

A children's book artist known for her colorful, exuberant style tells of her childhood on the run during World War II. Just five when the Nazis came to the door in Poland, she and her younger brother moved through a Benedictine convent into the concentration camps, and after the war, on to Sweden, where they recovered from tuberculosis before coming to the United States in 1952. The story is told plainly and powerfully, with precise detail and no sermonizing. Splendidly accessible for contemporary readers, it is one of the finest memoirs of a wartime childhood.

NOBODY'S FAMILY IS GOING TO CHANGE   [835]

Written and illustrated by Louise Fitzhugh

Cloth: Farrar, Straus & Giroux
Paper: Sunburst
Published: 1974

In this compelling story about expectations, stereotypes, and family pressures, Emma wants to be a lawyer, but it is her brother Willie who feels the career pressure. Moreover, Willie wants to dance on the stage like Uncle Dipsey. The Sheridan family is black, but the problems are universal. The novel was the basis of the musical *The Tap Dance Kid.*

THE NOONDAY FRIENDS   [836]

Written by Mary Stolz
Illustrated by Louis S. Glanzman

Cloth: HarperCollins
Paper: Harper Trophy
Published: 1965

A novel about school and family life in Greenwich Village as experienced by two eleven-year-old girls. Life was somewhat simpler in the olden days, but preadolescence remains a lot the same.

THE NOT-JUST-ANYBODY FAMILY

[837]

Written by Betsy Byars

Cloth: Delacorte
Paper: Dell Yearling
Published: 1986

The first in a series of books about the Blossom family, beset by goodwill and bizarre mishaps. Mother is away on the rodeo circuit, Pap managed to get arrested for dumping 2,147 soda cans, and Junior tried to fly and broke two legs. Adventures continue in *The Blossoms Meet the Vulture Lady* and *The Blossoms and the Green Phantom,* and end with *A Blossom Promise.*

NOTHING'S FAIR IN FIFTH GRADE

[838]

Written by Barthe DeClements

Cloth: Viking Press
Paper: Puffin
Published: 1981

Early adolescence is funny, sad, awkward, and consistently interesting, no less so if you are like Elsie, the "fat girl" in her class. The follow-up story, about "Bad Helen," is *Sixth Grade Can Really Kill You.*

NUMBER THE STARS   [839]

Written by Lois Lowry

Cloth: Houghton Mifflin
Paper: Yearling
Published: 1989   **Prizes: Newbery Medal**

The setting is Denmark in the fall of 1943 and the subject is the effort of Christian Danes to rescue Jews. The story is told from the perspective of Annmarie Johansen, whose best friend, Ellen Rosen, is Jewish. It is appropriate for middle grade readers. Another novel, *Lisa's War* by Carol Matas, for junior high school students, is on the same subject and addresses directly the enormity of the Nazi threat. If you are bringing up the Holocaust in discussions at home, also look for *Rescue: The Story of How Gentiles Saved Jews in the Holocaust* by Milton Meltzer.

THE NUTCRACKER   [840]

Written by E. T. A. Hoffman
Illustrated by Maurice Sendak

Cloth: Crown
Paper: Crown
Published: 1984   **Prizes: New York Times Best Illustrated Book**

Here is the ultimate *Nutcracker.* The text is the original story translated carefully by Ralph Manheim—far more complex than the familiar ballet versions such as the one George Balanchine choreographed for the New York City Ballet. The lavish illustrations derive from the Seattle Ballet's *Nutcracker,* which was designed by Maurice Sendak. A stunning and exciting book, it is much too complex for most youngsters going to the ballet for the very first time. There are many, many other editions telling the story thisaway and thataway.

OLIVER TWIST [841]

Written by Charles Dickens
Illustrated by Don Freeman

Cloth: Morrow Junior Books
Published: 1994

The illustrations to this handsome edition of Dickens's beloved story of the orphan boy led into and then rescued from a life of crime were done by the artist best known for the little bear Corduroy. These period drawings done decades earlier but never seen before, however, are well researched and filled with an energy that suits the tale. If only there could have been more, please.

ONE-EYED CAT [842]

Written by Paula Fox

Cloth: Bradbury
Paper: Dell Yearling
Published: 1984   **Prizes: Newbery Honor**

In this powerful novel about maturation, Ned, a rather isolated boy, has an invalid mother and a remote father. Ned believes he shot out the eye of a wildcat and must come to terms with the guilt he cannot express. The writing is both simple and eloquent, which increases the impact of the story.

ONION JOHN [843]

Written by Joseph Krumgold
Illustrated by Symeon Shimin

Cloth: HarperCollins
Paper: Harper Trophy
Published: 1959   **Prizes: Newbery Medal**

The story of a friendship between a twelve-year-old boy and an immigrant handyman that is misunderstood by well-intentioned townspeople. A didactic but well-written novel.

OUR ONLY MAY AMELIA [844]

Written by Jennifer L. Holm

Cloth: HarperCollins
Paper: Harper Trophy
Published: 1999   **Prizes: Newbery Honor**

A first novel based on the life of the author's great-aunt, the first Finnish-American girl born on the Naselle River in Washington in 1887. After seven boys, she was considered a miracle. Engaging and filled with details of farm life and the Finnish community.

THE OUTLAWS OF SHERWOOD [845]

Written by Robin McKinley

Cloth: Greenwillow
Paper: Ace
Published: 1988

Young readers today often arrive at the sequels to stories without knowing, let alone loving, the originals. Yet this imaginative and compelling novel about Robin Hood, his band of followers in the forest, and Maid Marian can be read alone or in sequence with library versions, comics, or movies. The tart, modern tone comes not least from Robin's temperamental personality and Marian's feisty independence.

THE OXFORD BOOK OF POETRY FOR CHILDREN [846]

Written by Edward Blishen
Illustrated by Brian Wildsmith

Cloth: Oxford Books
Paper: Bedrick
Published: 1986

An anthology of English poems for children, many of them, since there is a little of everything from Chaucer to Eliott, of course familiar to adults. *The Oxford Book of Story Poems* is very good for bedtime reading, too. The illustrations are exuberant.

PETER PAN [847]

Written by J. M. Barrie
Illustrated by Jan Ormerod

Cloth: Viking Press
Paper: Puffin
Published: 1987

These are the well-known, albeit mostly from adaptation, adventures of the Darling children, the little lost boy Peter Pan, and the faithful fairy Tinker Bell. The language of the original, while formal, is not so difficult that it cannot be read at full length by an average middle grade reader. There is no need for abridged-text editions, although there are some charming picture-book versions available for younger children. Until the copyright expired, the only full-length edition available had illustrations by Nora Unwin. A number of others have been published recently. This one has striking full-color plates, and Tinker Bell decorates nearly every text page. Incidentally, Barrie based the novel on his own play; the various Disney versions take liberties.

THE PHANTOM TOLLBOOTH [848]

Written by Norman Juster
Illustrated by Jules Feiffer

Cloth: Random House
Paper: Random House
Published: 1961

Milo drives his little car through what looks like a regular tollbooth, but it leads into enchanted lands of science, logic, and order as well as mystery and threat that surround the Mountains of Ignorance. A deserved classic. This brilliant story is perfectly illustrated in Feiffer's distinctive and timeless style. Great for reading aloud to or with, middle grade listeners.

[848]

PHILIP HALL LIKES ME.
I RECKON MAYBE [849]

Written by Bette Greene
Illustrated by Charles Lilly

Cloth: Dial
Paper: Dell Yearling
Published: 1974   **Prizes: Newbery Honor**

Beth is a bright, sassy eleven-year-old black girl living in rural Arkansas. She is the smartest girl in the class, and has a crush on the smartest boy in the class. The sequel is *Get On Out of Here, Philip Hall.*

PILGRIM'S PROGRESS [850]

Written by John Bunyan
Illustrated by Barry Moser

Cloth: Eerdmans
Published: 1994

Once known by most English reading youngsters, this account of faith and challenge has become remote and inaccessible despite the inherent power of the story. This remarkably lucid version is made better still by the intense, lush, painterly illustrations. Worth reading with older children who loved Narnia, went on to *The Golden Compass,* and are concerned with faith.

THE PINBALLS [851]

Written by Betsy Byars

Cloth: HarperCollins
Paper: HarperCollins
Published: 1977

Three children, unwanted and unconnected, one battered, one maimed, one lost, meet and join forces in a warm and caring foster home. Sounds awful, but in the hands of such a careful writer, it works and is actually inspiring.

POLLYANNA [852]

Written by Jean Stratton Porter

Paper: Puffin
Published: 1913

After years out of print, the story of the most relentlessly cheerful heroine in American literature, the inventor of the Glad Game, is available again. In fact it is easy to see why, in simpler days, she was such a popular heroine.

THE POWER OF LIGHT: EIGHT STORIES FOR HANUKKAH

[853]

Written by Isaac Bashevis Singer
Illustrated by Irene Lieblich

Cloth: Farrar, Straus & Giroux
Paper: Sunburst
Published: 1980

A collection of eight stories by the Nobel Prize–winning author to mark the eight nights of Hanukkah. The stories are set mostly in Poland in a time that seems very long ago. Very good for reading aloud.

THE PRINCESS IN THE PIGPEN [854]

Written by Jane Resh Thomas

Cloth: Clarion
Published: 1989

Most time-travel stories start here and now, and move back to then; this one begins in October 1600, in London, when Elizabeth, the duke's nine-year-old daughter, is being put to bed. She wakes up on a farm in Iowa in 1988. Surprises everywhere . . . the biggest being, guess what? Modern medicine. Nicely done.

A PROUD TASTE FOR SCARLET AND MINIVER [855]

Written and illustrated by E. L. Konigsburg

Cloth: Atheneum
Paper: Yearling
Published: 1973

A very witty and imaginative fictionalized biography of Eleanor of Aquitaine. The queen and others, including her mother-in-law and priest, are in heaven waiting for King Henry II to arrive. Good readers will find source material to answer their questions.

THE PUSHCART WAR [856]

Written by Jean Merrill
Illustrated by Ronni Solbert

Cloth: Addison-Wesley
Paper: Dell Yearling
Published: 1964

This fictional account of a "war" between pushcart peddlers and truckers in New York City is told in a light and breezy way but raises serious political and social issues middle and upper grade students can address.

RABBIT HILL [857]

Written and illustrated by Robert Lawson

Cloth: Viking Press
Paper: Puffin
Published: 1941   **Prizes: Newbery Medal**

Life among the creatures who live on Rabbit Hill is consistently entertaining. "New Folk" are coming to live in the Big House. This has been a popular favorite with middle grade readers for generations, and reads aloud particularly well.

RABBLE STARKEY [858]

Written by Lois Lowry

Cloth: Houghton Mifflin
Paper: Dell Yearling
Published: 1987

Her real name is Parable Ann, she's twelve and lives with her very young mother and her grandmother in a small town in Appalachia. Both smart and proud, she deals with the complexities of her life in a determined and persuasive way.

THE RAINBOW PEOPLE [859]

Written by Laurence Yep
Illustrated by David Wiesner

Cloth: HarperCollins
Paper: HarperCollins
Published: 1989

Chinese immigrants in the nineteenth and early twentieth centuries told their children folktales reflecting the stories of their own youth, spent mostly in a dozen provinces in China, but adapted to their new circumstances in American Chinatowns. As part of a WPA project in the 1930s, Jon Lee collected stories in Chinatown in Oakland, California. This collection is based on sixty-nine of those tales, all but one of which were set in China, and are retold here from a fascinating contemporary perspective. *Tales from Gold Mountain* by Paul Yee, recounts eight stories heard in Vancouver's Chinatown and has stunning illustrations by Simon Ng.

RAMONA THE PEST [860]

Written by Beverly Cleary

Cloth: Morrow Junior Books
Paper: Camelot
Published: 1952–1999

Ramona is a national treasure and an institution. This series of novels about the Quimby family and their neighbors, written over nearly half a century but bringing Ramona only to the fourth grade, is a mine of information about loving, ordinary day-to-day family life, told with increasing skill and laced with irresistible humor. Read one, read 'em all, learn to love Ramona, Beezus, and the rest.

Enjoy kindergarten and the early grades again. It's not all sunshine, but it rings true. These books may be slightly difficult to read alone at first, but if you begin them as read-aloud books, they will surely be reread independently for years to come. The illustrations by Louis Darling in the early books, and Allen Tiegreen in the later ones, are a perfect fit. Some of the best are *Henry and Beezus, Beezus and Ramona, Ramona the Brave,* and *Ramona Quimby, Age 8. Ramona's World* is the latest title.

THE RANDOM HOUSE BOOK OF POETRY FOR CHILDREN [861]

Written by Jack Prelutsky
Illustrated by Arnold Lobel

Cloth: Random House
Published: 1983

This large and distinctly optimistic anthology of poetry includes many familiar gems and has zestful illustrations of distinctly Arnold Lobelish owls, cats, and frogs, among other creatures.

THE RED PONY [862]

Written by John Steinbeck
Illustrated by Wesley Dennis

Cloth: Viking Press
Paper: Penguin
Published: 1937

A boy and his horse. A classic. Is there more to say?

RED SCARF GIRL: A MEMOIR OF THE CULTURAL REVOLUTION [863]

Written by Ji-li Jang

Cloth: HarperCollins
Paper: Harper Trophy
Published: 1997

The autobiographical account of the corrosive effects of the Cultural Revolution on one bourgeois family in Shanghai as seen by a twelve-year-old schoolgirl. She was a self-absorbed young adolescent, a good student, and a talented gymnast when the movement to crush the four "olds"—old ideas, old customs, old culture, and old habits—uprooted her family. Very powerful.

THE RELUCTANT DRAGON [864]

Written by Kenneth Grahame
Illustrated by Ernest H. Shepard

Cloth: Holiday House
Paper: Holiday House
Published: 1938

In this timeless story with its perfect line-drawing illustrations, a little boy makes friends with a very peaceful dragon. It's a good fantasy, with implicit moral lessons. Other editions are available but inadequate.

ROLL OF THUNDER, HEAR MY CRY

[865]

Written by Mildred Taylor

Cloth: Dial
Paper: Puffin
Published: 1976   **Prizes: Newbery Medal**

This bitter, memorable, and beautifully written story of a close-knit poor black family in Mississippi during the Depression is drawn from stories from the author's family. Cassie Logan's story continues in *Let the Circle Be Unbroken* and *The Road to Memphis*, which brings her to the end of high school in Jackson at the beginning of World War II.

RONIA, THE ROBBER'S DAUGHTER

[866]

Written by Astrid Lindgren

Cloth: Viking Press
Paper: Puffin
Published: 1983

Brave and adventurous Ronia is the only child of Matt, the robber chief. They live deep in a forest, and the girl causes trouble when she

befriends the son of a rival chief. A rich and complex novel by the author of *Pippi Longstocking,* but for older readers.

SARAH, PLAIN AND TALL   [867]

Written by Patricia MacLachlan

Cloth: HarperCollins
Paper: Harper Trophy
Published: 1985   **Prizes: Newbery Medal**

In the sparest prose, Anna tells how her father placed an ad for a wife in an eastern newspaper, and Sarah replied. Their mother died when Caleb was born, and the children want Sarah, who is "plain and tall" and comes from Maine with her cat, Seal, to stay with them and consider their proposal. A flawless piece of storytelling that touches so many aspects of longing, self-esteem, and raw family needs. Wonderful to read aloud, but have tissues handy. In *Skylark,* Sarah takes the children to Maine during the drought on the plains, but they return to their father and the farm.

THE SECRET GARDEN   [868]

Written by Frances Hodgson Burnett
Illustrated by Tasha Tudor

Cloth: HarperCollins
Paper: HarperCollins
Published: 1912

One of the greatest novels ever written for children, and one of the greatest novels about gardening and health, is the story of Mary Lennox, a spoiled orphan sent to live a solitary life on her guardian's estate on the Yorkshire moors. She encounters Dickon, a free-spirited country boy, Colin, the willful, ailing scion of the estate, and a secret walled garden. For many years this pretty edition was the only one available; however, the copyright on Burnett's work expired in 1987 and nearly a dozen illustrated editions appeared in both hardcover and paperback. They all show essentially the same scenes in the same fashion, emphasizing the Victorian setting. Choose whichever version appeals, but do not choose one with an abridged text. Despite some bits of dialogue in dialect, the prose is not difficult. Rather, it is quite splendid as it carries

Mary from her sallow self-absorption to radiant health. A thrilling book to read aloud. If you begin in late March, spring comes as you reach the garden.

SECRET OF THE ANDES   [869]

Written by Ann Nolan Clark
Illustrated by Jean Charlot

Cloth: Viking Press
Paper: Puffin
Published: 1952   **Prizes: Newbery Medal**

The exciting story of Cusi, an Incan boy living in a hidden valley in the mountains of Peru with Chuto, a llama herder, is a perennial favorite. It is an exciting introduction to another, remote culture.

SEEING EARTH FROM SPACE   [870]

Written by Patricia Lauber

Cloth: Orchard Books
Paper: Orchard Books
Published: 1990

In one sense, this is a sophisticated picture book, a well-edited selection of full-color photographs of earth taken from satellites, space shuttles, and rockets. The individual photographs are stunning and worth poring over for their details and for the cumulative information about the earth and the ways humans continue to change it. The text is spare and clear. It is of great interest to schoolchildren, who can detect features and ask questions. Though not exactly a read-aloud book, it is certainly one to talk about.

SHILOH   [871]

Written by Phyllis Reynolds Naylor

Cloth: Atheneum
Published: 1991   **Prizes: Newbery Honor**

The first of three novels about eleven-year-old Marty Preston, who rescues Shiloh, a maltreated dog, from a mean and cruel master. In this first installment, the boy finally solves the payment problem by going to work for wicked Judd Travers. The other titles are *Saving Shiloh* and *Shiloh Season*.

SING A SONG OF POPCORN: EVERY CHILD'S BOOK OF POEMS

[872]

Written by Beatrice Schenk de Regniers

Cloth: Scholastic
Published: 1988

This jolly collection of mostly familiar poetry to read aloud or quietly is organized thematically and illustrated with great style and wit by nine American artists, all winners of the Caldecott Medal. A family treat.

SING DOWN THE MOON   [873]

Written by Scott O'Dell

Cloth: Houghton Mifflin
Paper: Dell Yearling
Published: 1970   **Prizes: Newbery Honor**

A historical novel about Bright Morning, a fifteen-year-old Navajo girl whose tribe has been evicted from their homes. She tells about the forced march and her capture by Spanish slavers.

SKELLIG   [874]

Written by David Almond

Cloth: Delacorte
Published: 1999   **Prizes: Carnegie Medal**

It's a strange and miserable time in Michael's life. His family has moved into a new house, his infant sister is terribly ill, he's not getting much attention, and there is much to fear. And then, in the garage, he finds a strange man covered with dust and insects. The man is called Skellig, and as the story of his mysterious relationship to Michael and his new friend Mina unfolds, there is an everyday magic that is rich and rewarding.

SMOKE AND ASHES: THE STORY OF THE HOLOCAUST [875]

Written by Barbara Rogasky

Cloth: Holiday House
Paper: Holiday House
Published: 1988

Telling the story of the Nazi Holocaust to children and young adults is a formidable task and cannot be entrusted to a single book. This, however, is an unusually careful text, illustrated with powerful historic photographs. The author gives facts, asks tough questions, and discusses other crimes against masses of people in the twentieth century as well. Books such as this one deserve and indeed require discussion in the home. Parents and grandparents seeking out a book such as this one surely care enough to supervise the way it is read. In addition to *Anne Frank: The Diary of a Young Girl,* there are a number of novels for young readers dealing with aspects of the Holocaust across Europe and in the United States. *Rescue: The Story of How Gentiles Saved Jews in the Holocaust,* by Milton Meltzer, addresses a question children often raise.

SO FAR FROM THE BAMBOO GROVE [876]

Written by Yoko Kawashima Watkins

Cloth: Bradbury
Paper: Beech Tree Books
Published: 1986

This is the story of the life of a Japanese family in Korea during World War II. The sequel is *My Brother, My Sister, and I* in which Yoko, her older sister, Ko, and their mother fled their home in Korea after World War II and made their way back to Japan, their homeland. After their mother's death, the children are joined by their brother, Hideyo.

SOUNDER [877]

Written by William H. Armstrong
Illustrated by James Barkley

Cloth: HarperCollins
Paper: Harper Trophy
Published: 1969   **Prizes: Newbery Medal**

In this novel, set in the rural South in the late nineteenth century, a poor black sharecropper's family is struggling to get by. The father steals in order to feed his family and is arrested in front of them. His dog, Sounder, is wounded. Battered, the family does not fall. A related title, *Sour Land,* picks up the story when the son is an old man and helps three white children.

SOUP [878]

Written by Robert Newton Peck
Illustrated by Charles Gehm

Cloth: Knopf
Paper: Dell Yearling
Published: 1974

Soup, the author's childhood pal, stars in a popular series of novels. The setting is rural Vermont in the 1920s; the style is terse and funny. Other titles include *Soup on Ice, Soup on Wheels, Soup's Goat,* and *Soup and Me.*

SQUIDS WILL BE SQUIDS: FRESH MORALS, BEASTLY FABLES [879]

Written by Jon Scieszka
Illustrated by Lane Smith

Cloth: Viking Press
Published: 1998

Are children you know too old (they think) for Aesop, too young for Machiavelli, yet searching for parables for behavior? These sardonic fables just might suit. The snappy tone (morals such as "It takes one to know one") is in keeping with much classroom conversation.

STORIES FOR CHILDREN   [880]

Written by Isaac Bashevis Singer

Cloth: Farrar, Straus & Giroux
Paper: Sunburst
Published: 1984

This splendid collection of short fiction, some never previously published in book form, is ostensibly for children but is actually appropriate for all ages. The tales allow every reader to have a Polish-Jewish grandfather from whom to hear stories to think about at night.

THE STORY OF KING ARTHUR AND HIS KNIGHTS   [881]

Written and illustrated by Howard Pyle

Cloth: Scribner
Paper: Dover
Published: 1903

A four-volume retelling of the Arthurian legends begins with this book, which is fine, lushly illustrated, and in a large format that feels secure in the hand. The other titles are *The Story of Sir Lancelot & His Companions, The Story of the Champions of the Round Table,* and *The Story of the Grail & the Passing of Arthur.* There are, of course, many editions of individual stories.

STRAWBERRY GIRL   [882]

Written and illustrated by Lois Lenski

Cloth: HarperCollins
Paper: Harper Trophy
Published: 1945   **Prizes: Newbery Medal**

Birdie Boyer, a so-called Cracker girl, lived with her farming family in the rural Florida lake country more than half a century ago. The compelling and well-written novel tells of strawberry crops and neighborly strife. The region still grows strawberries, but the way of life described is gone.

A STRING IN THE HARP [883]

Written by Nancy Bond

Cloth: Margaret K. McElderry
Paper: Aladdin
Published: 1976 **Prizes: Newbery Honor**

A dandy fantasy novel about three American children living in Wales and a harp-tuning key that transports a boy back to the sixth century and the life of the bard Taliesin.

STUART LITTLE [884]

Written by E. B. White
Illustrated by Garth Williams

Cloth: HarperCollins
Paper: HarperCollins
Published: 1945

The Littles were surprised when their second son looked a great deal like a mouse. Stuart, a dignified chap, has some impressive adventures growing up, helping around the house, and exploring New York City. Eventually, he leaves his home and family to follow Margalo, a lovely wren who has flown north. This elegant fantasy is a prized example of fine writing, and is a considerable distance from the movie or movie tie-ins in book or toy form. A classic case of the book being far better than, or at least very different from, the movie.

THE SUMMER OF THE SWANS [885]

Written by Betsy Byars
Illustrated by Ted Coconis

Cloth: Viking Press
Paper: Puffin
Published: 1970 **Prizes: Newbery Medal**

All on a summer's day, a fourteen-year-old deals with her conflicts about herself, her beloved but retarded younger brother, who is lost, and the attentions of a boy who offers to help. And in the end, she finds her wings. This is a compelling and powerful story for older grade readers.

TALES OF A FOURTH GRADE NOTHING   [886]

Written by Judy Blume
Illustrated by Roy Doty

Cloth: Dutton
Paper: Dell Yearling
Published: 1972

One of the early and brighter titles in the Blume canon, this is accessible and user-friendly fiction for middle-class children. Peter Hatcher, a nine-year-old, describes his life and problems with his little brother, the truly terrible two-year-old known as Fudge. In the sequels, *Superfudge* and *Fudge-A-Mania,* the boys and their friends are older but still full of mischievous and original ways of dealing with life.

THE TALES OF UNCLE REMUS: THE ADVENTURES OF BRER RABBIT   [887]

Written by Julius Lester
Illustrated by Jerry Pinkney

Cloth: Dial
Paper: Puffin
Published: 1987

There are three slim, handsome volumes in this contemporary retelling of the Brer Rabbit stories by a distinguished black writer. They are sharp and colloquial and read aloud well. The watercolor illustrations, full of dappled light and sunshine, are sweeter than the tales. The other two are: *More Tales of Uncle Remus* and *Further Tales of Uncle Remus.* There is also a single-volume collection.

A TASTE OF BLACKBERRIES [888]

Written by Doris Buchanan Smith
Illustrated by Charles Robinson

Cloth: HarperCollins
Paper: Harper Trophy
Published: 1973

In this short, thoughtful novel, a young boy describes his friendship with Jamie and Jamie's sudden death. This is not a substitute for parental support in real life; it is a good novel and not bibliotherapy.

THEO [889]

Written by Barbara Harrison

Cloth: Clarion
Published: 1999

Americans in general, let along young readers, know very little about the Greek resistance to the Nazis during World War II, and a great many incidents are packed into a slim novel about a brave and honorable orphan boy named Theo. He and his brother Socrates have been living in an abandoned puppet workshop in Athens when a notice is posted that orphans will be sent to German work farms. What follows is a harrowing journey.

THEY SAW THE FUTURE: ORACLES, PSYCHICS, SCIENTISTS, GREAT THINKERS, AND PRETTY GOOD GUESSERS [890]

Written by Kathleen Krull
Illustrated by Kyrsten Brooker

Cloth: Atheneum
Published: 1999

Here are sketches of the lives and work of a dozen visionaries and their talent to predict. They are a mixed group, beginning with the oracle at Delphi and the sibyls and moving briskly past the Maya, Leonardo da Vinci, and Nostradamus, to Jules Verne and H. G.

Wells, and on to Edgar Cayce, Jeane Dixon, and Marshall McLuhan. The text is clear and thoughtful ("Mixed in with all the science, writing, thinking and paying attention was a lot of luck"), and there is a helpful bibliography.

THROUGH MY EYES [891]

Written by Ruby Bridges

Cloth: Scholastic
Published: 1999

The little girl who integrated her New Orleans elementary school in 1960, reporting to her first grade classroom alone, guarded by federal marshals, looks back on her experiences with simplicity and elegance. It's an inspiring story, handsomely organized with photographs, newspaper clippings, and other interesting materials.

[887]

TITUBA OF SALEM VILLAGE   [892]

Written by Ann Petry

Cloth: HarperCollins
Paper: Harper Trophy
Published: 1964

In this novel about Tituba, a slave from Barbados, she, along with her husband, is sold into the household of a Puritan minister and endures the hysteria of the Salem witchcraft trials. Vivid and frightening.

TO BE A SLAVE   [893]

Written by Julius Lester
Illustrated by Tom Feelings

Cloth: Dial
Paper: Scholastic
Published: 1968   **Prizes: Newbery Honor**

This landmark anthology of original material describing the experience of slavery is annotated with helpful commentary. An important and original book for older readers of all races.

TOM'S MIDNIGHT GARDEN   [894]

Written by Philippa Pearce
Illustrated by Susan Einzig

Cloth: HarperCollins
Paper: Dell Yearling
Published: 1958   **Prizes: Carnegie Medal**

A time-tripping novel, and a dandy one. In a magical garden, Tom can go back to meet a mysterious girl in Victorian England. This particular plot device, often copied, works best when it combines realism with inherent, convincing fantasy, as it does in this now-classic title.

TOMI UNGERER'S HEIDI   [895]

Written by Johanna Spyri
Illustrated by Tomi Ungerer

Cloth: Delacorte
Published: 1880; 1990

The lavish illustrations are so much a part of this hardcover edition
of the story of the Swiss orphan girl taken to live with her gruff and
solitary grandfather, who lives in a simple cottage high on the Alm
Mountain in the Swiss Alps, that the artist's name has gone into the
title. No sooner is Heidi happily settled than it's off to Frankfurt
and the invalid Klara. There are many abridged editions, and a plain
pocket-size paperback is available.

TRACES OF LIFE: THE ORIGINS
OF HUMANKIND   [896]

Written by Kathryn Lasky
Illustrated by Whitney Powell

Cloth: Morrow Junior Books
Published: 1990

Young scientists interested in the people who have been studying
the origins of people will meet some interesting folks in this account.
It is an introduction to the world of paleoanthropologists organized
chronologically from the discovery of the Lucy fossil in 1974, but
flashing back to the earlier work of scientists including Raymond
Dart and Mary and Louis Leakey.

TREASURE ISLAND   [897]

Written by Robert Louis Stevenson
Illustrated by N. C. Wyeth

Cloth: Scribner
Published: 1911

Here is a reissue of the elegant 1911 edition of that splendid adventure story dominated by Long John Silver, the pirate of all pirates.
There are nearly a dozen other editions, some with illustrations,
many abridged, but this one is peerless.

THE TROLL WITH NO HEART IN HIS BODY: AND OTHER TALES OF TROLLS, FROM NORWAY [898]

Written by Lise Lunge-Larsen
Illustrated by Betsy Bowen

Cloth: Houghton Mifflin
Published: 1999

You know about trolls, of course, starting with the Billy Goats Gruff. But they come in many forms and do many kinds of mischief. Here are nine Norwegian stories, carefully annotated and illustrated with distinctive woodcuts.

THE TROLLS [899]

Written by Polly Horvath

Cloth: Farrar, Straus & Giroux
Published: 1999

At the very last minute Aunt Sally comes from Canada to babysit for Melissa, Amanda, and Pee Wee in Ohio when their parents leave on a trip to Paris. She turns out to be a larger-than-life character who tells amazing, outrageous stories about their father's family, even one about leaving their father on the beach as an offering to the trolls . . . if there are trolls. Under the humor are layers of insight about family dynamics.

THE TRUMPET OF THE SWAN [900]

Written by E. B. White
Illustrated by Edward Frascino

Cloth: HarperCollins
Paper: Harper Trophy
Published: 1970

The third but not necessarily the least of E. B. White's classic books for children tells the story of Louis, a trumpeter swan born without a voice. The nature writing is splendid, the illustrations charming.

THE TRUMPETER OF KRAKOW [901]

Written by Eric P. Kelly
Illustrated by Janina Domanska

Cloth: Macmillan
Paper: Aladdin
Published: 1928   **Prizes: Newbery Medal**

This exciting tale of a courageous boy and a precious jewel, set in Poland's most beautiful city in the fifteenth century, was handsomely reillustrated in 1966.

TUCK EVERLASTING [902]

Written by Natalie Babbitt

Cloth: Farrar, Straus & Giroux
Paper: Sunburst
Published: 1975

The best children's books address the most serious questions in life in ways that make them manageable to readers. The title of this novel is a clue to its rich contents. The Tuck family drank from a magical spring and has been blessed (or is it cursed?) with eternal life. They try to live very inconspicuously, but ten-year-old Winnie Foster discovers their secret. An enthralling fantasy that is good to read aloud with early and middle grade listeners.

UNBROKEN [903]

Written by Jessie Haas

Cloth: Greenwillow
Published: 1999

The setting is 1910 in Vermont, and when Harriet (Harry) is orphaned, her only inheritance is an unbroken colt. The girl is sent to live with embittered elderly relatives whose secrets she gradually learns and whose hearts open to her.

UNDERGROUND [904]

Written and illustrated by David Macaulay

Cloth: Houghton Mifflin
Paper: Houghton Mifflin
Published: 1976

Here is everything you really want to know about what happens underneath the pavement of a city street, told in clear pen-and-ink illustrations and spare, precise text. A book to study endlessly and enjoyably.

UNDERSTOOD BETSY [905]

Written by Dorothy Canfield Fisher
Illustrated by Kimberly Bucklin Root

Cloth: Henry Holt
Published: 1916/1999

One of the classic American stories of childhood transformation takes place early in the twentieth century and tells how Elizabeth, a frail, anxious orphan, is sent from an unfriendly unnamed city to live with cousins in rural Vermont. Gently guided by some crusty New England characters, she is transformed into a sturdy, independent, understood girl. There's wit and humor, and curiously, the novel is also a virtual manual of the principles of Montessori education. Out of print for a long time, the new edition has pretty illustrations. Good for reading aloud.

UPON THE HEAD OF A GOAT: A CHILDHOOD IN HUNGARY, 1939–1944 [906]

Written by Aranka Siegal

Cloth: Farrar, Straus & Giroux
Paper: NAL
Published: 1981

Prizes: Newbery Honor

A remarkable autobiographical novel in which the author, as Piri Davidowitz, describes her Jewish childhood and the destruction of her family in World War II. The sequel, *Grace in the Wilderness: After the Liberation, 1945–48,* carries her from the Bergen-Belsen concentration camp through quarantine in Sweden and on to embarkation for the United States. The two books are suitable companions to Anne Frank.

THE UPSTAIRS ROOM   [907]

Written by Johanna Reiss

Cloth: HarperCollins
Paper: HarperCollins
Published: 1982   **Prizes: Newbery Honor**

This is an autobiographical novel about a Dutch-Jewish family during World War II. The narrator, the youngest of three sisters, tells how a peasant family, the Oostervelds, hid her and one sister for more than two years. *The Journey Back* tells what happened after the war.

VICTOR: A NOVEL BASED ON THE LIFE OF THE SAVAGE OF AVEYRON   [908]

Written by Mordicai Gerstein

Cloth: Farrar, Straus & Giroux
Published: 1998

In 1800 in the woods of Aveyron in the south of France, a naked, filthy boy was captured. Was he a "noble savage"? He could not speak, had no family. He was taken to Paris where Jean-Marc Itard, an idealistic doctor, eventually "civilized" the boy he named Victor to the point of his wearing clothes, eating with cutlery, and understanding a few written words. It's a story that has been retold in fiction and film repeatedly and remains fascinating. This eloquent novel is wonderfully complemented by Gerstein's rich story book for grade school readers, *The Wild Boy: Based on the True Story of the Wild Boy of Aveyron."*

THE VIEW FROM SATURDAY   [909]

Written by E. L. Konigsburg

Cloth: Atheneum
Paper: Aladdin
Published: 1996   **Prizes: Newbery Medal**

A two-tiered novel about Mrs. Olinski's sixth grade Academic Bowl team. In the foreground is the story of the team and how it wins the state finals. There's a cast of grandparents, mostly in Century Village, Florida, who have connections the youngsters can't imagine. A deft confection, full of wit and astute observations of bright children and their forebears.

VOLCANO: THE ERUPTION AND HEALING OF MOUNT ST. HELENS

[910]

Written by Patricia Lauber

Cloth: Bradbury
Published: 1986   **Prizes: Newbery Honor**

A fine photo essay about the eruption of the Mount St. Helens volcano. The text and color photographs capture and explain with unusual clarity the healing abilities of nature in the years that followed.

WALK TWO MOONS   [911]

Written by Sharon Creech

Cloth: HarperCollins
Paper: Harper Trophy
Published: 1994   **Prizes: Newbery Medal**

In this classical tale of spiritual quest, Salamanca Tree Hiddle is thirteen years old, proud of the "Indianness in her blood" and heading west with her grandparents on a 2,000-mile journey from Ohio to Idaho in search of the mother who left her. Sal is only part Indian and her parents actually got her name wrong, but she loves the Indian stories and the tales she hears on the trip.

THE WATSONS GO TO BIRMINGHAM—1963   [912]

Written by Christopher Paul Curtis

Cloth: Delacorte
Paper: Bantam
Published: 1995   **Prizes: Newbery Honor**

Half of this solid and appealing family story is set in Flint, Michigan, where it's bitter, bitter cold and Kenny Watson, the ten-year-old, struggles with winter, school, and family. The rest takes place in Alabama as all the Watsons bring big brother Byron to spend the summer with Grandma Sands, who is going to discipline him. The fiction is deftly merged with the actual bombing of the 16th Street Baptist Church in which four girls were killed.

THE WAY THINGS WORK [913]

Written and illustrated by David Macaulay

Cloth: Houghton Mifflin
Published: 1988/1998

[913]

An enormous, imaginative, and witty exploration of the science of our lives was revised in 1998 to incorporate the communications revolutions that shape our twenty-first-century lives. In it, the author/illustrator uses his drafting skill and a friendly mastodon to guide readers of every age through the processes of scientific invention from lever to laser. This is a family book, not to read from cover to cover, but to look at a few pages and poke around together. It's also a private browsing and study treasure. There is no need to proceed chronologically.

THE WESTING GAME [914]

Written by Ellen Raskin

Cloth: Dutton
Paper: Avon/Puffin
Published: 1978

Prizes: Newbery Medal

A very sophisticated mystery novel for older readers in which sixteen heirs of an eccentric millionaire are assembled, organized, and given clues, which they believe will lead them to their inheritance.

THE WHEEL ON THE SCHOOL [915]

Written by Meindert DeJong
Illustrated by Maurice Sendak

Cloth: HarperCollins
Paper: Harper Trophy
Published: 1954

Prizes: Newbery Medal

[913]

All because Lina wondered why there were no storks in Shora, a tiny Dutch village on the dikes, things began to happen. Six schoolchildren set out to learn about birds, but everyone becomes involved. The rescue of two storks caught on a sandbar after a mighty storm and the race against the turning of the powerful tide are so thrilling you have to finish the chapter and continue to the end. This marvelous novel is best read aloud today, but once begun, older children may choose to finish or reread it themselves. A great deal of natural science about storks and dikes and tides is conveyed effortlessly.

WHEN BIRDS COULD TALK & BATS COULD SING [916]

Written by Virginia Hamilton
Illustrated by Barry Moser

Cloth: Scholastic
Paper: Scholastic
Published: 1996 **Prizes: Newbery Medal**

Eight stories collected by Martha Young, a nineteenth-century folk-lorist and contemporary of Joel Chandler Harris, are retold in contemporary language. They are engaging fables about why bats don't have feathers, about brown wren and blue jay. The illustrations show realistic painterly birds and creatures wearing top hats and bonnets. Read aloud.

WHEN ZACHARY BEAVER CAME TO TOWN [917]

Written by Kimberly Willis Holt

Cloth: Henry Holt
Published: 1999 **Prizes: National Book Award**

Not much is happening in Antler, Texas, although the Vietnam War is raging half a world away, and Toby Wilson's mom has run away to Nashville to be a country music star. Then a trailer decked with Christmas lights arrives, and folks line up to pay to see 643-pound Zachary Beaver, billed by his guardian as the world's fattest boy. A remarkably deft novel about small-town life and deceiving appearances.

WHERE THE FLAME TREES BLOOM [918]

Written by Alma Flor Ada
Illustrated by Antonio Martorell

Cloth: Atheneum
Paper: Aladdin
Published: 1995

A collection of eleven short and charming stories, mostly about the author's childhood in Camaguey, are set in a small city in rural Cuba at mid-century. The subtle black-and-white watercolor illustrations are appealing. The second volume, *Under the Royal Palms: A Childhood in Cuba,* adds another ten stories and photographs of the author's family.

WHERE THE RED FERN GROWS

[919]

Written by Wilson Rawls

Cloth: Doubleday
Paper: Bantam
Published: 1961

A young boy in the Ozark Mountains during the Depression earns the money to buy, and then train, a fine pair of coonhounds—Old Dan and Little Ann. It is a fine coming-of-age novel, with dreams and values tested and justified. The book's enduring popularity among middle grade and older readers has been reinforced by a motion picture.

WHERE THE SIDEWALK ENDS: POEMS AND DRAWINGS [920]

Written and illustrated by Shel Silverstein

Cloth: HarperCollins
Published: 1974

This wildly popular collection of poems and drawings for children and adults ranges from silly to sad and back again.

[920]

THE WHIPPING BOY [921]

Written by Sid Fleischman
Illustrated by Peter Sis

Cloth: Greenwillow
Paper: Troll
Published: 1986   **Prizes: Newbery Medal**

The theme is akin to that of the Prince and the Pauper, and done with a fine hand and a light heart. Jemmy is the whipping boy to Prince Brat, who deserves his name. The prince runs away, taking Jemmy with him, and their adventures with a motley bunch of silly and unsavory sorts teach them both good lessons. The black-and-white illustrations are deft and witty. Good for reading aloud.

THE WHITE STAG [922]

Written and illustrated by Kate Seredy

Cloth: Viking Press
Paper: Puffin
Published: 1938   **Prizes: Newbery Medal**

Here is the story of Attila and the migration of the Huns and Mag-
yars from Asia to Europe. Bold and sweeping historical fiction of
the timeless variety. The author also wrote two novels set in early
twentieth-century Hungary, *The Good Master* and *The Singing
Tree,* that stand up well and are worth finding.

THE WHITE STALLION [923]

Written by Elizabeth Shub
Illustrated by Rachel Isadora

Cloth: Greenwillow
Paper: Bantam
Published: 1982

As her family heads across Texas in a Conestoga wagon, Gretchen
falls asleep tied onto the back of an old mare. She awakens in the
midst of a band of wild horses. It's a thrilling story, beautifully illustrated.

[925]

WIDER THAN THE SKY: POEMS TO GROW UP WITH   [924]

Written by Scott Elledge

Cloth: HarperCollins
Published: 1990

This unusually varied anthology of two hundred poems by British and American writers, mostly written for adults, is intended for older children who are independent readers—say, those reaching their double-digit birthdays and chomping for something grown up. No illustrations at all, but helpful notes at the end. Splendid.

THE WIND IN THE WILLOWS   [925]

Written by Kenneth Grahame
Illustrated by Ernest H. Shepard

Cloth: Scribner
Published: 1908/1933

The riverbank adventures of those fine fellows Rat, Mole, Toad, and Badger. The stories celebrate a golden time just before the modern world. (Was it ever really so golden?) Somehow, the 1933 edition, with Shepard's illustrations, captures the story so perfectly it seems pointless to consider others. However, the language is difficult, so younger readers may prefer to hear it rather than read it to themselves. There are many abridged editions.

THE WINDOW   [926]

Written by Michael Dorris

Cloth: Hyperion
Published: 1997

When Raynona Taylor's mother goes into a detox program, her dad, who is well-meaning but not well organized, moves her around until eventually taking her from Seattle to Louisville, Kentucky to meet his side of the family. Raynona appears in the adult novels *A Yellow Raft in Blue Water* and *Cloud Chamber*. She's a memorable child and her story, her acceptance and her anger, are powerfully moving.

WINNIE-THE-POOH [927]

Written by A. A. Milne
Illustrated by Ernest H. Shepard

Cloth: Dutton
Paper: Dell Yearling
Published: 1926

Winnie-the-Pooh is the bear of little brain who belongs to Christopher Robin, a proper English boy hero of not so very long ago. Their adventures in and around Pooh Corner, with Eeyore, Piglet, Tigger, and the rest of their friends, continue in *The House at Pooh Corner* and have been beloved for generations. They are small whimsical adventures, but however charming the stories, some adults find the prose cloying. A fine early chapter book for reading aloud. The line drawings are enchanting. By the way, most of the Disney films are only distantly related to the original stories.

THE WONDERFUL WIZARD OF OZ [928]

Written by L. Frank Baum
Illustrated by W. W. Denslow

Cloth: Morrow Junior Books
Paper: Dover
Published: 1900

It is often called the original American fairy tale, and it certainly marked Kansas forever, because "There's no place like home." As a result of the film, it is hard to find a child who doesn't know the story, but as is often the case, the books are better. Much better. This is a facsimile of the handsome first edition. Most of the series—involving several writers and running to dozens of volumes—is available in large-format paperback from Dover and small paperback from Ballantine. Start with Dorothy, Toto, and that first trip to Oz, but don't miss *Ozma of Oz* or *The Patchwork Girl of Oz.* Grand for reading aloud to middle grade and younger children.

[927]

WRINGER [929]

Written by Jerry Spinelli

Cloth: HarperCollins
Published: 1997

A tightly structured and provocative novel about individuals and collective pressure. There's a grim coming-of-age ritual in the town of Waymer, where Palmer Larue is growing up. Every ten-year old boy is expected to join the crew snapping the necks of pigeons wounded in the annual Pigeon Day shoot. It's an important charity event, and nine-year-old Palmer is in dread of it. Skillfully told.

[927]

A WRINKLE IN TIME [930]

Written by Madeleine L'Engle

Cloth: Farrar, Straus & Giroux
Paper: Dell Yearling
Published: 1962   **Prizes: Newbery Medal**

The first of the fine, and very popular, quartet of fantasy novels about the Murray family, especially Meg and Charles Wallace. In the first book they go on a dangerous mission in search of their scientist father. The other titles are *A Wind in the Door* and *A Swiftly Tilting Planet* (these three are available in a boxed edition) and *Many Waters,* which follows the twins, Sandy and Dennys, back into biblical times.

THE YEARLING [931]

Written by Marjorie Kinnan Rawlings
Illustrated by N. C. Wyeth

Cloth: Scribner
Paper: Collier
Published: 1938/1985

In the backwoods of Florida, a boy named Jody struggles to save the animals he loves, especially the yearling. The memorable N. C. Wyeth illustrations were rephotographed for the 1985 edition.

YOUNG, BLACK, AND DETERMINED: A BIOGRAPHY OF LORRAINE HANSBERRY [932]

Written by Patricia C. McKissick

Cloth: Holiday House
Published: 1998

The American playwright was just twenty-eight years old when *A Raisin in the Sun* was produced on Broadway and only thirty-four when she died in 1965. This thoughtful biography places her life and work in the political context of the changing times in which she lived.

ZLATEH THE GOAT AND OTHER STORIES [933]

Written by Isaac Bashevis Singer
Illustrated by Maurice Sendak

Cloth: HarperCollins
Paper: Harper Trophy
Published: 1966

**Prizes: Newbery Honor
New York Times Best Illustrated Book**

Seven traditional Middle European folktales are told and illustrated by modern masters with unusual poignancy in this fine collection. It appeals to children and adults and is splendid to read aloud.

Young Adult Books

This is a small selection of titles written for adolescent readers and generally concerned with coming of age, self-awareness, role models, and personal possibility. The serious-sounding fare is leavened with humor.

ANNIE ON MY MIND [934]

Written by Nancy Garden

Cloth: Farrar, Straus & Giroux
Paper: Sunburst
Published: 1982

Here is an unusually strong and unsentimental novel that involves a lesbian relationship. Liza, the narrator, met Annie at the Metropolitan Museum of Art in New York City when they were in high school, before she had any understanding of her own sexuality.

ANTHONY BURNS: THE DEFEAT AND TRIUMPH OF A FUGITIVE SLAVE [935]

Written by Virginia Hamilton

Cloth: Knopf
Published: 1988

This is a novel about property, ownership, and law. Anthony Burns was raised a slave in Virginia. In 1854, when he was about twenty, he ran away to Massachusetts, was captured, and was tried under the Fugitive Slave Act. His incarceration and his master's suit were hotly debated and marked a turning point in the northern antislavery movement. The chapters of the novel alternate between objective and subjective chronicles—the "facts" and Burns's inner thoughts. A stunning achievement, this is a book to be discussed within families.

ART ATTACK: A SHORT CULTURAL HISTORY OF THE AVANT-GARDE [936]

Written by Marc Aronson

Cloth: Clarion
Published: 1998

As the twentieth century recedes, here's a helpful introduction into the multifaceted avant-garde movement in the visual arts, music, and dance written specifically for adolescent readers whose worlds are enlarging. There are a number of nimble connections made between culture and politics and ample reference material to texts and other media.

ATHLETIC SHORTS: SIX SHORT STORIES [937]

Written by Chris Crutcher

Cloth: Greenwillow
Published: 1991

Sports stories plus. These are not insensitive jocks; rather, they are athletes facing big questions about life as well as sports. Honest and good-natured as well.

THE BEDUINS' GAZELLE [938]

Written by Frances Temple

Cloth: Orchard Books
Paper: HarperCollins
Published: 1996

The setting is Fez, the year is 1302. Aitayah and Helimi, cousins, were betrothed at birth, separated, and are ultimately reunited. At one point she is lost in a sandstorm and rescued by a rival tribe. Etienne, the young French pilgrim from the novel *The Ramsay Scallop*, appears in this short elegant novel as well.

BELLE PRATER'S BOY [939]

Written by Ruth White

Cloth: Farrar, Straus & Giroux
Paper: Yearling
Published: 1996

In Coal Station, Virginia, one summer in the 1950s, everyone is talking about Belle Prater, who just walked out of her house one morning six months ago and hasn't been seen since. Her niece, Gypsy, wonders as well, and then Belle's son Woodrow also comes to live in Coal Station. The developing relationship between the children is at the core of the novel, but it is a rich depiction of a small town not so long ago.

BEYOND THE MANGO TREE [940]

Written by Amy Bronwen Zemser

Cloth: Greenwillow
Paper: Harper Trophy
Published: 1998

The narrator is a young girl living in Liberia in West Africa. Her father is largely absent, her mother ill and unbalanced, and her friendship with a Liberian boy tentative at first, but rewarding. That relationship is misunderstood in ways that demonstrate social inequality and underscore the importance of thinking for oneself.

THE CHANGEOVER: A SUPERNATURAL ROMANCE [941]

Written by Margaret Mahy

Cloth: Margaret K. McElderry
Paper: Scholastic
Published: 1984   **Prizes: Carnegie Medal**

A remarkably clever and stylishly written novel about witchcraft, family ties, and romance by the inventive New Zealand writer. When Laura's little brother becomes deathly ill, she realizes that the cause is witchcraft and that her only chance to save him is to "change over" herself.

THE CHOCOLATE WAR [942]

Written by Robert Cormier

Cloth: Pantheon
Paper: Dell
Published: 1974

One of the best contemporary young adult novels deals with power struggles and the misuse of power at a boys' boarding school in New England. The worthy sequel is *Beyond the Chocolate War*.

THE CONTENDER [943]

Written by Robert Lipsyte

Cloth: HarperCollins
Paper: Harper Trophy
Published: 1967

This fine novel about Alfred, a seventeen-year-old boy in Harlem who almost accidentally begins training to be a professional fighter, doesn't seem dated. The issues—entrapment, education, escape, drugs—are ever-present in society. Engrossing sports writing, too. Years later, the author turned to two other sport themes for novels about coming-of-age: *The Brave* and *The Chief.*

A DAY NO PIGS WOULD DIE [944]

Written by Robert Newton Peck

Cloth: Knopf
Paper: Dell Yearling
Published: 1973

A thirteen-year-old Shaker boy living on a farm in Vermont is the central figure in this compelling novel as he takes on many of the responsibilities of an adult. Graphic scenes of farm life, beginning with the opening chapter, offer a view of rural reality that may shock urban teens. The author wrote the popular, and lighter, *Soup* series for younger readers.

DINKY HOCKER SHOOTS SMACK! [945]

Written by M. E. Kerr

Cloth: HarperCollins
Paper: Harper Trophy
Published: 1972

Dinky doesn't use drugs, but she is fat and miserable and longs for attention. This novel from the wave of provocative young adult titles of the 1970s holds up very well. The adolescent issues are timeless, and the dialogue remains sharp and funny.

DOGSONG [946]

Written by Gary Paulsen

Cloth: Bradbury
Paper: Puffin
Published: 1985   **Prizes: Newbery Honor**

An Eskimo boy sets out on a dogsled, turning his back on his modern village, and makes a journey of physical and spiritual self-discovery. Exciting reading for older grade readers of both sexes. *Woodsong* is a first-person account of a challenging time in the woods. *Cookcamp* is about time nearly alone at a logging camp.

THE FACTS SPEAK
FOR THEMSELVES [947]

Written by Brock Cole

Cloth: Front Street
Paper: Puffin
Published: 1997

This is among the bleakest and best written of the dark adolescent novels of the last 1990s, and not a book for every reader. It begins with a murder and involves rape and desperate actions. It is told in the voice of Linda, a sexually abused thirteen-year-old who is trying to explain her circumstances to a social worker. Multigenerational dysfunction precedes her, but she seems to be a survivor.

FALLEN ANGELS [948]

Written by Walter Dean Myers

Cloth: Scholastic
Paper: Scholastic
Published: 1988

A historical novel of the Vietnam War, in which young soldiers band together in hopes of getting home alive. The tragic tale of two brothers holds up well.

FLOUR BABIES   [949]

Written by Anne Fine

Cloth: Little, Brown
Paper: Laureleaf
Published: 1994   **Prizes: Carnegie Medal**

To begin to grasp the complexities of being a parent, the class of fourteen-year-old boys in this British novel are assigned to look after six-pound bags of flour for three weeks as if they were their own babies and keep a diary of their experiences. It manages to be a comic novel about an earnest subject, deft and well written.

FORBIDDEN LOVE: THE SECRET HISTORY OF MIXED-RACE AMERICA   [950]

Written by Gary B. Nash

Cloth: Henry Holt
Published: 1999

The title to this very formal but useful book is a bit misleading. It is a history that concentrates not on intimate details, but on the social themes of mixed race in the United States, demonstrating that the phenomenon has always existed and has almost always been misunderstood. An interesting companion book is *What Are You? Voices of Mixed-Race Young People.*

FOREVER   [951]

Written by Judy Blume

Cloth: Bradbury
Paper: Pocket
Published: 1975

A first sexual relationship, entered into in good faith but outgrown in the course of ordinary events, is described by an author who has earned the trust and faith of her readers.

FRANKENSTEIN [952]

Written by Mary Shelley

Cloth: Viking Press
Published: 1818/1998

Undoubtedly the best romantic novel ever written by an eighteen-year-old, the tale of Victor Frankenstein and his monster is vaguely known to most young adults, if only from the movies. It's immensely readable, and this particular edition comes with annotations and period artwork that makes it particularly accessible. There's also an illustrated, cartoony edition better suited to grade school readers.

A GIRL FROM YAMHILL: A MEMOIR [953]

Written by Beverly Cleary

Cloth: Morrow Junior Books
Published: 1988

Beverly Bunn, who grew up first on a farm in Yamhill, Oregon, and later in Portland during the 1920s, has written some of the most warmhearted stories of American childhood in the Ramona and Henry Huggins books. Her own story, though told lightly, has dark undertones that her fans in the years of their greatest enthusiasm for her work may not catch. Older children, loving her as they do, may find this memoir, which carries her through high school and departure for Southern California in the Great Depression, surprising. It is memorable and worth rereading. *My Own Two Feet* carries the story forward into her married adult life.

GO AND COME BACK [954]

Written by Joan Abelove

Cloth: DK Publishing
Paper: Puffin
Published: 1998

Alicia, the narrator, lives in a village in the Peruvian jungle, and in this sharp-eyed first novel, she observes two strange white women who come and stay for a year. They are anthropologists and the learning goes both ways as Joanna and Margarita learn a great deal from their hosts. For self-absorbed young adolescent readers, it is a shrewd, possibly eye-opening work of fiction.

HABIBI [955]

Written by Naomi Shihab Nye

Cloth: Simon & Schuster
Paper: Aladdin
Published: 1997

This autobiographical novel set in the 1970s is about cultural change and confusion. Liyana Abboud has been raised in St. Louis, but now her Palestinian father moves the family, his American wife and their children, back to his homeland. They settle just outside Jerusalem, where he works, and Ramallah, where his family lives. For an apolitical fourteen-year-old, everything is new and challenging. She confronts roiling history everywhere, and of course makes friends with a nice Jewish boy.

THE HAUNTING [956]

Written by Margaret Mahy

Cloth: Margaret K. McElderry
Paper: Dell
Published: 1982

Prizes: Carnegie Medal

The New Zealand novelist is such a good storyteller that even people who actively dislike ghost stories read her books. Barney, a boy who is afraid to tell about the messages he receives from a dead relative, is the center of this prizewinning tale.

A HERO AIN'T NOTHIN' BUT A SANDWICH [957]

Written by Alice Childress

Cloth: Coward
Paper: Puffin
Published: 1973

This harrowing novel about Benjie, a thirteen-year-old black boy who is using heroin, is told from the perspectives of many of the people who know him. The ending is problematic but holds promise. Recognized at once when it was published, it remains one of the best of the socially aware young adult novels of the 1970s.

I AM THE CHEESE [958]

Written by Robert Cormier

Cloth: Knopf
Paper: Dell Yearling
Published: 1977

This is a complex and suspenseful novel of psychological exploration. Adam Farmer describes his bicycle trip to see his father in Vermont, deals with a psychiatric interview, and confronts some memories. Very well written.

I FEEL A LITTLE JUMPY AROUND YOU: A BOOK OF HER POEMS AND HIS POEMS COLLECTED IN PAIRS [959]

Edited by Naomi Shihab Nye and Paul B. Janeczko

Cloth: Simon & Schuster
Paper: Aladdin
Published: 1996

Here's a skillful anthology of 196 poems about perspective, 98 comparative views of aspects of the human condition as seen by men and women, boyfriends and girlfriends, fathers and daughters, mothers and sons, a first kiss, siblings. Entertaining and surprisingly provocative. Especially fine for browsing.

I HADN'T MEANT TO TELL YOU THIS [960]

Written by Jacqueline Woodson

Cloth: Delacorte
Paper: Laureleaf
Published: 1994

The setting is a small town in Ohio, and Marie is the middle-class black girl who is accused of being an Uncle Tom when she becomes friends with Lena, the new girl others call white trash. Marie's mother has left the family, but Lena's situation is even more complicated. A novel about friendship and incest, carefully written and thought-provoking.

I RODE A HORSE OF
MILK WHITE JADE   [961]

Written by Diane Lee Wilson

Cloth: Orchard Books
Paper: Harper Trophy
Published: 1998

Oyuna's shamaness grandmother has chosen her for an unspecified mission. It's thirteenth-century Mongolia and our heroine, who is lame, is brave and resourceful as she treks across the Gobi Desert and then along the Great Wall of China. It's a very complicated plot full of fascinating details.

THE INK-KEEPER'S APPRENTICE

[962]

Written by Allen Say

Paper: Houghton Mifflin
Published: 1974/1996

The autobiographical novel of an esteemed illustrator tells of his lonely coming-of-age in post–World War II Japan. While just a schoolboy, he moved, all alone, from Yokohama to Tokyo to be apprenticed to a famous cartoonist and was caught up in student politics as well as commercial art. Powerful.

IRONMAN   [963]

Written by Chris Crutcher

Cloth: Greenwillow
Paper: Laureleaf
Published: 1995

Bo Brewster, a high school senior, is in training for a triathlon and in search of self-understanding, self-possession, and self-respect. He's got a lot of problems at home and at school, and an imagined confidant in the television host Larry King. Perhaps too many plot points, but such strong writing the reader cares what happens to Bo.

JACK [964]

Written by A. M. Homes

Cloth: Macmillan
Paper: Vintage
Published: 1990

The doggedly funny fifteen-year-old protagonist is a good guy caught in difficult circumstances. Jack is still grieving for the end of his parents' marriage when his father tells him that his roommate, Bob, is actually his lover. His friend Max's parents, whom Jack has perceived as the most stable adults in his world, turn out to have problems, too.

JACOB HAVE I LOVED [965]

Written by Katherine Paterson

Cloth: HarperCollins
Paper: Harper Trophy
Published: 1980   **Prizes: Newbery Medal**

Sara Louise, her relationship with her twin sister, adolescence, and, incidentally, the Chesapeake Bay area, are the heroine and themes of this well-written and thought-provoking novel.

KISSING THE WITCH: OLD TALES IN NEW SKINS [966]

Written by Emma Donoghue

Cloth: HarperCollins
Paper: HarperCollins
Published: 1997

None of the women in these thirteen stories have names. They are spinsters—that is, they spin tales. They are also recognizable, even if the familiar fairy tales have been turned inside out—Cinderella stays with her fairy godmother, Rapunzel retreats to the tower. Brilliantly written but dense and challenging.

LETTERS FROM THE INSIDE [967]

Written by John Marsden

Cloth: Houghton Mifflin
Paper: Dell
Published: 1994

Mandy answers Tracey's ad for a pen pal, and initially both girls fabricate stories making their lives appear idyllic, but gradually they develop suspicions. When Mandy discovers that Tracey is in fact in prison, she does not abandon the correspondent who has become her friend.

THE LONG SEASON OF RAIN [968]

Written by Helen Kim

Cloth: Henry Holt
Paper: Henry Holt
Published: 1996

In this closely observed domestic novel set in Korea in 1969, generations of women are struggling, each in their own way, with the weight of a patriarchal tradition. An orphaned boy is brought into the family, and in the long wet season that follows, it slowly becomes clear that the autocratic father is not merely remote, he has a mistress.

THE LORD OF THE RINGS TRILOGY [969]

Written by J. R. R. Tolkien

Cloth: Houghton Mifflin
Paper: Houghton Mifflin
Published: 1954

The trilogy—*The Fellowship of the Ring, The Two Towers,* and *The Return of the King*—is a saga of good and evil, cast as the War of the Ring set in a mysterious Middle Earth. The writing is lush and fast-paced. There are many imitations of this formula and style, but none so riveting. It's a leap up in tone and complexity from *The Hobbit.*

MAKE LEMONADE   [970]

Written by Virginia Euwer Wolff

Cloth: Henry Holt
Paper: Point Signature
Published: 1993

Jolly, a single mother, tells the improbable story of her life with two young children and LaVaughn, the fourteen-year-old who becomes their babysitter. It's a fine novel that supports the old saying about having lemons and making lemonade.

MISSING GIRLS   [971]

Written by Lois Metzger

Cloth: Viking Press
Published: 1999

It's New York in 1967 and thirteen-year-old Carrie is ashamed of Muti, her grandmother, with whom she has lived since her mother's death. Circumstances combine to help Carrie come to terms and grow up. The Scots beekeeper who took in her mother when she had fled Vienna after the Nazi invasion comes to New York, and Carrie learns more about her own family as well as her friend Mona's, the family Carrie thinks is just perfect.

MONSTER   [972]

Written by Walter Dean Myers
Illustrated by Christopher Myers

Cloth: HarperCollins
Published: 1999   **Prizes: Michel L. Printz**

Steve Harmon is a sixteen-year-old accused of murder. He was the lookout when a drugstore owner was killed, and now he copes with his trial by transforming it into a screenplay that he films in his mind. What really happened? How did Steve get involved, and is he innocent? Gripping. A lighter teenage novel by the same author is *Motown and Didi*.

THE MOVES MAKE THE MAN [973]

Written by Bruce Brooks

Cloth: HarperCollins
Paper: Harper Trophy
Published: 1984

Prizes: Newbery Honor

This fine novel about growing up and friendship is also a very good novel about basketball, as both a game and a metaphor. Jerome Foxworthy is the first black at his high school, and Bix is the best white athlete he's ever seen.

MY BROTHER STEALING SECOND

[974]

Written by Jim Naughton

Cloth: HarperCollins
Paper: Harper Trophy
Published: 1989

The title of this affecting novel of emotional recovery refers to Bobby's favorite memory of his older brother, Billy, who died in an accident before the story begins. The author, a sportswriter, uses baseball scenes deftly.

NIGHT KITES [975]

Written by M. E. Kerr

Cloth: HarperCollins
Paper: Harper Trophy
Published: 1986

Erick Rudd has a difficult, provocative girlfriend, a rather pompous father, and a kind older brother, who, it turns out, has AIDS. The novel deals with the problem of AIDS within a family, and acknowledging the sexual orientation of an adult child with skill and tact as the background to Erick's own maturation.

NOTHING BUT THE TRUTH: A DOCUMENTARY NOVEL [976]

Written by Avi

Cloth: Orchard Books
Paper: Flare
Published: 1991   **Prizes: Newbery Honor**

Phillip Malloy, a bright ninth grader, brings on a school crisis by humming along with the national anthem. The story is told through a pastiche of sources—letters, diaries, memos, reports—and is, in light of events in American schools in the late nineties, benign. Engaging and good for discussion about what really goes on in school.

ONE FAT SUMMER [977]

Written by Robert Lipsyte

Cloth: HarperCollins
Paper: Harper Trophy
Published: 1977

The first of three books about Bobby Marks, who starts out, at fourteen in the 1950s, fat and insecure. This one tells about his first job. He deals with first love in *Summer Rules* and, when he is eighteen, hazardous working conditions in a laundry where he works in *The Summerboy*.

THE OTHER SHEPARDS [978]

Written by Adele Griffin

Cloth: Hyperion
Paper: Hyperion
Published: 1998

The setting is contemporary Greenwich Village. The siblings who died before they were born haunt two sisters who are trying to grow up as normally as possible in the modern world. This deftly written novel indirectly addresses the adolescent issue of separation.

THE OUTSIDERS [979]

Written by S. E. Hinton

Cloth: Viking Press
Paper: Dell
Published: 1967

A classic gang novel, filled with suspense and action. It is writ large and compelling in a story that details both the relationships of the city gang members to each other and their remove from social conventions. Successive generations of high school readers have been discovering it with stunned delight for more then thirty years. The companion tales are *Rumble Fish* and *That Was Then, This Is Now. Tex* has a rural setting.

PARROT IN THE OVEN: MI VIDA [980]

Written by Victor Martinez

Cloth: HarperCollins
Paper: Harper Trophy
Published: 1996

A coming-of-age novel set in a Chicano community in the Central Valley of California describes a year in the life of Manuel (Manny) Hernandez. His situation is problem-ridden—his father is an alcoholic and unemployed, his sister gets pregnant, his mother shows near superhuman strength in holding the family together. The writing is sharp and focused and makes the vignettes believable and often moving.

THE RUBY IN THE SMOKE [981]

Written by Philip Pullman

Cloth: Knopf
Paper: Knopf
Published: 1985

Sally Lockhart's search for clues to solve the puzzle of her father's death and to take revenge for it leads the young woman through the seamy byways of mid-Victorian London. It is 1872 and the fog is thick with menace. The story continues in *Shadow in the North* and *Tiger in the Well*.

SCORPIONS [982]

Written by Walter Dean Myers

Cloth: HarperCollins
Paper: Harper Trophy
Published: 1988   **Prizes: Newbery Honor**

Jamal Hicks is twelve years old, lives in Harlem, and seems to be becoming the leader of the Scorpion street gang. There's pressure everywhere—at home, at school, and in the street. A grim, haunting novel that reflects real events and situations in American cities. A sunnier view is in his novel *The Mouse Rap*—a summery novel about kids who find release in music despite the wrenching details of their lives.

SHABANU [983]

Written by Suzanne Fisher Staples

Cloth: Knopf
Paper: Knopf
Published: 1989   **Prizes: Newbery Honor**

In a remote part of modern Pakistan, in a corner of the Cholistan desert, the idea of an arranged marriage for Shabanu, the twelve-year-old daughter in the household of a camel driver, is appropriate. But due to convulsive circumstances, her eventual betrothal to the brother of the hateful landowner (who already has three wives) presents a dilemma. Shabanu's bravery is memorable in this skillfully written and affecting novel. The sequel is *Haveli;* another novel, *Shiva's Fire*, is also recommended.

SLAKE'S LIMBO [984]

Written by Felice Holman

Cloth: Margaret K. McElderry
Paper: Aladdin
Published: 1974

A novel about homelessness published well ahead of widespread awareness of the problem, this is the story of Artemis Slake, a thirteen-year-old runaway who goes down into the New York City subway system at a time when it was an overwhelmingly unsafe and terrifying place.

THE SLAVE DANCER   [985]

Written by Paula Fox

Cloth: Bradbury
Paper: Dell
Published: 1973   **Prizes: Newbery Medal**

A stunning novel about a boy called Jessie Bollier, in which he recalls the summer of 1840, when he was press-ganged aboard a slave ship bound for Africa and played his flute while the slaves were exercised.

SOLDIER'S HEART: BEING THE STORY OF THE ENLISTMENT AND DUE SERVICE OF THE BOY CHARLEY GODDARD IN THE FIRST MINNESOTA VOLUNTEERS   [986]

Written by Gary Paulsen

Cloth: Delacorte
Published: 1998

A short, stark, persuasive novel of combat in the Civil War. Charley Goddard was a real fifteen-year-old who traveled by train to the eastern front, observed the discipline and boredom of camp life, served at Bull Run and Gettysburg, witnessed the horrors of combat, and suffered greatly. An epilogue explains that the title comes from a condition we would now call post-traumatic stress syndrome and that Goddard died at the age of twenty-three. Very powerful.

SOMEHOW TENDERNESS SURVIVES: STORIES OF SOUTHERN AFRICA   [987]

Written by Hazel Rochman

Cloth: HarperCollins
Paper: Harper Trophy
Published: 1988

Here is a thoughtful, now historical collection of autobiographical stories and fiction by Southern African writers who generally address adult audiences, dealing with aspects of life under apartheid. It comes with useful notes on the contributors, among them Doris Lessing, Nadine Gordimer, Gcina Mhlope, and Mark Mathabane.

STAYING FAT FOR SARAH BYRNES

[988]

Written by Chris Crutcher

Cloth: Greenwillow
Paper: Laureleaf
Published: 1993

The title refers to a loyal friendship between two outsiders, Eric Calhoune and Sarah Byrnes, as adolescence offers them room to change. The plot veers toward melodrama—she was horribly burned, he was fat, there are hideous family problems—but is balanced by believable character development and dialogue.

THE SUMMER OF MY GERMAN SOLDIER   [989]

Written by Bette Greene

Cloth: Dial
Paper: Bantam
Published: 1973

A Jewish storekeeper's daughter living in Arkansas during World War II befriends an escaped German prisoner of war. It is a poignant coming-of-age story in which Patty confronts a number of subtle issues.

SWEET WHISPERS, BROTHER RUSH   [990]

Written by Virginia Hamilton

Cloth: Philomel
Paper: Avon
Published: 1982   **Prizes: Newbery Honor**

Tree, a fourteen-year-old girl, is alone most of the time and in charge of her older, retarded brother. In this well-written novel, Tree comes to terms with her family's tragic history and with her memories and fantasies of a dead uncle. For older readers.

TIGER EYES [991]

Written by Judy Blume

Cloth: Bradbury
Paper: Laurel Leaf
Published: 1981

One of the most serious of the Blume novels, addressed to older readers, is about a girl called Davey. Her father was killed in a holdup of his store, and she must cope with grief and fear and learn to go on. Davey and her mother head west to visit relatives in New Mexico, where Davey is befriended by a boy called Wolf.

THE TRICKSTERS [992]

Written by Margaret Mahy

Cloth: Margaret K. McElderry
Paper: Scholastic
Published: 1987

Perhaps the most sophisticated of the imaginative New Zealand novelist's efforts, this is the story of a family Christmas holiday at the beach and the arrival of three handsome strangers. Harry, the seventeen-year-old who is secretly writing a novel, has a special sense of who they are and their powers.

THE TRUE CONFESSIONS OF CHARLOTTE DOYLE [993]

Written by Avi

Cloth: Orchard Books
Paper: Avon (1992)
Published: 1990   **Prizes: Newbery Honor**

In 1832, Charlotte Doyle, then thirteen years old, was sent on a transatlantic voyage by herself. No sooner was she on board than the cook slipped her a knife. Before the trip was over, she was tried for murder. A galloping thriller from the first page to the last, with a skillfully controlled plot.

THE TULIP TOUCH   [994]

Written by Anne Fine

Cloth: Little, Brown
Paper: Bantam
Published: 1997

Natalie, who is a "good" girl, is entranced by Tulip, her new friend who, it emerges, comes from an abusive family and is hurtling into disaster herself. Ultimately, but just barely, Natalie survives.

VANISHING   [995]

Written by Bruce Brooks

Cloth: HarperCollins
Paper: Harper Trophy
Published: 1999

Alice has been in the hospital for seven weeks. She's starving herself in a pediatric ward and doesn't much care who knows. Doctors and hallucinations, despair and annoyance bombard her. But her new friend Rex, who may or may not be dying, is the person who makes real, affecting contact with Alice. The 1999 paperback edition of Deborah Hautzig's 1981 novel about anorexia, *Second Star to the Right* contains a powerful personal afterword by the author.

WEETZIE BAT   [996]

Written by Francesca Lia Block

Cloth: HarperCollins
Paper: Harper Trophy
Published: 1989

Postmodern, hip, chic, glittering, glitzy, but still just a kid, Weetzie Bat is coming of age in eighties L.A. She's best friends with Dirk, finds a Secret Agent Lover Man, and dreams of a little house and living happily ever after. There's sex, drugs, rock and roll, and everything else you might imagine or fear, all deftly told, and ultimately the stories are affirming. A very stylish writer whose other books about the enlarging cast of characters include *Baby BeBop, Cherokee Bat and the Goat Boys, Missing Angel Juan,* and *Witch Baby.* There's a collected set called *The Weetzie Bat Books.*

WHAT JAMIE SAW [997]

Written by Carolyn Coman

Cloth: Front Street
Paper: Puffin
Published: 1995   **Prizes: Newbery Honor**

A finely written domestic novel about a family that is somehow getting by. Life isn't easy for Jamie, who is nine years old, or for his mom and little sister, but somehow, there is optimism. The adult characters—Patty, the mother; Earl, her friend; and Mrs. Desrochers, Jamie's teacher—are particularly well drawn.

WHIRLIGIG [998]

Written by Paul Fleischman

Cloth: Henry Holt
Published: 1998

In this stunning short novel, seventeen-year-old Brent is asked to make restitution for killing a girl while driving drunk. He must build whirligigs with her image on them and place them at the four corners of the United States. The issues skillfully addressed include change and perspective.

THE WITCH OF BLACKBIRD POND [999]

Written by Elizabeth George Speare

Cloth: Houghton Mifflin
Paper: Dell
Published: 1958   **Prizes: Newbery Medal**

The setting is Puritan New England and the subject is the coming-of-age and trial of an independent-minded young woman.

SHIZUKO'S DAUGHTER [1000]

Written by Kyoko Mori

Cloth: Henry Holt
Paper: Juniper
Published: 1993

A stunning and painful coming-of-age novel set in Japan about Yuki, who was twelve years old in 1969 when her mother, Shizuko, an artist, committed suicide. The story is mostly told retrospectively. Her father quickly remarried; the girl was sent to her grandparents and found her way to become an artist in remembrance of an artist. Elegantly written.

ZEL [1001]

Written by Donna Jo Napoli

Cloth: Dutton
Paper: Puffin
Published: 1996

The setting is medieval Switzerland and the story is told in three voices, those of the thirteen-year-old Zel, her mother, and the young nobleman who falls in love with the girl. It's a persuasive and affecting novelization of Rapunzel, with all its insights about growing up, possessive love, and change. *The Magic Circle* by the same author is a fictional contemplation of Hansel and Gretel.

INDEX TO INDEXES

[64]

INDEX TO ALL TITLES

Wordless Books [1–16]

Picture Books [17–270]

Story Books [271–584]

Early Reading Books [585–648]

Middle Reading Books [649–933]

Young Adult Books [934–1001]

Wordless Books [1–16]
Picture Books [17–270]
Story Books [271–584]
Early Reading Books [585–648]
Middle Reading Books [649–933]
Young Adult Books [934–1001]

Wordless Books [1–16]

Picture Books [17–270]

Story Books [271–584]

Early Reading Books [585–648]

Middle Reading Books [649–933]

Young Adult Books [934–1001]

[72]

Wordless Books [1–16]

Picture Books [17–270]

Story Books [271–584]

Early Reading Books [585–648]

Middle Reading Books [649–933]

Young Adult Books [934–1001]

[83]

Wordless Books [1–16]

Picture Books [17–270]

Story Books [271–584]

Early Reading Books [585–648]

Middle Reading Books [649–933]

Young Adult Books [934–1001]

[301]

Wordless Books [1–16]

Picture Books [17–270]

Story Books [271–584]

Early Reading Books [585–648]

Middle Reading Books [649–933]

Young Adult Books [934–1001]

[100]

Wordless Books [1–16]

Picture Books [17–270]

Story Books [271–584]

Early Reading Books [585–648]

Middle Reading Books [649–933]

Young Adult Books [934–1001]

[134]

Wordless Books [1–16]

Picture Books [17–270]

Story Books [271–584]

Early Reading Books [585–648]

Middle Reading Books [649–933]

Young Adult Books [934–1001]

Wordless Books [1–16]

Picture Books [17–270]

Story Books [271–584]

Early Reading Books [585–648]

Middle Reading Books [649–933]

Young Adult Books [934–1001]

[245]

Wordless Books [1-16]

Picture Books [17-270]

Story Books [271-584]

Early Reading Books [585-648]

Middle Reading Books [649-933]

Young Adult Books [934-1001]

[95]

Wordless Books [1-16]

Picture Books [17-270]

Story Books [271-584]

Early Reading Books [585-648]

Middle Reading Books [649-933]

Young Adult Books [934-1001]

[229]

INDEX OF AUTHORS

Wordless Books [1–16]

Picture Books [17–270]

Story Books [271–584]

Early Reading Books [585–648]

Middle Reading Books [649–933]

Young Adult Books [934–1001]

[543]

Wordless Books [1–16]
Picture Books [17–270]
Story Books [271–584]
Early Reading Books [585–648]
Middle Reading Books [649–933]
Young Adult Books [934–1001]

[255]

INDEX OF ILLUSTRATORS

[185]

Gag, Wanda [146]

Galdone, Paul [216], [720]

Gammel, Stephen [15], [170], [194], [327],
[477], [639]

Gannett, Ruth Chrisman [632]

Garns, Allen [755]

Gehm, Charles [878]

Geisert, Arthur [274], [497]

George, Jean Craighead [831]

Gerstein, Mordicai [458], [530], [554]

Glanzman, Louis S. [637], [836]

Goble, Paul [120], [360], [362], [599]

Goembel, Ponder [472]

Goffstein, M.B. [364]

Gonzales [351]

Goodall, John S. [9]

Goode, Diane [256]

Gorey, Edward [641], [648], [772]

GrandPré, Mary [760]

Graston, Arlene [564]

Grifalconi, Ann [128], [345]

Grossman, Nancy [606]

Guettier, Benedicte [74]

Haas, Irene [140]

Hague, Michael [515], [654], [768]

Hale, James Graham [227]

Hallensleben, Georg [35]

Halperin, Wendy Anderson [604]

Hassett, John [53]

Hauman, George and Doris [131]

Hawkes [157]

Hawkes, Kevin [442]

Hays, Michael [751]

Haywood, Carolyn [593]

Heine Helme [87]

Henkes, Kevin [413], [421]

Heo, Yumi [208]

Hewitt, Kathryn [808]

Hill, Eric [257]

Himler, Ronald [304], [329], [519]

Wordless Books [1-16]
Picture Books [17–270]
Story Books [271–584]
Early Reading Books [585–648]
Middle Reading Books [649–933]
Young Adult Books [934–1001]

AGE-APPROPRIATE INDEXES

INFANTS

TODDLERS

PRESCHOOLERS

[128]

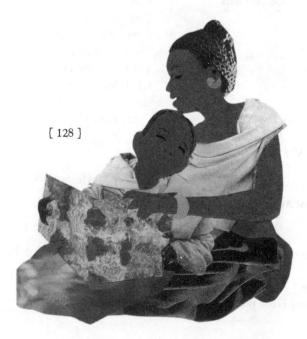

Wordless Books [1–16]

Picture Books [17–270]

Story Books [271–584]

Early Reading Books [585–648]

Middle Reading Books [649–933]

Young Adult Books [934–1001]

[26]

Wordless Books [1–16]

Picture Books [17–270]

Story Books [271–584]

Early Reading Books [585–648]

Middle Reading Books [649–933]

Young Adult Books [934–1001]

Prickly

[98]

Wordless Books [1–16]

Picture Books [17–270]

Story Books [271–584]

Early Reading Books [585–648]

Middle Reading Books [649–933]

Young Adult Books [934–1001]

Grand Canyon

[224]

EARLY READERS AND LOWER GRADES

Wordless Books [1–16]

Picture Books [17–270]

Story Books [271–584]

Early Reading Books [585–648]

Middle Reading Books [649–933]

Young Adult Books [934–1001]

[3]

Wordless Books [1-16]

Picture Books [17-270]

Story Books [271-584]

Early Reading Books [585-648]

Middle Reading Books [649-933]

Young Adult Books [934-1001]

[275]

Wordless Books [1–16]

Picture Books [17–270]

Story Books [271–584]

Early Reading Books [585–648]

Middle Reading Books [649–933]

Young Adult Books [934–1001]

[279]

MIDDLE GRADE READERS

Wordless Books [1–16]

Picture Books [17–270]

Story Books [271–584]

Early Reading Books [585–648]

Middle Reading Books [649–933]

Young Adult Books [934–1001]

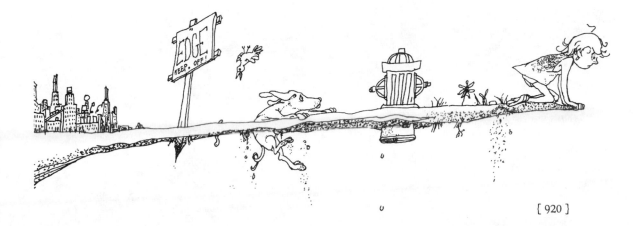

[920]

READ-ALOUD INDEX

Wordless Books [1–16]

Picture Books [17–270]

Story Books [271–584]

Early Reading Books [585–648]

Middle Reading Books [649–933]

Young Adult Books [934–1001]

SPECIAL SUBJECT INDEXES

[629]

Wordless Books [1–16]
Picture Books [17–270]
Story Books [271–584]
Early Reading Books [585–648]
Middle Reading Books [649–933]
Young Adult Books [934–1001]

ANTHOLOGY

AUTOBIOGRAPHY

BEARS

BEDTIME

[848]

American Folk Songs for Children [280]

Amos & Boris [24]

Anansi the Spider: A Tale from the Ashanti [283]

Angelina Ballerina [26]

Angry Arthur [27]

Animal Crackers [28]

The Animal Family [284]

Anno's Journey [1]

Arthur's Honey Bear [592]

Baba Yaga: A Russian Folktale [293]

Babushka: An Old Russian Folktale [294]

Bark, George [36]

The Bat-Poet [299]

Bea and Mr. Jones [301]

The Beautiful Christmas Tree [37]

The Beauty of the Beast: Poems From the Animal
    Kingdom [595]

Best Enemies [596]

The Best Town In the World [304]

The BFG [677]

Blackboard Bear [40]

Blueberries for Sal [41]

A Book of Americans [598]

The Borrowers [684]

Brave Irene [312]

Bread and Jam for Frances [313]

Bridge to Terabithia [686]

Brown Bear, Brown Bear, What Do You See? [44]

Buffalo Woman [599]

Building [4]

Can't Sleep [49]

The Carrot Seed [51]

The Cat in the Hat [601]

Cat is Sleepy [52]

Catch Me & Kiss Me & Say It Again [54]

Catwings [316]

A Chair for my Mother [317]

Changes, Changes [5]

Charlotte's Web [697]

A Child's Treasury of Poems [319]

The Children's Homer: The Adventures of Odysseus
    and the Tale of Troy [700]

The Christmas Miracle of Jonathan Toomey [324]

Cinderella [325]

City Dog [57]

Come Along Daisy! [60]

The Cricket in Times Square [711]

Danny the Champion of the World [714]

The Dark-Thirty: Southern Tales of the Supernatural
    [716]

Dawn [67]

Do Not Feed the Table [69]

Doctor De Soto [336]

A Dog on Barkham Street [719]

The Dragons Are Singing Tonight [338]

Drummer Hoff [70]

Wordless Books [1-16]

Picture Books [17-270]

Story Books [271-584]

Early Reading Books [585-648]

Middle Reading Books [649-933]

Young Adult Books [934-1001]

Wordless Books [1–16]
Picture Books [17–270]
Story Books [271–584]
Early Reading Books [585–648]
Middle Reading Books [649–933]
Young Adult Books [934–1001]

BIOGRAPHY

[716]

BOYS

CATS

COMING OF AGE

CONCEPTS

[252]

Wordless Books [1–16]

Picture Books [17–270]

Story Books [271–584]

Early Reading Books [585–648]

Middle Reading Books [649–933]

Young Adult Books [934–1001]

FAIRY TALES

FAMILY LIFE

Wordless Books [1–16]

Picture Books [17–270]

Story Books [271–584]

Early Reading Books [585–648]

Middle Reading Books [649–933]

Young Adult Books [934–1001]

FEAR

FOLKLORE

The Troll With No Heart in His Body: And Other
    Tales of Trolls From Norway [898]
Washday on Noah's Ark [241]
When Birds Could Talk & Bats Could Sing [916]
Why Mosquitoes Buzz in People's Ears: A West
    African Tale [578]
Why the Sun & Moon Live in the Sky [579]
Zel [1001]
Zlateh the Goat and Other Stories [933]

FRIENDSHIP

A, My Name Is Alice [586]
Alan and Naomi [656]
Amos & Boris [24]
Anna Banana and Me [285]
Best Friends [303]
Beyond the Mango Tree [940]
Bridge to Terabithia [686]
The Children of Green Knowe [699]
The Egypt Game [725]
Friends [87]
Frog and Toad Together [612]
George and Martha [359]
The Goats [750]
Harry Potter and the Sorcerer's Stone [760]
Hey, Al [382]
Horace and Morris But Mostly Dolores [109]
Horton Hatches the Egg [386]
The House With a Clock in Its Walls [772]
The Hundred Dresses [617]
I Hadn't Meant to Tell You This [960]
Leon and Bob [419]
Letters from the Inside [967]
Little Bear [621]
The Lord of the Rings Trilogy [969]
Lottie's New Beach Towel [430]
The Moves Make the Man [973]
The Noonday Friends [836]
Onion John [843]
The Outsiders [979]
The Pinballs [851]
Snow Bear [206]

Staying Fat for Sarah Byrnes [988]
We Were Tired of Living in a House [244]
Who Said Red? [260]
Will I Have a Friend? [263]

GHOSTS

The Children of Green Knowe [699]
The Dark-Thirty: Southern Tales of the Supernatural
    [716]
The Devil's Storybook [332]
Hob and the Goblins [767]
The Other Shepards [978]
Scary Stories to Tell in the Dark: Collected from
    American Folklore [639]
The Teeny-Tiny Woman: A Ghost Story [216]
The Three Robbers [563]

GIRLS

A Girl Named Disaster [649]
Afternoon of the Elves [655]
All-Of-A-Kind Family [657]
Amber Brown Is Not a Crayon [647]
Anastasia Krupnik [659]
Angelina Ballerina [26]
Anne Frank: The Diary of a Young Girl [662]
Anne of Green Gables [663]
Annie On My Mind [934]
Are You There, God? It's Me, Margaret [664]
"B" Is for Betsy [593]

Wordless Books [1–16]
Picture Books [17–270]
Story Books [271–584]
Early Reading Books [585–648]
Middle Reading Books [649–933]
Young Adult Books [934–1001]

GRANDPARENTS

GROWING UP

[479]

HOLIDAYS

Wordless Books [1–16]

Picture Books [17–270]

Story Books [271–584]

Early Reading Books [585–648]

Middle Reading Books [649–933]

Young Adult Books [934–1001]

Wordless Books [1–16]

Picture Books [17–270]

Story Books [271–584]

Early Reading Books [585–648]

Middle Reading Books [649–933]

Young Adult Books [934–1001]

IMMIGRANTS

[152]

MANNERS

MICE

MINORITIES

MUSIC

NATURE

OTHER EDITIONS

PETS

POETRY AND VERSE

Wordless Books [1–16]

Picture Books [17–270]

Story Books [271–584]

Early Reading Books [585–648]

Middle Reading Books [649–933]

Young Adult Books [934–1001]

[143]

PROBLEMS

RABBITS

RELIGION

SCHOOL

SCIENCE

Wordless Books [1-16]

Picture Books [17-270]

Story Books [271-584]

Early Reading Books [585-648]

Middle Reading Books [649-933]

Young Adult Books [934-1001]

SERIES

Wordless Books [1–16]

Picture Books [17–270]

Story Books [271–584]

Early Reading Books [585–648]

Middle Reading Books [649–933]

Young Adult Books [934–1001]

[268]

SIBLINGS

SPORTS

WAR AND PEACE

BIBLIOGRAPHY

There are a great many books about children's books and reading as they relate to child development. Here are a few tested and reliable guides.

Choosing Books for Children: A Commonsense Guide. By Betsy Hearne, with Deborah Stevenson. Urbana: University of Illinois Press (1999).

The New Read Aloud Handbook, 4th Edition. By Jim Trelease. New York: Penguin (1995).

Valerie & Walter's Best Books for Children: A Lively, Opinionated Guide. By Valerie V. Lewis, Walter M. Mayes. New York: Avon (1999).

If you are interested in reading regular, thoughtful reviews and commentary about children's books, you might want to consult:

The Bulletin of the Center for Children's Books
1325 S. Oak
Champaign, IL 61820-6903

The Horn Book
56 Roland Street, Suite 200
Boston, MA 02129
Magazine@hbook.com
www.hbook.com

The Riverbank Review
University of St. Thomas
1000 LaSalle Avenue MO- 217
Minneapolis, MN 55403-2009
www.riverbank.com

In addition, *Dear Genius: The Letters of Ursula Nordstrom,* collected and edited by Leonard S. Marcus, HarperCollins, 1998, is an engrossing introduction to twentieth-century American children's books through the scrupulously annotated correspondence of one of the key editors.

PERMISSIONS
ACKNOWLEDGMENTS

Grateful acknowledgment is made to the following for permission to reprint previously published artwork:

ON THE COVER:

HarperCollins Publishers: Illustration from *Ramona's World* by Beverly Cleary, illustrated by Alan Tiegreen (Morrow Junior Books). Illustrations copyright © 1999 by Beverly Cleary; illustration from *Little Bear* by Else Holmelund Minarik, pictures by Maurice Sendak. Copyright 1957 by Maurice Sendak; illustration from *Charlotte's Web* by E. B. White, illustrated by Garth Williams. Copyright © 1952 by Garth Williams. Copyright renewed © 1980 by Garth Williams; illustration from *Lilly's Purple Plastic Purse* by Kevin Henkes (Greenwillow Books). Copyright © 1996 by Kevin Henkes. Used by permission of HarperCollins Publishers.

Penguin/Putnam, Inc.: Illustration from *Make Way for Ducklings* by Robert McCloskey. Copyright 1941 by Robert McCloskey, renewed 1969 by Robert McCloskey; illustration from *Madeline* by Ludwig Bemelmans. Copyright 1939 by Ludwig Bemelmans, renewed © 1967 by Madeleine Bemelmans and Barbara Bemelmans Marciano; illustration from *Amazing Grace* by Mary Hoffman, illustrated by Caroline Binch. Illustrations copyright © 1991 by Caroline Binch. Used by permission of Penguin Putnam Books for Young Readers, a division of Penguin Putnam, Inc.

Random House, Inc.: Illustration from *Frederick* by Leo Lionni (Random House Children's Books). Copyright © 1967 by Leo Lionni; illustration from *How the Grinch Stole Christmas* by Dr. Seuss (Random House Children's Books). TM and copyright © by Dr. Seuss Enterprises, L.P. 1957, renewed 1985; illustration from *The Story of Babar* by Jean de Brunhoff (Random House Children's Books). Copyright © 1933 by Random House, Inc. Copyright renewed 1961 by Random House, Inc. Reprinted by permission of Random House Children's Books, a division of Random House, Inc.

Scholastic, Inc.: Illustration by Mary GrandPré from *Harry Potter and the Sorcerer's Stone* by J. K. Rowling. Published by Arthur Levine Books, an imprint of Scholastic Press, a division of Scholastic, Inc. Illustration copyright © 1998 by Mary GrandPré; illustration from *No, David!* by David Shannon. Published by Blue Sky Press, a division of Scholastic, Inc.

ON THE HALF TITLE
AND TITLE PAGES:

HarperCollins Publishers: Illustration on half-title page from *Little Bear* by Else Holmelund Minarik, pictures by Maurice Sendak. Copyright 1957 by Maurice Sendak. Used by permission of HarperCollins Publishers.

Penguin Putnam, Inc.: Illustration on title page from *Madeline* by Ludwig Bemelmans. Copyright 1939 by Ludwig Bemelmans, renewed © 1967 by Madeleine Bemelmans and Barbara Bemelmans Marciano. Used by permission of Penguin Putnam Books for Young Readers, a division of Penguin Putnam, Inc.

Random House, Inc.: Illustration on title page from *Frederick* by Leo Lionni. Copyright © 1967 by Leo Lionni. Copyright renewed 1995 by Leo Lionni. Reprinted by permission of Random House Children's Books, a division of Random House, Inc.

IN THE TEXT:

Chronicle Books: Illustration from *Mooses Come Walking* by Arlo Guthrie, illustrated by Alice Brock © 1995; illustration from *Ten Little Rabbits* by Virginia Grossman, illustrated by Sylvia Long © 1991; illustration from *Mama, Do You Love Me?* by Barbara M. Joosse, illustrated by Barbara Lavallee © 1991; illustration from *Olive, the Other Reindeer* by J. Otto Seibold and Vivian Walsh © 1997. Published by Chronicle Books, San Francisco. Used with permission.

Farrar, Straus & Giroux: Illustration from *Amos and Boris* by William Steig. Copyright © 1971 by William Steig; illustration from *Applebet* by Clyde Watson, illustrated by Wendy Watson. Illustration copyright © 1982 by Wendy Watson; illustration from *Cat Is Sleepy* by Satoshi Kitamura. Copyright © 1996 by Satoshi Kitamura; illustration from *Snow* by Uri Shulevitz. Copyright © 1998 by Uri Shulevitz; illustration from *The Winter Wren* by Brock Cole. Copyright © 1984 by Brock Cole; illustration from *Brave Irene* by William Steig. Copyright © 1986 by William Steig; illustration from *The Devil's Storybook* by Natalie Babbitt. Copyright © 1974 by Natalie Babbitt; illustration from *Doctor De Soto* by William Steig. Copyright © 1982 by William Steig; illustration from *The Gardener* by Sarah Stewart, illustrated by David Small. Illustrations copyright © 1997 by David Small; illustration from *I Once Was a Monkey* by Jeanne M. Lee. Copyright © 1999 by Jeanne M. Lee; illustration from *The Incredible Painting of Felix Clousseau* by Jon Agee. Copyright © 1988 by Jon Agee; illustration from *Puss in Boots* by Charles Perrault, illustrated by Fred Marcellino. Illustrations copyright © 1990 by Fred Marcellino; illustration from *Spinky Sulks* by William Steig. Copyright © 1988 by William Steig; illustration from *Starry Messenger* by Peter Sis. Copyright © 1996 by Peter Sis; illustration from *The BFG* by Roald Dahl, illustrated by Quentin Blake. Illustrations copyright © 1982 by Quentin Blake; illustration from *The Juniper Tree* by The Brothers Grimm, illustrated by Maurice Sendak. Copyright © 1973 by Maurice Sendak. Used with the permission of the publisher, Farrar, Straus and Giroux.

Harcourt, Inc.: Illustration from *The Little Prince* by Antoine de Saint-Exupéry. Copyright 1943 by Harcourt, Inc.; copyright renewed 1971 by Consuelo de Saint-Exupéry. English translation © 2000 by Richard Howard; illustration from *Stellaluna* by Janell Cannon. Copyright © 1993 by

Kellogg. Illustrations copyright © 1975 by Steven Kellogg; illustration from *Lon Po Po: A Red-Riding Hood Story from China* by Ed Young. Copyright © 1989 by Ed Young; illustration from *Merry Ever After* by Joe Lasker; illustration from *Miss Rumphius* by Barbara Cooney. Copyright © 1982 by Barbara Cooney Porter; illustration from *Mirette on the High Wire* by Emily Arnold McCully. Copyright © 1992 by Emily Arnold McCully; illustration from *Nana Upstairs & Nana Downstairs* by Tomie dePaola; illustration from *Officer Buckle and Gloria* by Peggy Rathmann. Copyright © 1995 by Peggy Rathmann; illustration from *Ox-Cart Man* by Donald Hall, illustrated by Barbara Cooney. Illustrations copyright © 1979 by Barbara Cooney Porter; illustration from *Ooh-La-La (Max in Love)* by Maira Kalman. Copyright © 1991 by Maira Kalman; illustration from *A Peaceable Kingdom: The Shaker Abecedarius*, illustrated by Alice and Martin Provensen. Illustrations copyright © 1978 by Alice and Martin Provensen; illustration from *Pink and Say* by Patricia Polacco. Copyright © 1994 by Patricia Polacco; illustration from *Rapunzel* by Paul O. Zelinsky. Copyright © 1997 by Paul O. Zelinsky; illustration from *Saving Sweetness* by Diane Stanley, illustrated by G. Brian Karas. Illustrations copyright © 1996 by G. Brian Karas; illustration from *Sayonara, Mrs. Kackleman* by Maira Kalman. Copyright © 1989 by Maira Kalman; illustration from *Seven Blind Mice* by Ed Young. Copyright © 1992 by Ed Young; illustration from *The Stinky Cheese Man and Other Fairly Stupid Tales* by Jon Scieszka, illustrated by Lane Smith. Illustrations copyright © 1992 by Lane Smith; illustrations from *The Story of Ferdinand* by Munro Leaf, illustrated by Robert Lawson. Copyright 1936 by Munro Leaf and Robert Lawson, renewed © 1964 by Munro Leaf and John W. Boyd; illustration from *The True Story of the Three Little Pigs* by Jon Scieszka, illustrated by Lane Smith. Illustrations copyright © 1989 by Lane Smith; illustration

from *Tomie dePaola's Favorite Nursery Tales* by Tomie dePaola. Copyright © 1986 by Tomie dePaola; illustration from *When We Were Very Young* by A. A. Milne, illustrated by Ernest H. Shepard; illustration from *Why Mosquitoes Buzz in People's Ears* by Verna Aardema, illustrated by Leo and Diane Dillon. Illustrations copyright © 1975 by Leo and Diane Dillon; illustration from *Amanda Pig and Her Big Brother Oliver* by Jean Van Leeuwen, illustrations by Ann Schweninger. Illustrations copyright © 1982 by Ann Schweninger; illustration from *Today Was a Terrible Day* by Patricia Reilly Giff, illustrated by Susanna Natti. Illustrations copyright © 1984 by Susanna Natti; illustration from *Pippi Longstocking* by Astrid Lindgren, illustrated by Louis S. Glanzman; illustration from *Amber Brown Is Not a Crayon* by Paula Danziger, illustrated by Tony Ross. Illustrations copyright © 1994 by Tony Ross; illustration from *Matilda* by Roald Dahl, illustrated by Quentin Blake. Illustrations copyright © 1988 by Quentin Blake; illustration from *The Tales of Uncle Remus* by Julius Lester, illustrated by Jerry Pinkney. Illustrations copyright © 1987 by Jerry Pinkney; illustration from *Winnie-the-Pooh* by A. A. Milne, illustrated by E. H. Shepard. Copyright 1926 by E. P. Dutton, renewed 1954 by A. A. Milne; illustration from *The Guinea Pig ABC* by Kate Duke. Copyright © 1983 by Kate Duke; illustration from *A Boy, a Dog and a Frog* by Martha Alexander. Copyright © 1972 by Martha Alexander. Reprinted by permission of Penguin Books for Young Readers, a division of Penguin Putnam, Inc.

Random House, Inc.: Illustrations from *Frederick* by Leo Lionni. Copyright © 1967 by Leo Lionni (Random House Children's Books). Copyright renewed 1995 by Leo Lionni; illustrations from *The Cat in the Hat* by Dr. Seuss (Random House Children's Books). ® & copyright © by Dr. Seuss Enterprises, L.P. 1957, renewed 1986; illustrations from *The Bear and the Fly* by Paula Winter

(Crown Children's Books). Copyright © 1976 by Paula Winter; illustration from *The Snowman* by Raymond Briggs (Random House Children's Books). Copyright © 1978 by Raymond Briggs; illustrations from *Angelina Ballerina* by Katherine Holabird and Helen Craig (Clarkson Potter/Publishers). Illustrations copyright © 1983 by Helen Craig; illustration from *One Fish Two Fish Red Fish Blue Fish* by Dr. Seuss (Random House Children's Books). ® & copyright © by Dr. Seuss Enterprises, L.P. 1960, renewed 1988; illustration from *Possum Come A-Knockin'* by Nancy Van Laan, illustrated by George Booth (Alfred A. Knopf Children's Books). Illustrations copyright © 1990 by George Booth; illustration from *Swimmy* by Leo Lionni (Random House Children's Books). Copyright © 1963 by Leo Lionni. Copyright renewed 1991 by Leo Lionni; illustration from *D'Aulaire's Book of Greek Myths* by Ingri and Edgar Parin D'Aulaire (Random House Children's Books). Copyright © 1962 by Ingri and Edgar Parin D'Aulaire; illustrations from *How the Grinch Stole Christmas* by Dr. Seuss (Random House Children's Books). TM and copyright © by Dr. Seuss Enterprises, L.P. 1957, renewed 1985; illustration from *In Coal Country* by Judith Hendershot, illustrated by Thomas B. Allen (Alfred A. Knopf Children's Books). Illustrations copyright © 1987 by Thomas B. Allen; illustration from *Noah's Ark* by Peter Spier (Doubleday). Copyright © 1977 by Peter Spier; illustration from *The People Could Fly: American Black Folktales* by Virginia Hamilton, illustrated by Leo and Diane Dillon (Alfred A. Knopf Children's Books). Illustrations copyright © 1985 by Leo and Diane Dillon; illustrations from *The Story of Babar* by Jean de Brunhoff (Random House Children's Books). Copyright © 1933 by Random House, Inc. Copyright renewed 1961 by Random House, Inc.; illustration from *Tar Beach* by Faith Ringgold (Crown Children's Books). Copyright © 1991 by Faith Ringgold; illustration from *Tasty Baby Belly Buttons* by Judy Sierra, illustrated by Meilo So (Alfred A. Knopf Children's Books). Illustrations copyright © 1999 by Meilo So; illustration from *The Beauty of the Beast* by Jack Prelutsky, illustrated by Meilo So (Alfred A. Knopf Children's Books). Illustrations copyright © 1997 by Meilo So; illustration from *My Father's Dragon* by Ruth Stiles Gannett (Random House Children's Books). Copyright © 1948 by Random House, Inc.; illustration from *The Dark Thirty: Southern Tales of the Supernatural* by Patricia C. McKissack, illustrated by Brian Pinkney (Alfred A. Knopf Children's Books). Illustrations copyright © 1992 by Brian Pinkney; illustrations from *The Phantom Tollbooth* by Norton Juster, illustrated by Jules Feiffer (Random House Children's Books). Illustrations copyright © 1961 by Jules Feiffer. Illustrations copyright renewed 1989 by Jules Feiffer. Reprinted by permission of Random House, Inc.

Scholastic Inc.: Illustrations by Mary GrandPré from *Harry Potter and the Sorcerer's Stone* by J. K. Rowling. Published by Arthur Levine Books, an imprint of Scholastic Press, a division of Scholastic Inc. Illustrations copyright © 1998 by Warner Bros. Used by permission; illustration from *Black Cat* by Christopher Myers. Published by Scholastic Press, a division of Scholastic Inc. Copyright © 1999 by Christopher Myers. Used by permission; illustration from *Goose* by Molly Bang. Published by the Blue Sky Press, an imprint of Scholastic Inc. Copyright © 1996 by Molly Bang. Used by permission; illustrations by Ann Grifalconi from *The Lion's Whiskers* by Nancy Raines Day. Illustration copyright © 1995 by Ann Grifalconi. Used by permission of Scholastic Inc.; illustrations from *No, David* by David Shannon. Published by the Blue Sky Press, an imprint of Scholastic Inc. Copyright © 1998 by David Shannon. Used by permission; illustration from *When Sophie Gets Angry—Really, Really Angry . . .* by Molly Bang. Published by the Blue Sky Press, an imprint of Scholastic Inc. Copyright © 1999 by Molly Bang. Used by permission; illustration by Bruce Degan from *The Magic School Bus at the Water Works* by Joanna Cole. Illustration copyright © 1986 by Bruce Degan. Used by permission of Scholastic Inc. *The Magic School Bus* is a registered trademark of Scholastic Inc.

Simon & Schuster: Illustration reprinted with the permission of Margaret K. McElderry Books, an imprint of Simon & Schuster Children's Publishing Division from *Naughty Nancy* by John S. Goodall. Copyright © 1975 John S. Goodall; illustration reprinted with the permission of Atheneum Books for Young Readers, a division of Simon & Schuster Children's Publishing Division from *Cloudy with a Chance of Meatballs* by Judy Barrett, illustrated by Ron Barrett. Illustrations copyright © 1970 Ron Barrett; illustration reprinted with the permission of Margaret K. McElderry Books, an imprint of Simon & Schuster Children's Publishing Division from *Friends* by Helme Heine. Illustrations copyright © 1982 Gertraud Middelhauve Verlag, Koln; illustration reprinted with the permission of Simon & Schuster Books for Young Readers, an imprint of Simon & Schuster Children's Publishing Division from *Happy Birthday, Moon* by Frank Asch. Copyright © 1982 Frank Asch; illustration reprinted with the permission of Atheneum Books for Young Readers, an imprint of Simon & Schuster Children's Publishing Division from *Horace and Morris but Mostly Delores* by James Howe, illustrated by Amy Walrod. Illustrations copyright © 1999 Amy Walrod; illustration reprinted with the permission of Atheneum Books for Young Readers, an imprint of Simon & Schuster Children's Publishing Division from *May I Bring a Friend?* by Beatrice Schenk de Regniers, illustrated by Beni Montresor. Illustrations copyright © 1964 Beni Montresor; illustration reprinted with the per-

mission of Margaret K. McElderry Books, an imprint of Simon & Schuster Children's Publishing Division from *Not So Fast, Songololo* by Niki Daly. Copyright © 1985 Niki Daly; illustration reprinted with the permission of Simon & Schuster Books for Young Readers, an imprint of Simon & Schuster Children's Publishing Division from *The Relatives Came* by Cynthia Rylant, illustrated by Stephen Gammell. Illustrations copyright © 1985 Stephen Gammell; illustrations reprinted with the permission of Margaret K. McElderry Books, an imprint of Simon & Schuster Children's Publishing Division from *We're Going on a Bear Hunt* by Michael Rosen, illustrated by Helen Oxenbury. Illustrations copyright © 1989 Helen Oxenbury. Canadian rights administered by Candlewick Press, Inc., Cambridge, MA, on behalf of Walker Books Ltd., London; illustration reprinted with the permission of Margaret K. McElderry Books, an imprint of Simon & Schuster Children's Publishing Division from *Who Said Red?* by Mary Serfozo, illustrated by Keiko Narahashi. Illustrations copyright © 1988 Keiko Narahashi; illustrations reprinted with the permission of Atheneum Books for Young Readers, an imprint of Simon & Schuster Children's Publishing Division from *Alexander and the Terrible, Horrible, No Good, Very Bad Day* by Judith Viorst, illustrated by Ray Cruz. Illustrations copyright © 1972 Ray Cruz; illustrations reprinted with the permission of Simon & Schuster Books for Young Readers, an imprint of Simon & Schuster Children's Publishing Division from *Bea and Mr. Jones* by Amy Schwartz. Copyright © 1982 Amy Schwartz; illustration reprinted with the permission of Simon & Schuster Books for Young Readers, an imprint of Simon & Schuster Children's Publishing Division from *Eloise* by Kay Thompson, illustrated by Hilary Knight. Copyright © 1955 Kay Thompson; copyright renewed © 1983 Kay Thompson; illustration reprinted with the permission of Simon & Schuster Books

ABOUT THE AUTHOR

Eden Ross Lipson is the children's book editor of *The New York Times*. A native New Yorker with a B.A. in political science from the University of California at Berkeley, she joined the newspaper as an editor of *The Book Review* in 1974 and took over the children's section in 1984. She wrote the first edition of *The New York Times Parent's Guide to the Best Books for Children* in 1988 and the second in 1991. She is also the editor of *Times Talk*, the paper's in-house magazine. She and her family live in lower Manhattan in a house built when Andrew Jackson was president of the United States.

NOTES

NOTES

NOTES

NOTES

NOTES